IMAGES
of America

LAKEPORT

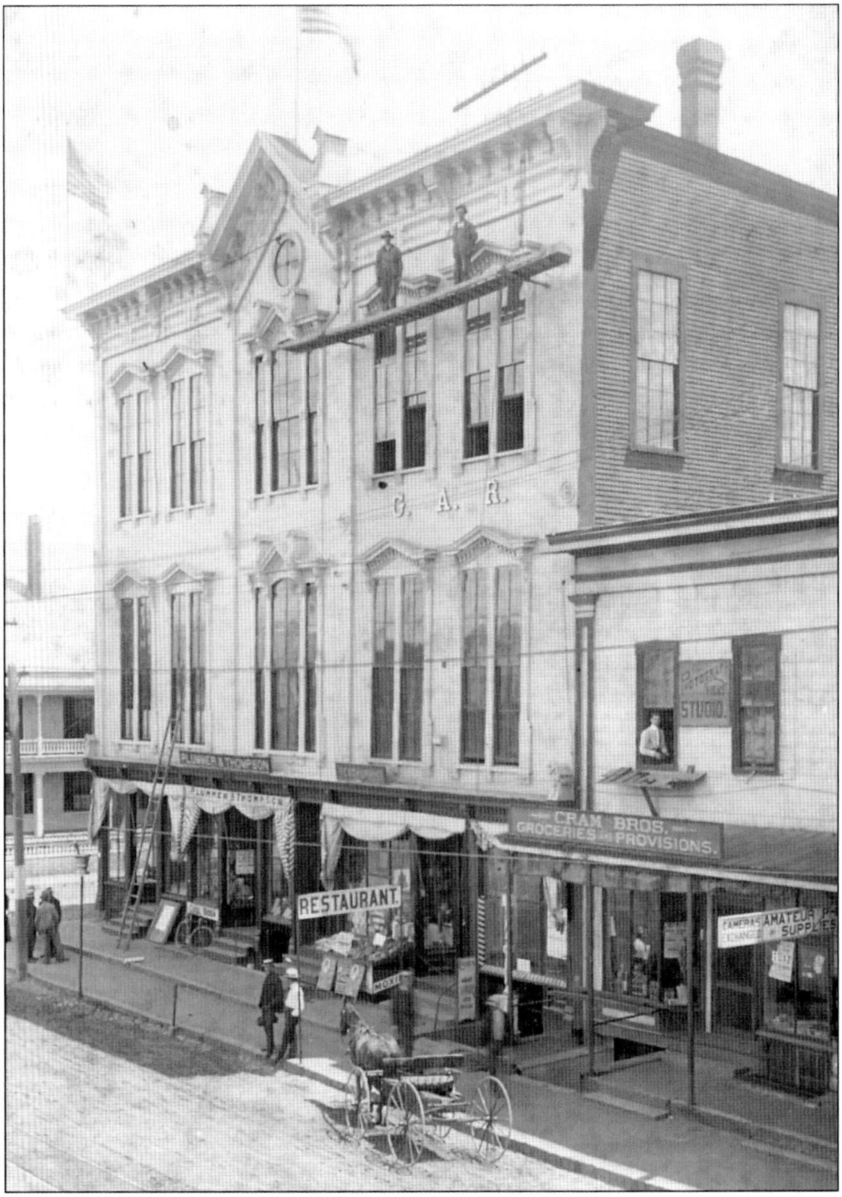

OPERA HOUSE BLOCK, C. 1900. High above Lakeport (later Webster) Square, two well-dressed "painters" survey the scene, while at right, the photographer appears to be tending his natural-light exposures on the slanting shelf. Built by Drs. David F. and Joseph C. Moore on the site of the Weeks Block, which was destroyed by fire in 1881, the Opera House Block has been the centerpiece of Lakefront Square since 1885. An association of Odd Fellows acquired the building in 1893 and the lodge remained in these quarters until 1967. For many years, the Lakeport Post Office occupied the left storefront. In the adjoining two-story Osgood Block, above the Cram Bros. grocery store, Chester D. Andrews's photography studio produced many views of local scenes. The Osgood Block was "reduced to an ice-coated shell" in January 1939, and was replaced by a modern brick First National Store. For many years after the First National closed, Henry Rogers operated the Lakeport 5 Cents to a Dollar Store in this space until his death in 1992.

IMAGES
of America

LAKEPORT

Warren Huse

ARCADIA
PUBLISHING

ISBN 978-0-7385-XXXX-X

Published by Arcadia Publishing
Charleston, South Carolina

Printed in the United States of America

Library of Congress Catalog Card Number: 99-60799

For all general information contact Arcadia Publishing at:
Telephone 843-853-2070
Fax 843-853-0044
E-mail sales@arcadiapublishing.com
For customer service and orders:
Toll-Free 1-888-313-2665

Visit us on the Internet at www.arcadiapublishing.com

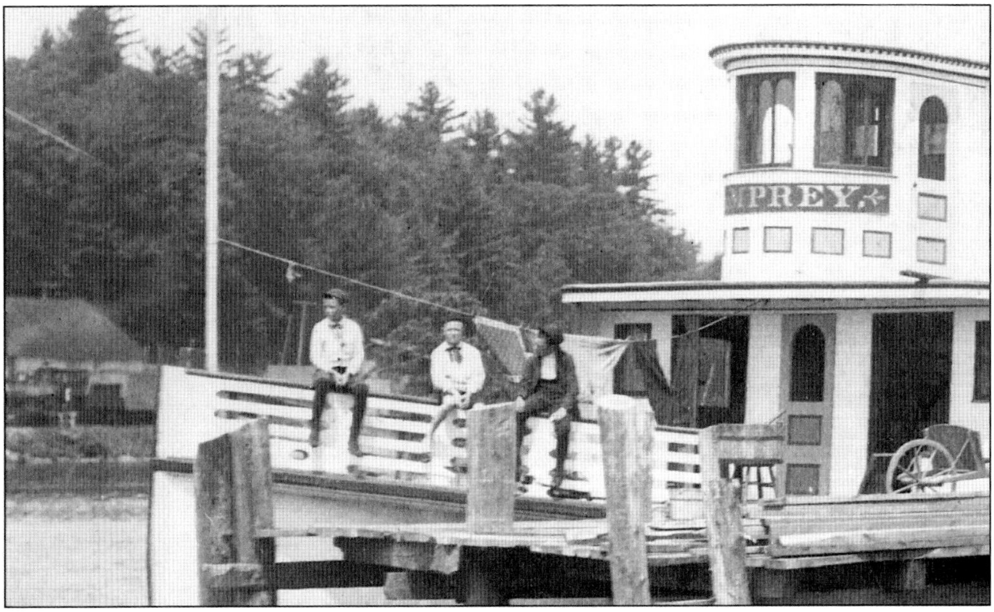

DETAIL, FROM THE PHOTOGRAPH AT THE TOP OF PAGE 117. Three youthful boaters enjoy some leisure at the bow of the steamer *Lamprey* at her dock in Lakeport, *c.* 1890. Meanwhile, a locomotive of the Boston, Concord & Montreal Railroad moves freight on the opposite shore. Built at Long Island in 1882 by Alanson and Robert Lamprey, the vessel burned at her mooring on the Moultonboro Shore in 1892.

COVER *PHOTOGRAPH*: LAKEPORT SQUARE, EARLY 1920S. Trolley car No. 27 of the Laconia Street Railway pauses in front of the Opera House Block. Purchased in 1920 from the Wason Manufacturing Co., of Springfield, Mass., this car was one of only four not manufactured for the line by the Laconia Car Co. The Laconia Street Railway ceased rail operations on August 9, 1925.

Contents

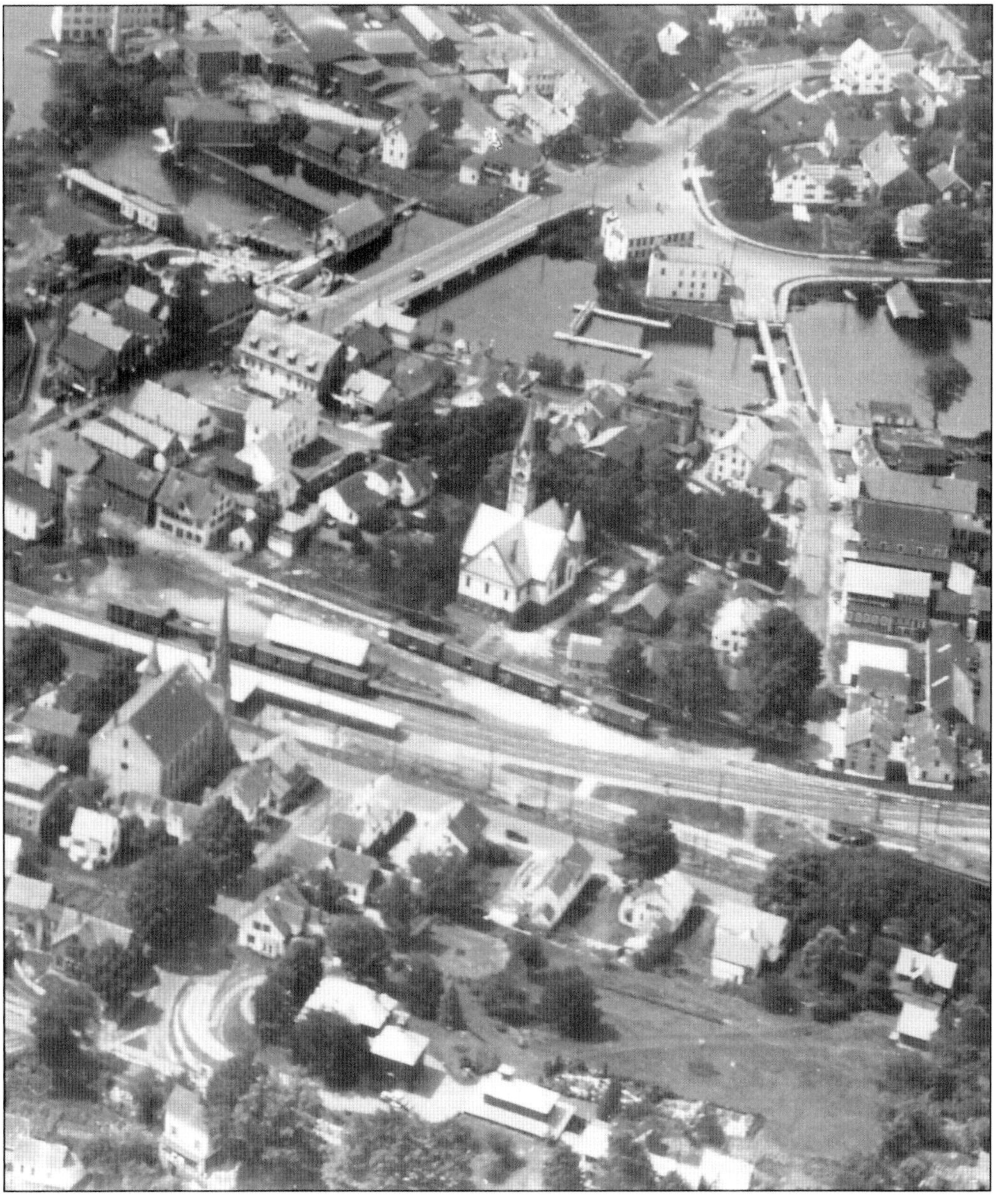

Aerial View, early 1930s, Looking West. The United Baptist Church appears at center, with the Union Avenue Baptist Church (torn down 1940) at left on the near side of the railroad tracks and Union Avenue. The Gold Street Bridge is at upper right, with the GAR Hall at the far end of the bridge. The Piper Block (with mansard roof) is visible on Fore Street, west of the Park Street Church. The Lakeport Dam is just downstream from the Elm Street Bridge. The new Wood's Mill (later Sweaterville) is visible in the upper left corner. Lakeport Square is off the photograph at center left and Lake Paugus is off the photograph at center right.

INTRODUCTION

This volume completes an initial Arcadia trilogy depicting the city of Laconia, New Hampshire. Earlier books have been devoted to Laconia (1995) and The Weirs (1996). As with the previous volumes, the emphasis here is on Lakeport to around 1900, although some later views are included.

Lakeport began as Folsom's Mills when Abraham Folsom settled here in 1766. The area around the outlet from Lake Paugus (earlier called Long Bay) was known to early explorers as the "Lower Weirs," due to Native American fish traps at that location. (The "Upper Weirs" were at today's Weirs Channel.) Nathan Batchelder acquired property and the water privilege in the 1820s and, for a number of years, the settlement was known as Batchelder's Mills. Because of the quantity of logs sawed at the mills, the hamlet was also known for a time as "Slab City." Around the middle of the 19th century, it began to be called Lake Village. In 1892 it renamed itself Lakeport, and in 1893 it became part of the new city of Laconia.

Beginning in the late 1820s, Batchelder and others began the construction of textile mills and, by the 1860s, the manufacture of hosiery, knitting machines, and knitting machine needles had commenced. Meanwhile, the arrival of the Boston, Concord & Montreal Railroad in 1848 opened up the area to greater industrial expansion. Israel Cole and his son Benjamin, among others, began producing heavy machinery. In addition, the railroad located repair shops here, which flourished until close to the end of the century. Lake Village became a retail and professional, as well as an industrial center—rivaling the nearby village of Meredith Bridge (now Downtown Laconia).

Originally divided by the river, between Meredith on the west and Gilford on the east, Lake Village saw the western part of its territory ceded to the new town of Laconia in 1855, then to Gilford in 1876, before the entire village finally became part of the new city of Laconia in 1893.

In 1882, Lake Village and Laconia had been connected by a horse railroad, which was electrified in 1898 and extended to The Weirs in 1899. With its own newspapers, the *Lake Village Times* (begun in 1868) and the successor *Belknap Republican* (early 1900s), the community expressed its own strong identity. Site of several boat-building enterprises, the village was an important steamer port well into the 20th century. Laconia's waterworks and reservoir were built here in the mid-1880s. In 1890, the Lake Shore Railroad began operations, connecting Lake Village with Alton Bay until the mid-1930s, when the line was abandoned.

An event that changed the face of the neighborhood forever was the Great Fire of 1903, which leveled most of the area from Bayside Court and Franklin Street to Belvidere Hill. Lakeport rebuilt and today there is little evidence of the widespread devastation of that long ago day in May.

In the early 1900s, the Scott & Williams Corp. took over much of the real estate occupied by the railroad shops, the Cole Manufacturing Co., Halifax, and other mills. Today, Scott & Williams and its successors are also gone—leaving largely empty space where, once, mighty industrial engines turned out products shipped across the United States and around the world. Today, while essentially a residential section of Laconia, Lakeport has a proud industrial and commercial history and retains its own special identity.

In addition to *The Illustrated Laconian* (1899), I am indebted to Horace G. Whittier's *Historic Sketches of Lakeport* (1915), Major John Aldrich's *Lakeport's Ancient Homes* (1917), Carl F. Blaisdell's *Meredith Parade* (1960), and Theodore Steinberg's *Nature Incorporated: Industrialization and the Waters of New England* (1991). In addition, Elizabeth Durfee Hengen's historical inventory of the Elm Street Bridge area, for the New Hampshire Department of Transportation (November 1996), and the notes of John M. Cox and Theo S. Jewett have been of great assistance.

The work of Ward & Munsey, C.J. Lane, Chester D. Andrews, Harrison Morin, G.H. Tebbetts, and a host of unknown photographers over the years should be recognized for their part in making this book possible.

Among the many who have contributed to this book, I wish to thank especially Richard L. Shetler for photographic support, Robert C. Fay, Arthur A. Tilton, Dana Philbrook, Charles O. Hopkins, Laconia Fire Chief George Landry, Laurence W. Leonard, Jim Dodge, Gordon A. Dubois, the United Baptist Church of Lakeport, Ridgely Mauck, Mrs. Norman S. Weeks, and the late Marge Lachance, among a host of others who have helped with research and provided images. Specific acknowledgments are provided on p. 128.

As always, Gilbert S. Center and Julie Upham have been unstinting in their assistance.

The enthusiastic support and cooperation of the staff of the Laconia Public Library, its director, Carol Sykes, and board of trustees, and the officers and directors of the Laconia Historical and Museum Society are profoundly appreciated.

I also wish to acknowledge the unwavering support of my editors at Arcadia, Sarah Maineri, Rebecca Heflin, Cindy Byrd, Heather Roy, and Michael Joseph Guillory, and the technicians who input the photographs, Paul Webb and Hazel Devera. Kirsty Sutton's encouragement has again been instrumental in the completion of this project.

To the memory of Robert F. Dearborn (1932–1996), organizer of the city's centennial observances in 1992–1993, founder of the Laconia Museum Society, and president at the time of his death of the Laconia Historical Society, this volume is dedicated.

Warren D. Huse

One

Laconia to Lakeport Square

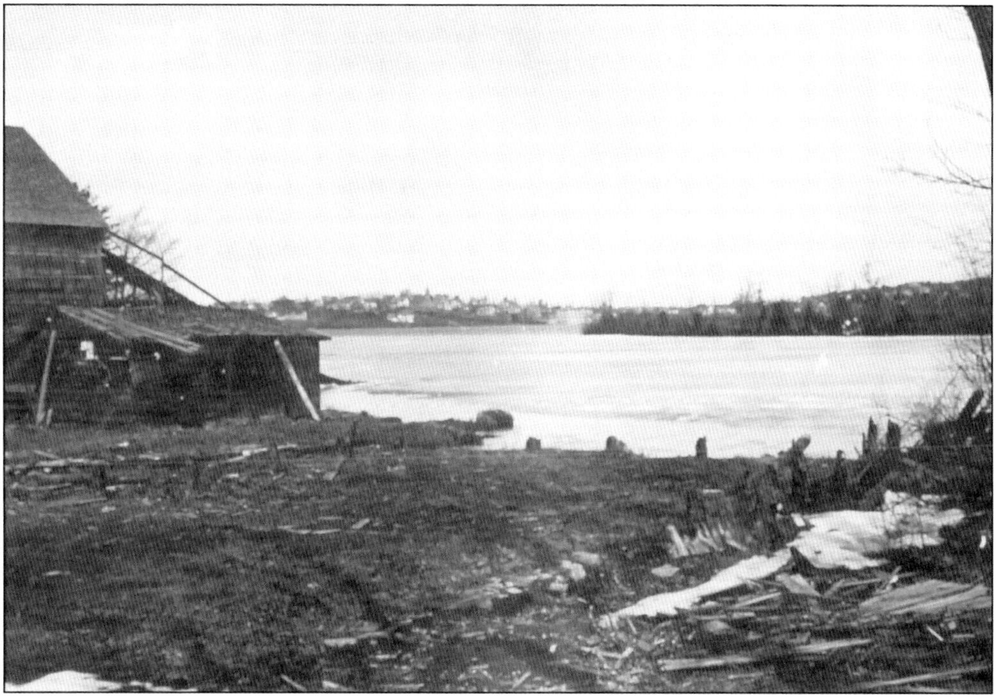

Lakeport (in Distance) from North Main Street, Laconia, c. 1930. Wood's Mill is the white building at center on the far shore. The Wilcox & McGowan Icehouse on the near shore of Lake Opechee, left foreground, represented the thriving ice industry of the late 1880s through World War II, after which electromechanical refrigeration replaced the annual winter ice harvests. This icehouse was destroyed in the Great Hurricane of 1938 but was rebuilt. It was ultimately torn down in 1943. The Opechee Park bathing beach is off the photograph at right.

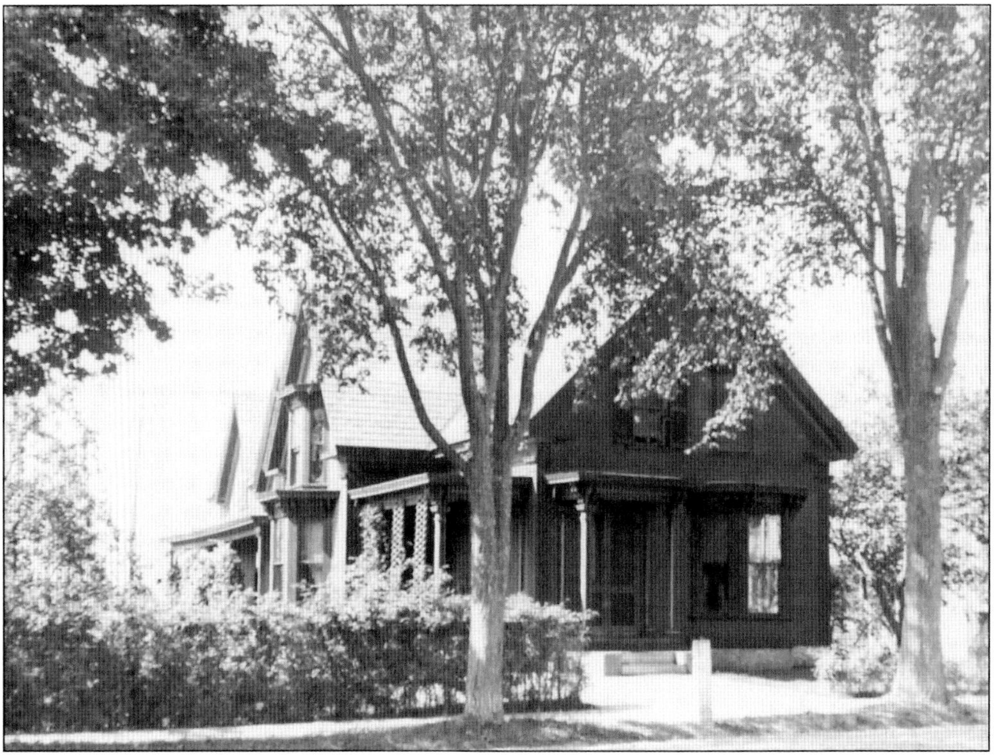

Dr. Joseph C. Moore House, 594 Union Avenue. In addition to his career as a physician, Dr. Moore founded the *Manchester Union* newspaper and owned the Halifax Hosiery Mills in Lakeport, among other interests.

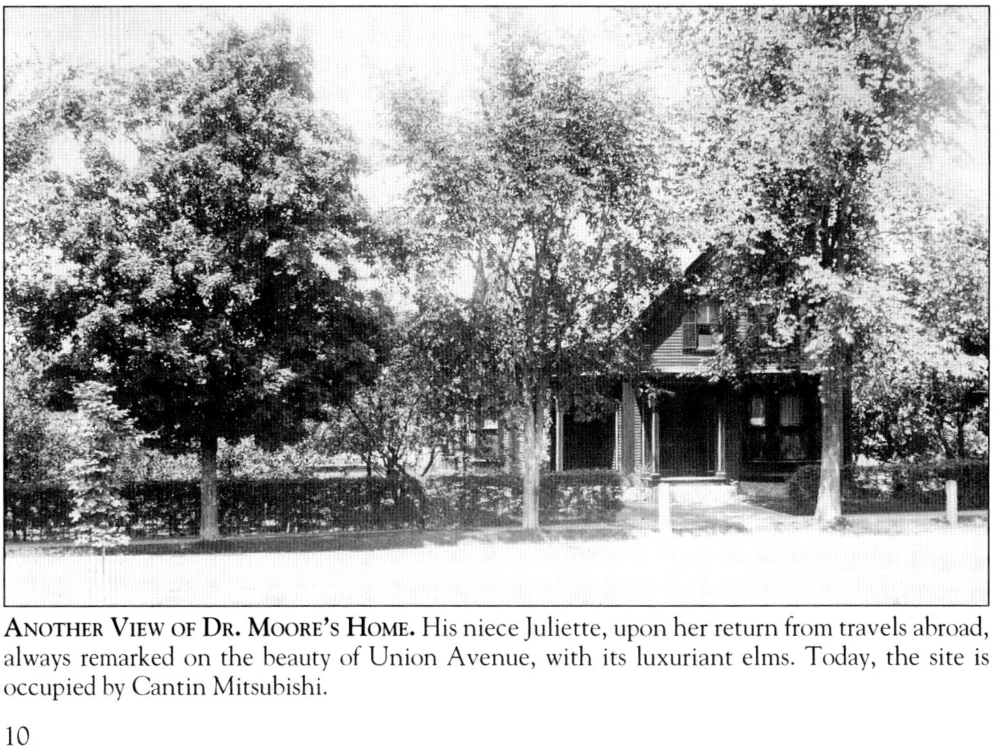

Another View of Dr. Moore's Home. His niece Juliette, upon her return from travels abroad, always remarked on the beauty of Union Avenue, with its luxuriant elms. Today, the site is occupied by Cantin Mitsubishi.

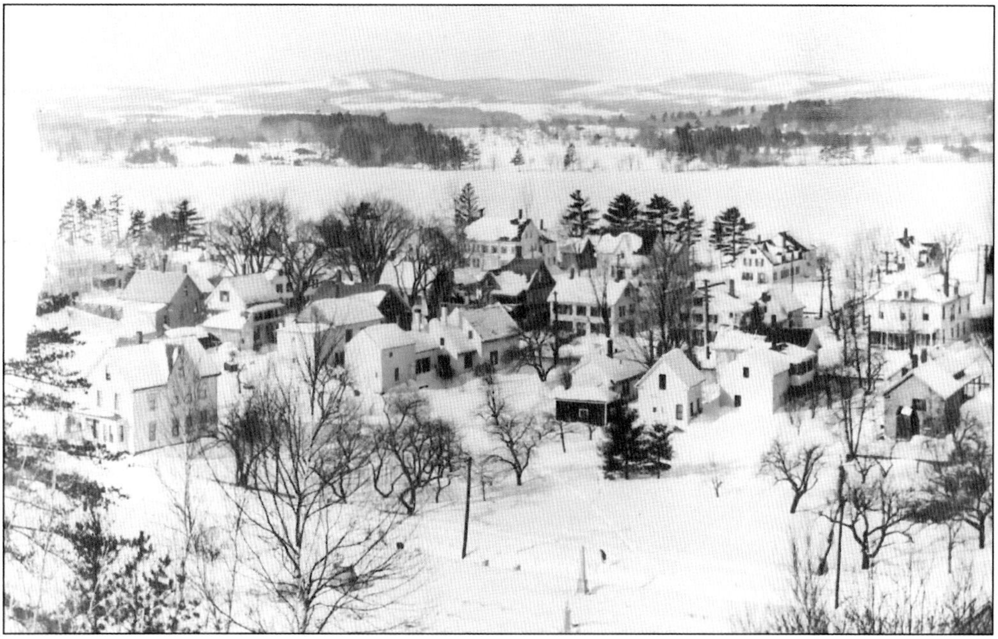

MECHANIC STREET, UNION AVENUE, AND THE MOULTON STREET NEIGHBORHOOD FROM ABOVE HILLSIDE CEMETERY. Lake Opechee and its northwestern shore are at the top of the photograph. Today, although most of the open space in the foreground still remains, the residential neighborhood has been largely replaced by commercial development. Cantin Chevrolet is now just off the photograph at left.

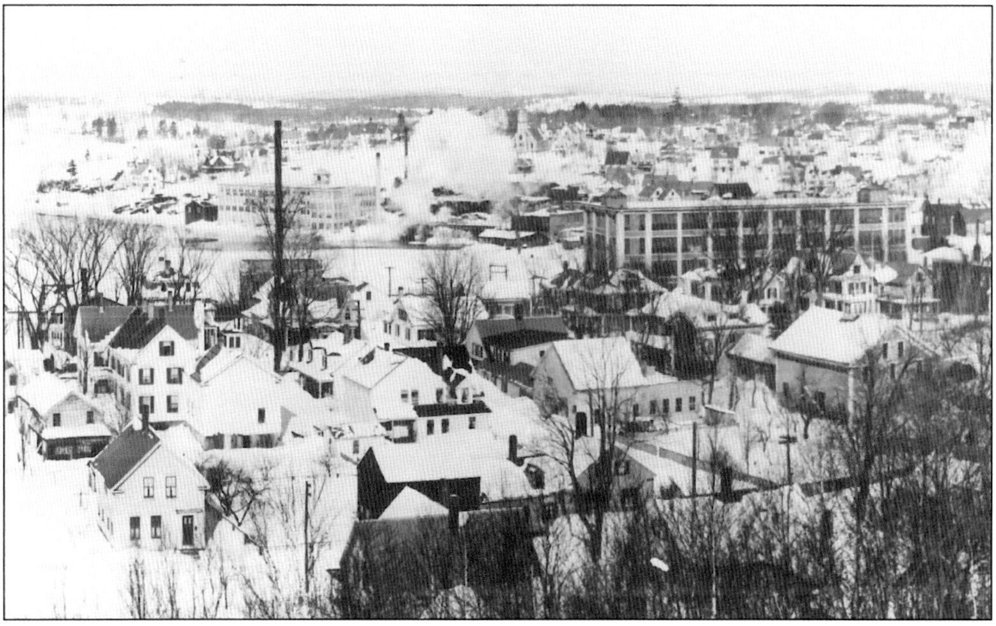

MECHANIC STREET AND UNION AVENUE, SOUTH OF LAKEPORT SQUARE. Wood's Mill appears at the upper left, on the far shore of Lake Opechee; Building 25 of Scott & Williams Inc. dominates the upper right. Original Our Lady of the Lakes Church is visible at the upper center.

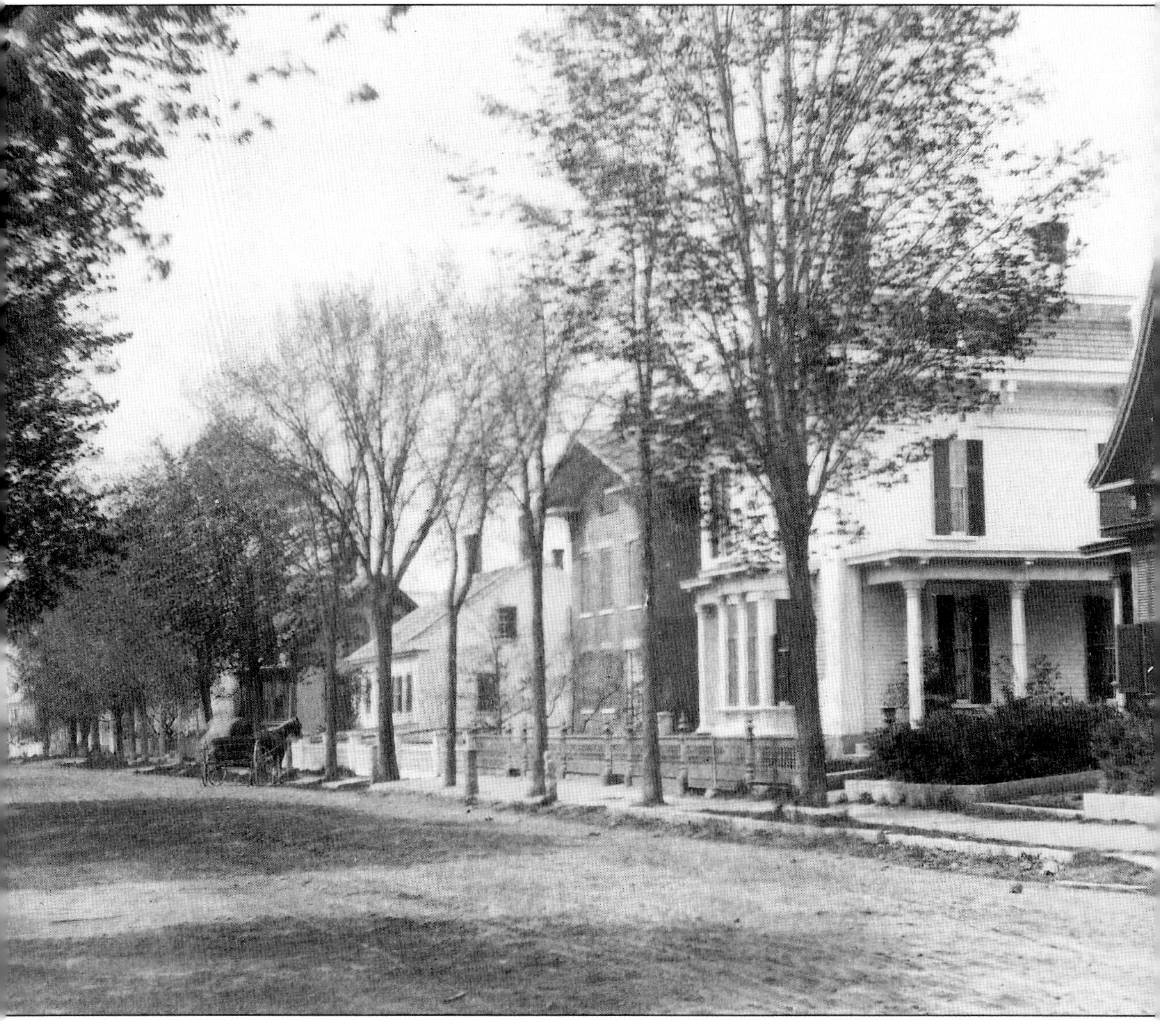

UNION AVENUE, LOOKING SOUTH IN THE 1870S. Lakeport Square is off the photograph at right. The imposing frame residence of Stephen B. Cole, at center right (see next page), burned in 1997. Cole, a nephew of industrialist Benjamin J. Cole, was captain of the steamer *Lady of the Lake* on Lake Winnipesaukee for a number of years. He was also cashier of the Lakeport National Bank and treasurer of the Citizens' Telephone Company.

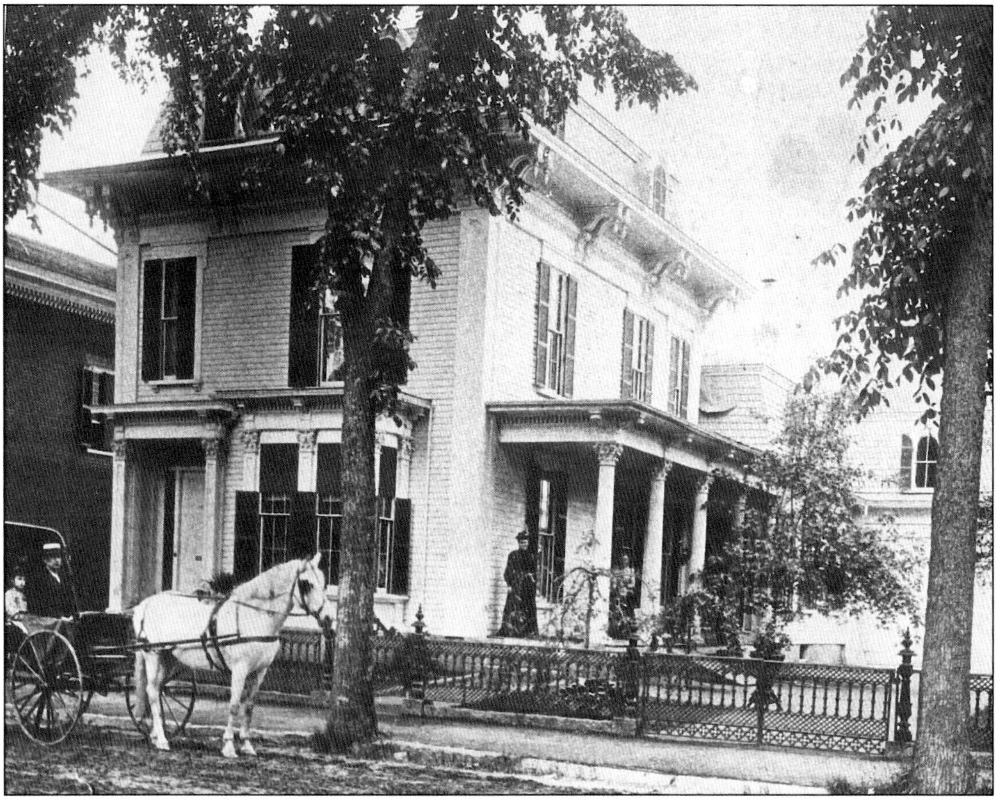

STEPHEN B. COLE HOUSE, 688 UNION AVENUE. Cole and his daughter Virginia occupy the horse-drawn buggy while figures in their Sunday best watch from the Italianate piazza.

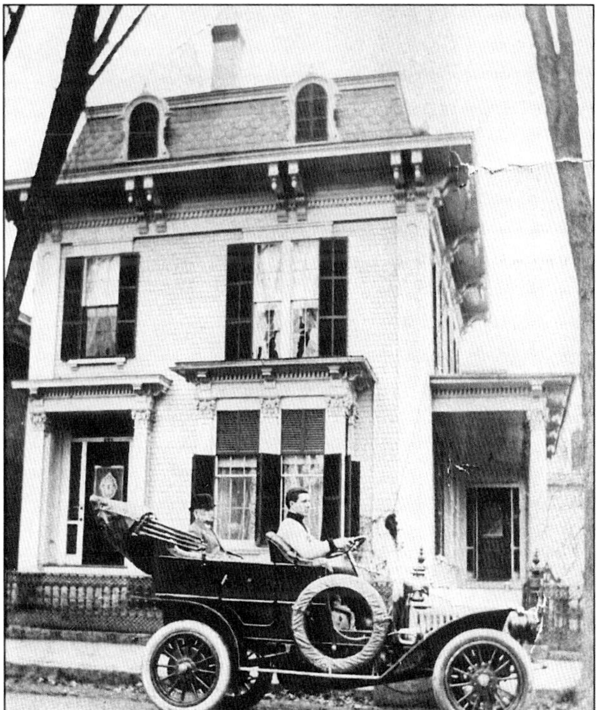

STEPHEN B. COLE. In later years, Cole was chauffeured by Walter "Bucky" Boyson. Bucky ultimately married his employer's daughter, Virginia.

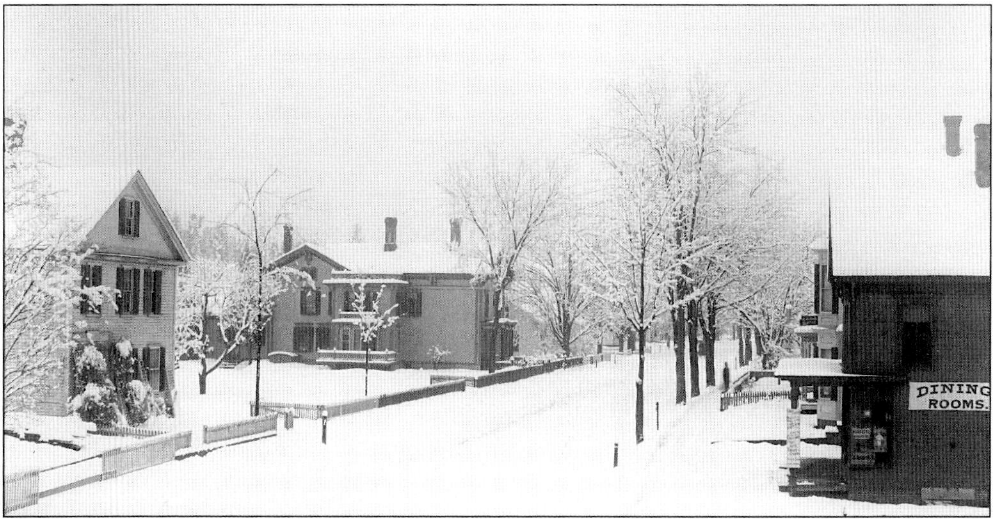

Union Avenue, Looking South from Mount Belknap House (off photo, left) and Quimby Block (off photo, right). The Adams-Moulton House is at left, with the Cole-Quinby House at center left. The building at right has survived through a multitude of occupancies.

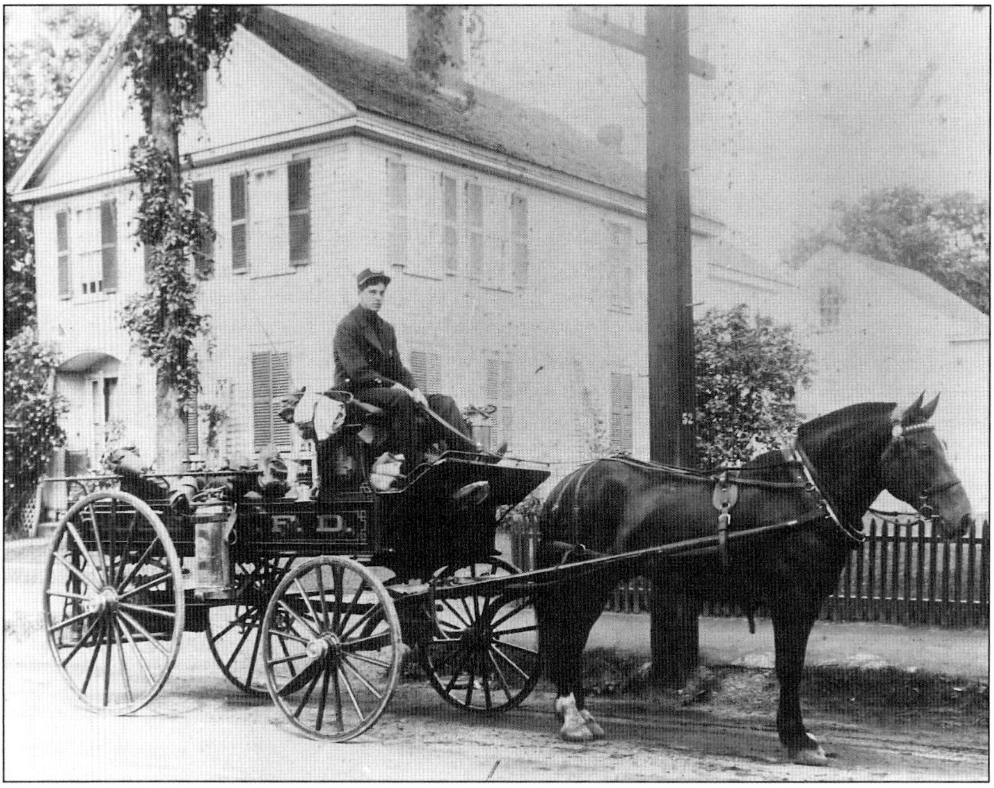

Carl E. Wallace, Age 16, later Proprietor of the Foxy Excursion Boats, at Reins of Lakeport's Hose Co. 4 Wagon. The Adams-Moulton House at 743 Union Avenue (in the background) still exists with its outbuildings, between today's Lake Village Apartments high-rise and the Robbins Auto Parts store.

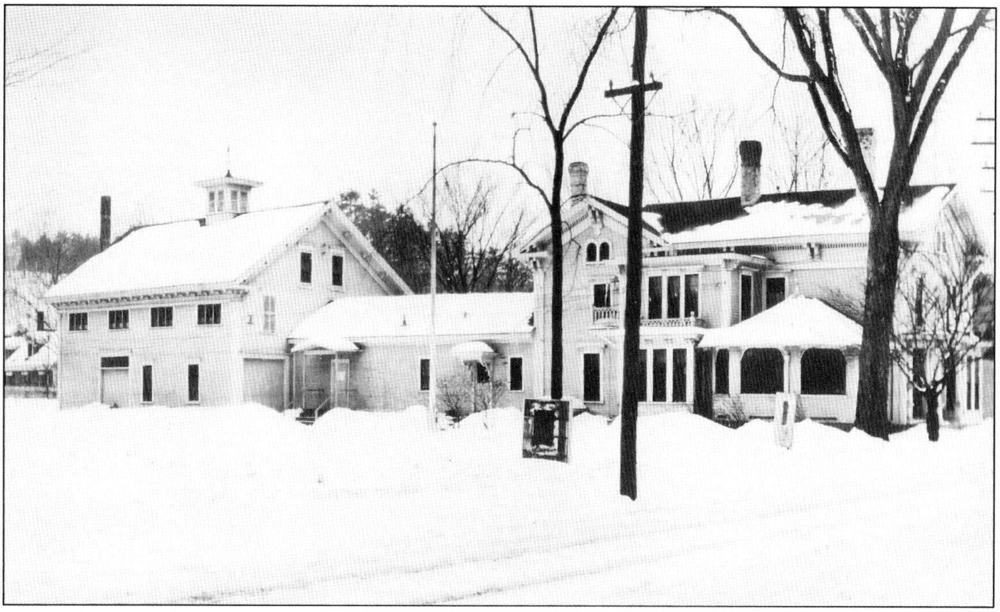

Cole-Quinby House at 713 Union Avenue. The son-in-law of prominent industrialist Benjamin J. Cole (see p. 67), Henry B. Quinby was governor of New Hampshire from 1909 to 1911.

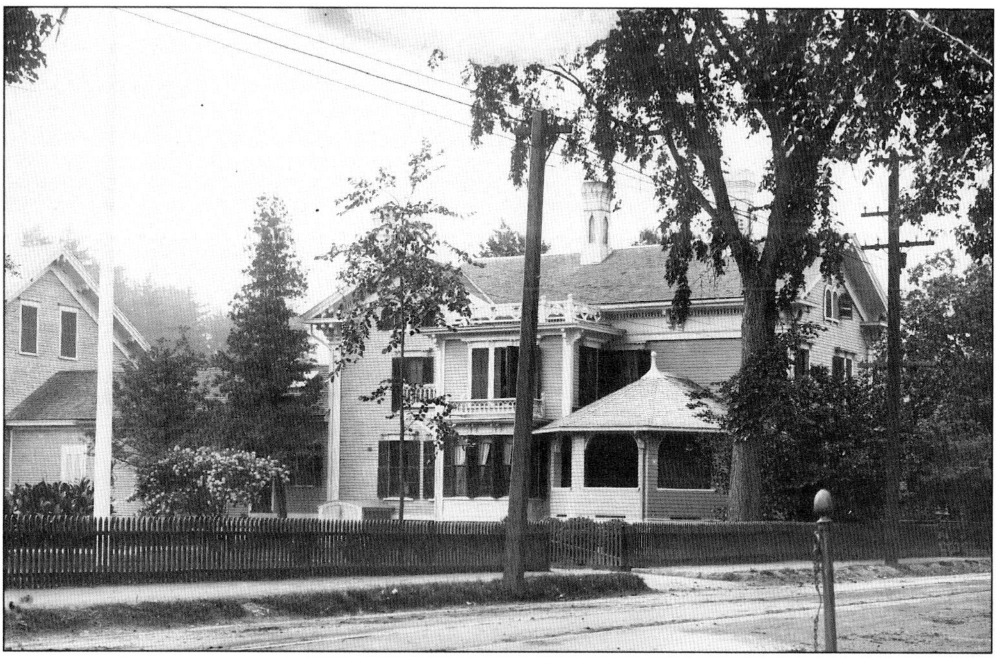

Another View of the Cole-Quinby House. In later years, the property was occupied by the Knights of Pythias and is today site of the Robbins Auto Parts store.

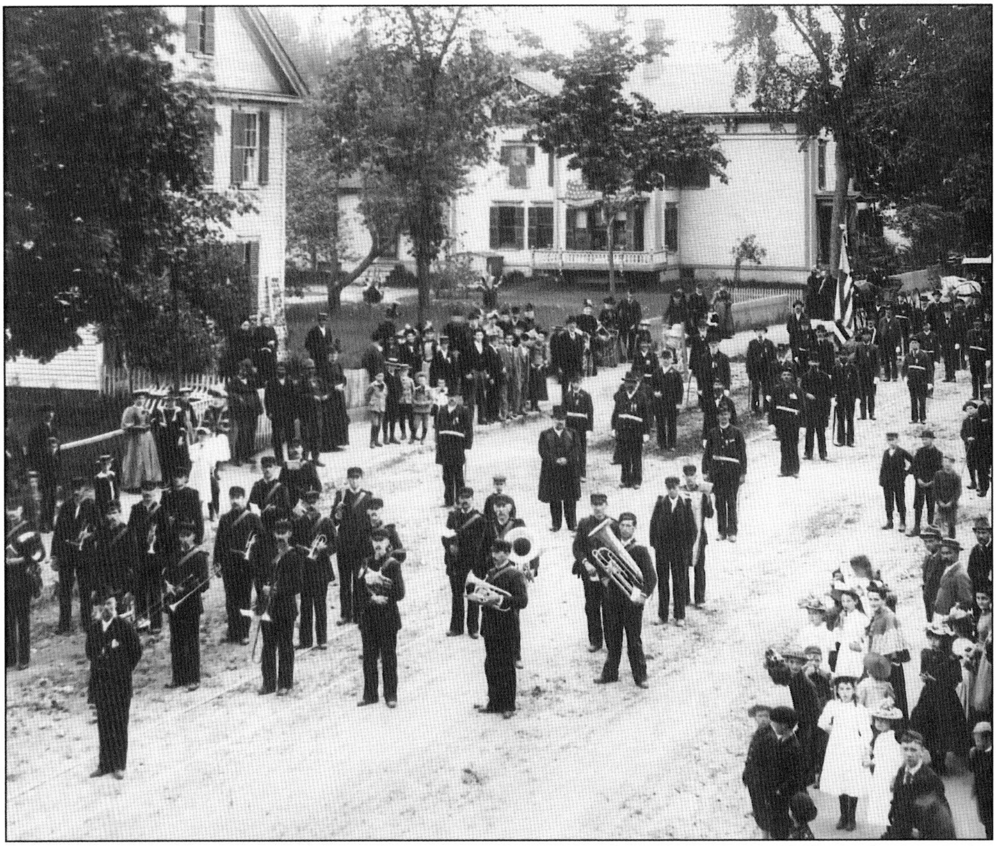

A PARADE PAUSES ON UNION AVENUE. The Adams-Moulton House is at left, with the Cole-Quinby House at top center.

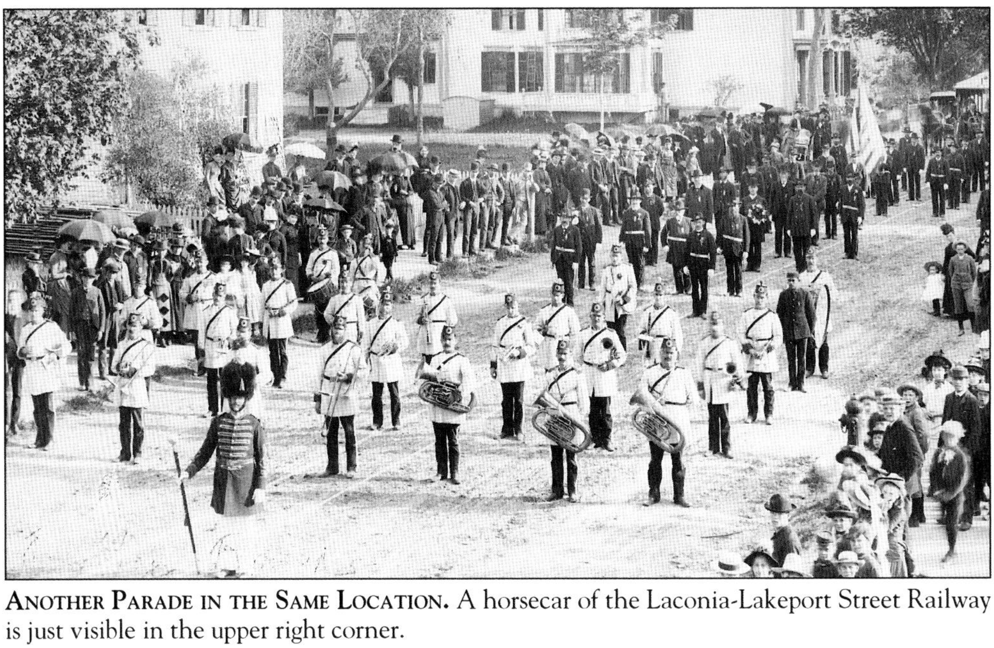

ANOTHER PARADE IN THE SAME LOCATION. A horsecar of the Laconia-Lakeport Street Railway is just visible in the upper right corner.

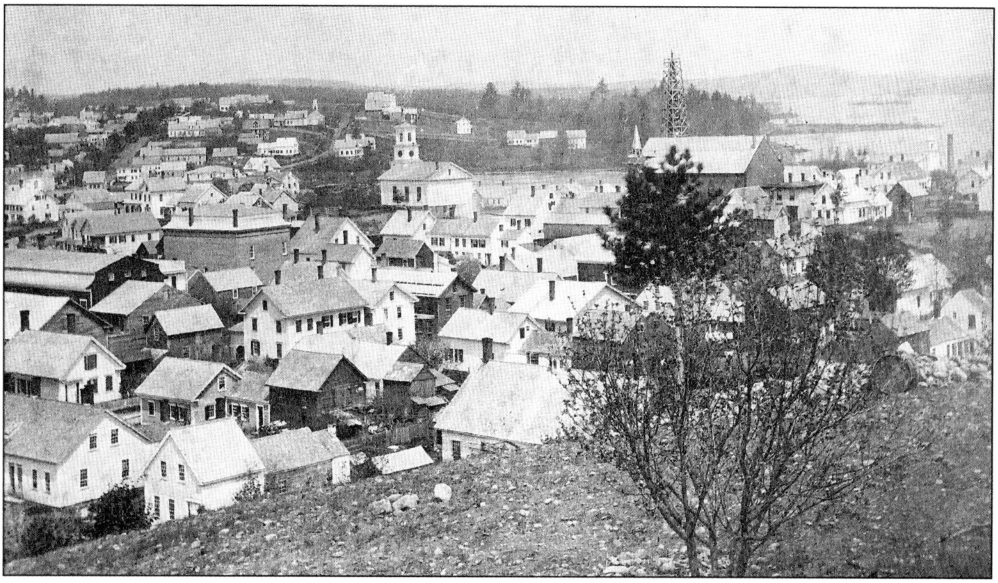

Lake Village, c. 1871. The Free Will Baptist Church (burned 1890) is at top center. The Union Avenue Baptist Church (demolished 1940) appears at right, with construction of its Gothic Revival spire in progress.

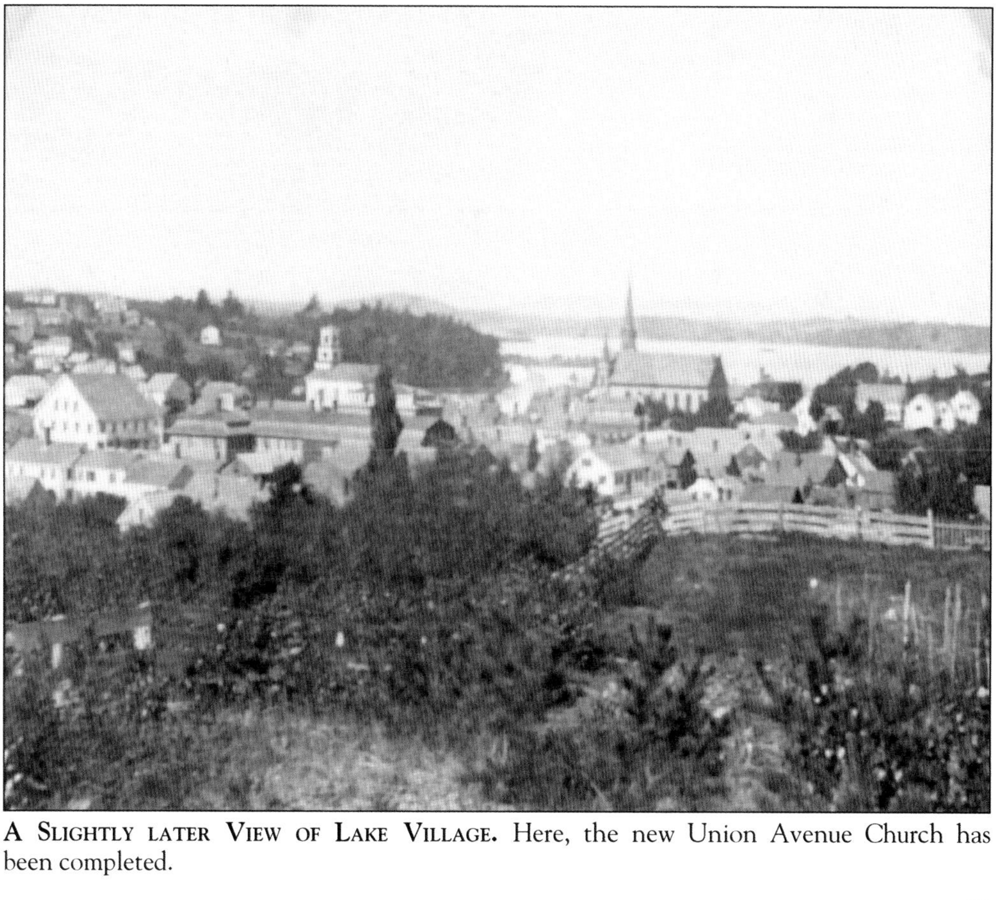

A Slightly later View of Lake Village. Here, the new Union Avenue Church has been completed.

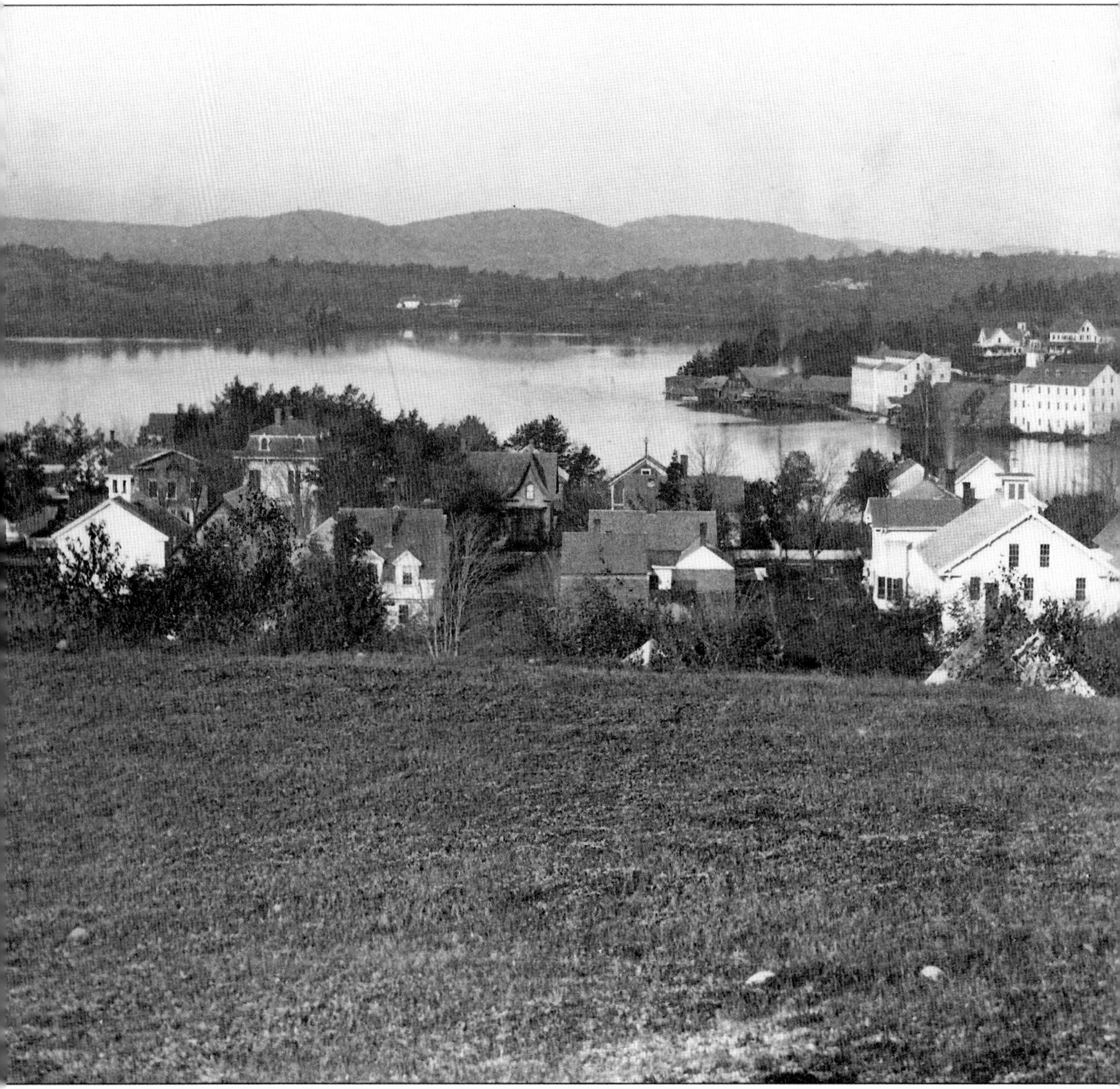

LAKE VILLAGE, C. 1870S. Early-19th-century mills on the west side appear at center right. Wood's Mill is the white building with the bell tower, upriver from the white mill structure with clerestory roofs (see pp. 72–73.) Today's Mechanic Street and Union Avenue run from left to right in the center of the photograph, with Lake Opechee beyond.

Two

Lakeport (Webster) Square

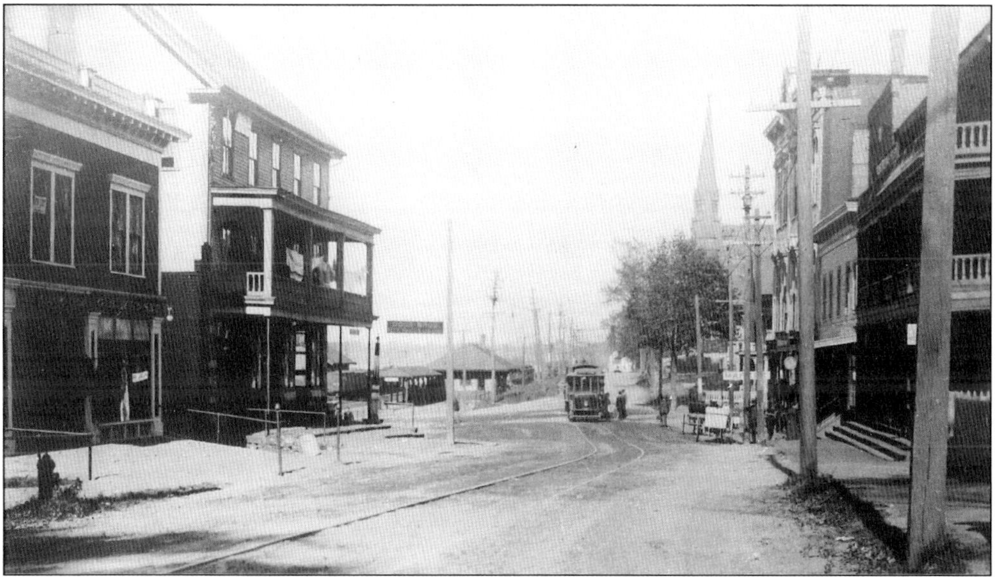

Lakeport (now Webster) Square, Looking North, c. 1905. The railroad station, opened February 7, 1900, is at left beyond the trolley car. The Quimby and Morgan Blocks are at near left; the Mount Belknap House is at near right, with the Opera House Block beyond the two-story Osgood Block at center right. Following a major fire, December 17, 1911, the Mount Belknap House (see p. 22) was remodeled, removing the mansard roof and porches and substituting two two-story bow windows on each side of the entrance. The square at the intersection of Union Avenue, Clinton, and Elm Streets was designated Webster Square in 1922, honoring the memory of Bugler Earl A. Webster, killed in the Argonne while serving with Company E of the 103rd Infantry during World War I. Earlier, he had served with the First New Hampshire Regiment on the Mexican border.

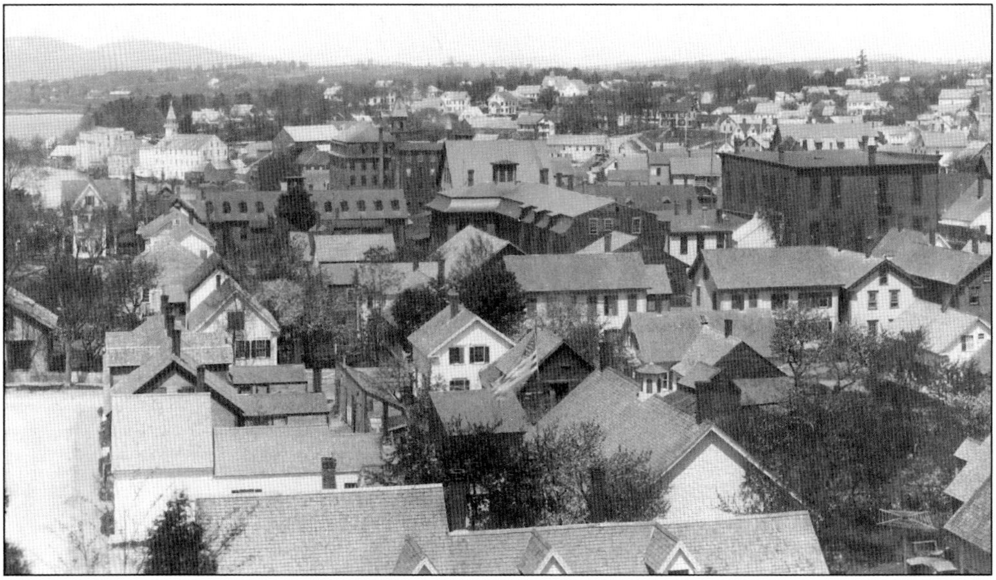

LAKEPORT SQUARE AREA, LOOKING WEST FROM COLE'S HILL, C. 1895. The Opera House Block is at right and the Mount Belknap House is at center, with the Morgan Block just beyond. Wood's Mill (with bell tower) is visible on the shore of Lake Opechee, upper left.

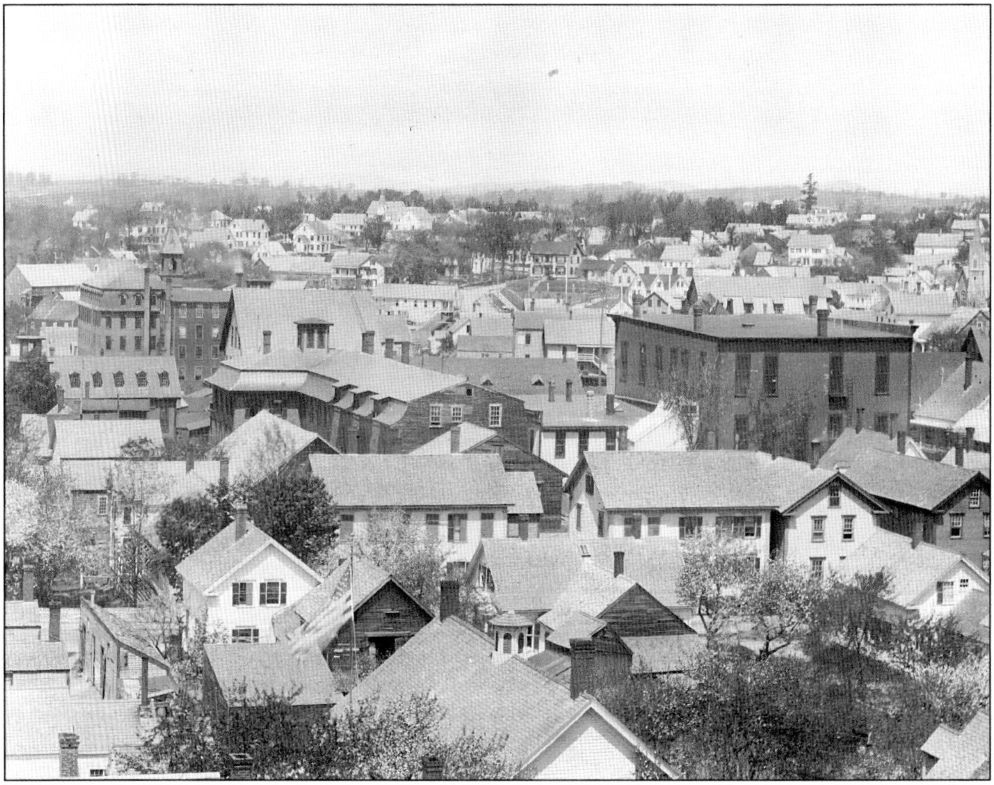

A CLOSE-UP OF THE SAME VIEW. The cupola of the Mount Belknap House partly obscures the roof of the Morgan Block. Beyond the low building with the dormers of the Cole Manufacturing Co., at left, was the Bayside Mill. The Morgan Block obscures most of the Halifax Mill.

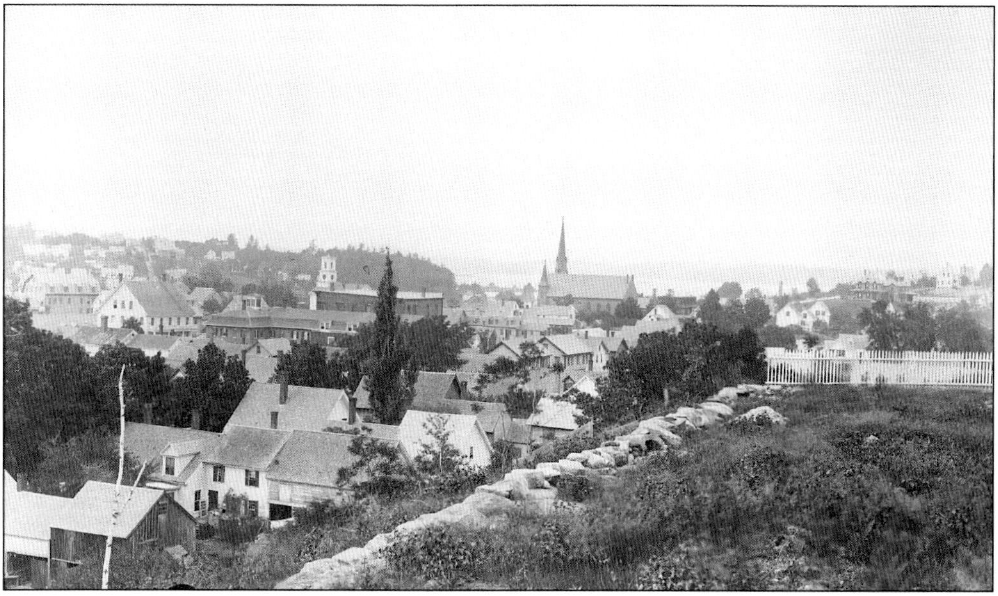

Lakeport from Cole's Hill, Looking Northwest, c. 1880. The Free Will Baptist Church, left of center, burned in December 1890 and was rebuilt as today's Park Street (United Baptist) Church. The Union Avenue Baptist Church, center, had been rebuilt in Gothic Revival style, 1868–1871.

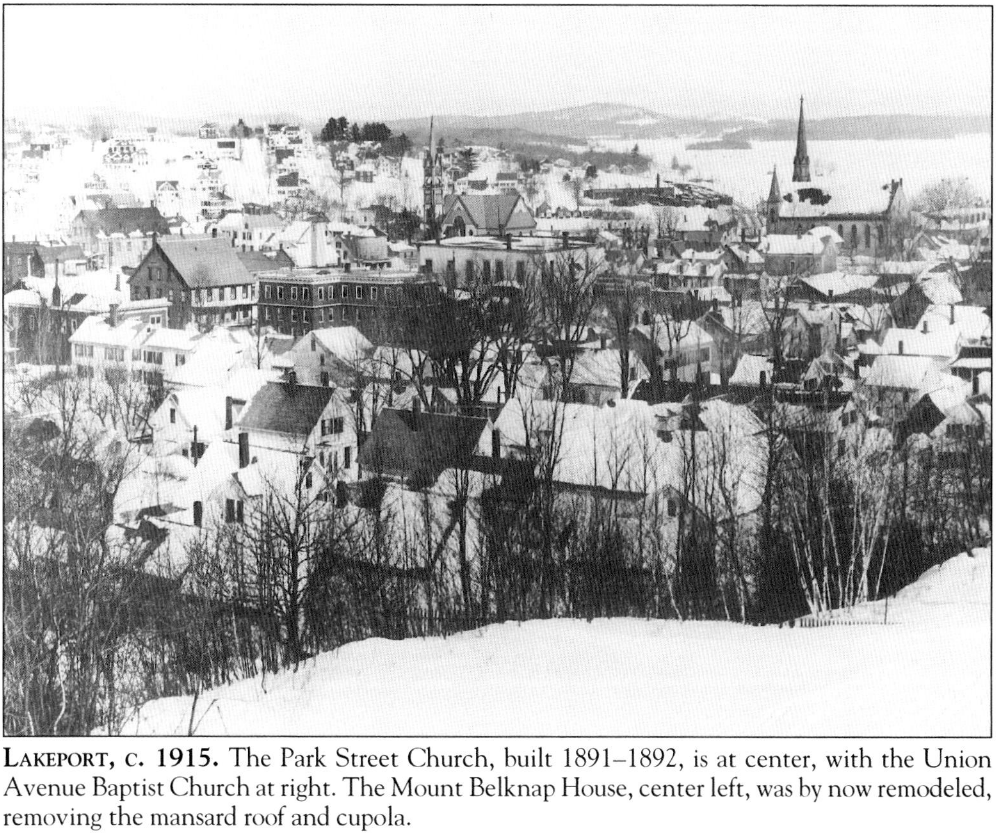

Lakeport, c. 1915. The Park Street Church, built 1891–1892, is at center, with the Union Avenue Baptist Church at right. The Mount Belknap House, center left, was by now remodeled, removing the mansard roof and cupola.

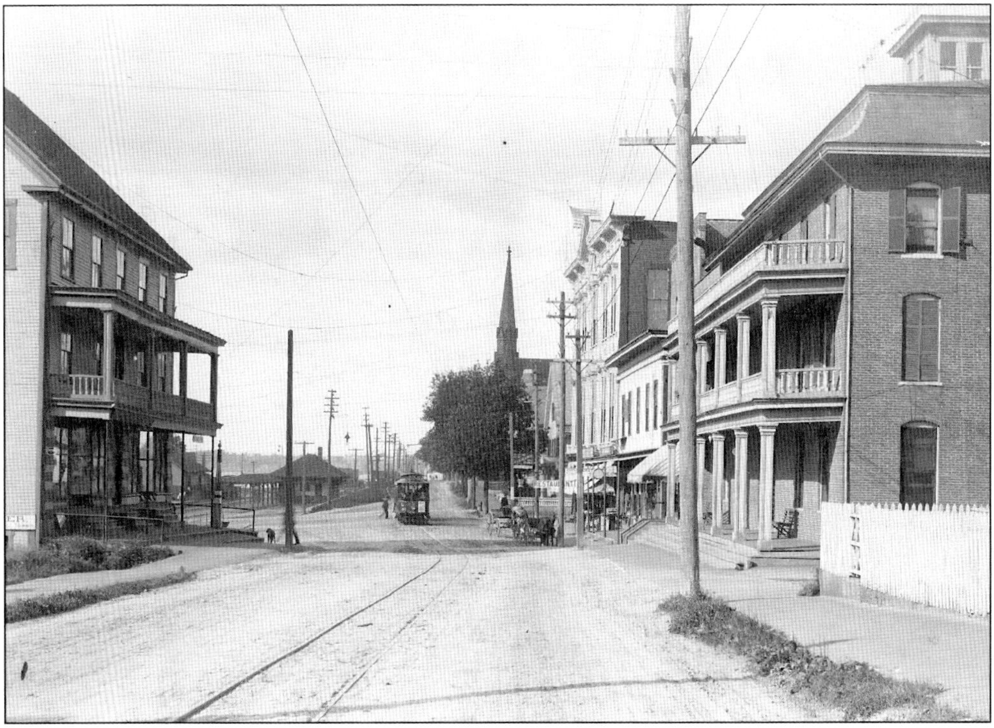

Another View of Lakeport Square, c. 1905. The Cushing and Osgood Blocks are visible at right between the Mount Belknap House and the Opera House.

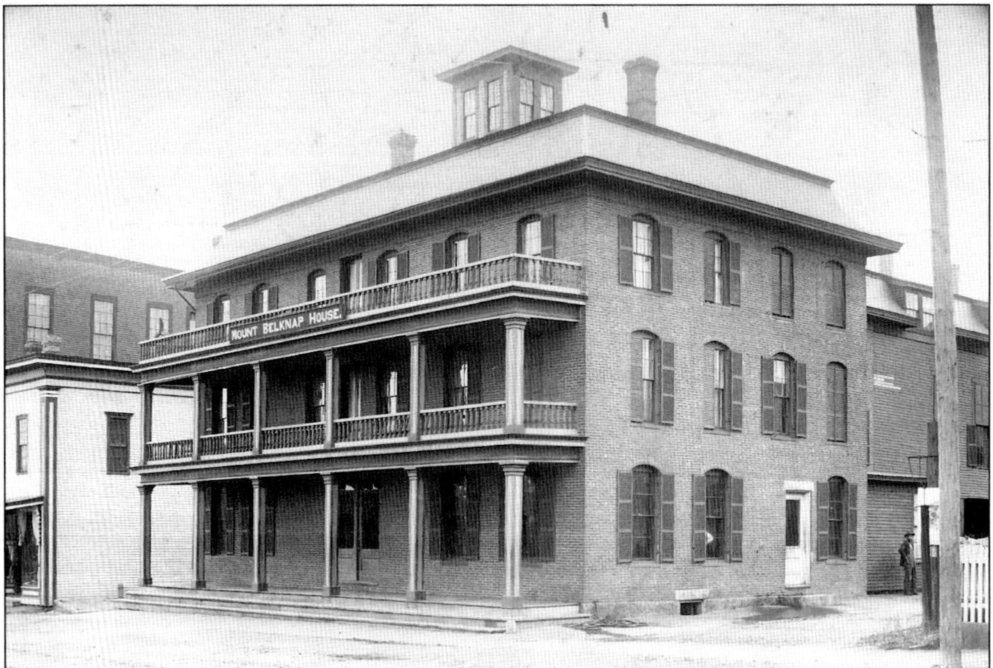

Mount Belknap House before Construction of Cushing Block.

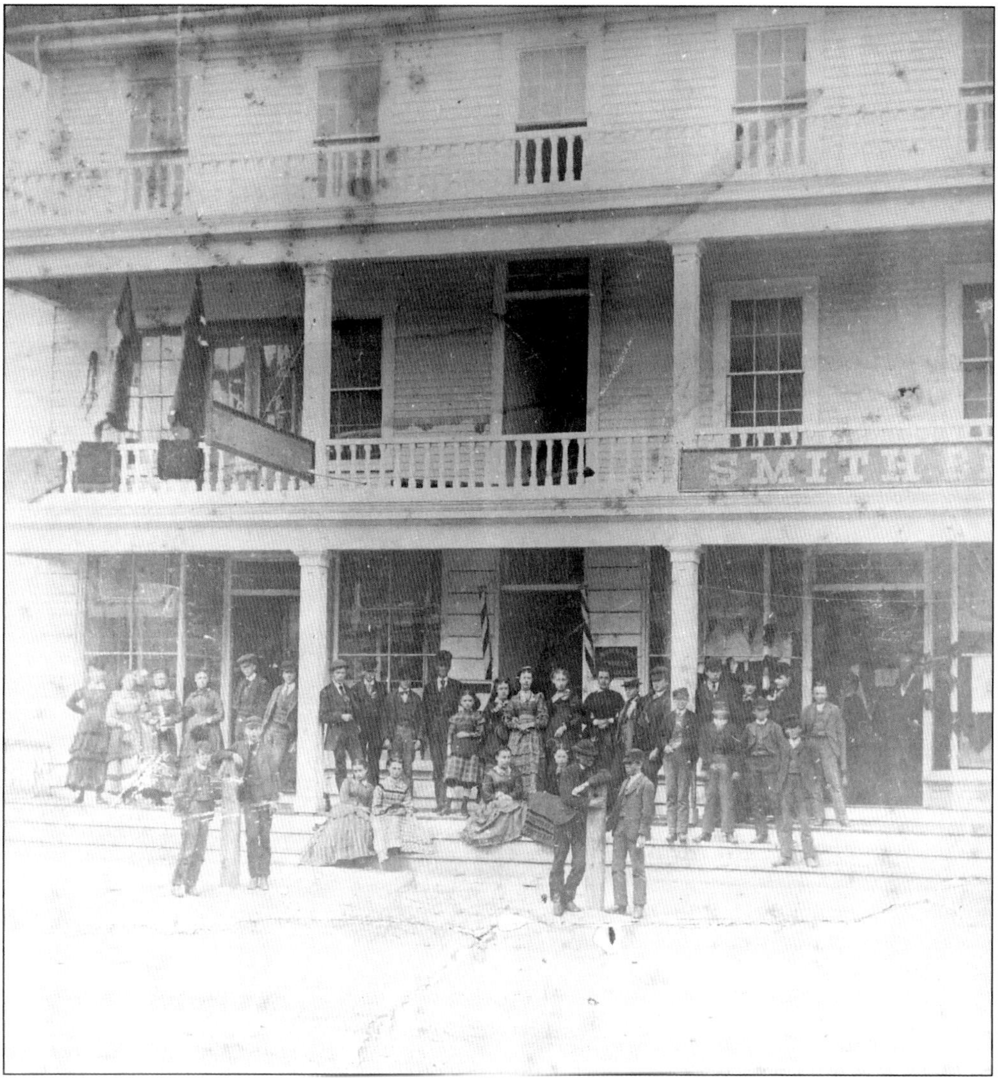

Morgan Block. Built in 1849 by Langdon G. Morgan, it was raised up in 1868 and an additional story put under it by then-owners James H. Plummer and George W. Sanders. Among tenants of the hall on the top floor were the *Lake Village Times* in 1868 and, later, the Darius A. Drake Post No. 36 of the GAR. In the late 1890s, the exterior of the building was treated to a coat of startling chrome yellow paint. The basement was used for a time as the railroad waiting room until construction of the new passenger depot, 1899–1900. The structure, vacant for several years, was razed in 1965. Today, the site is part of Torrey Park.

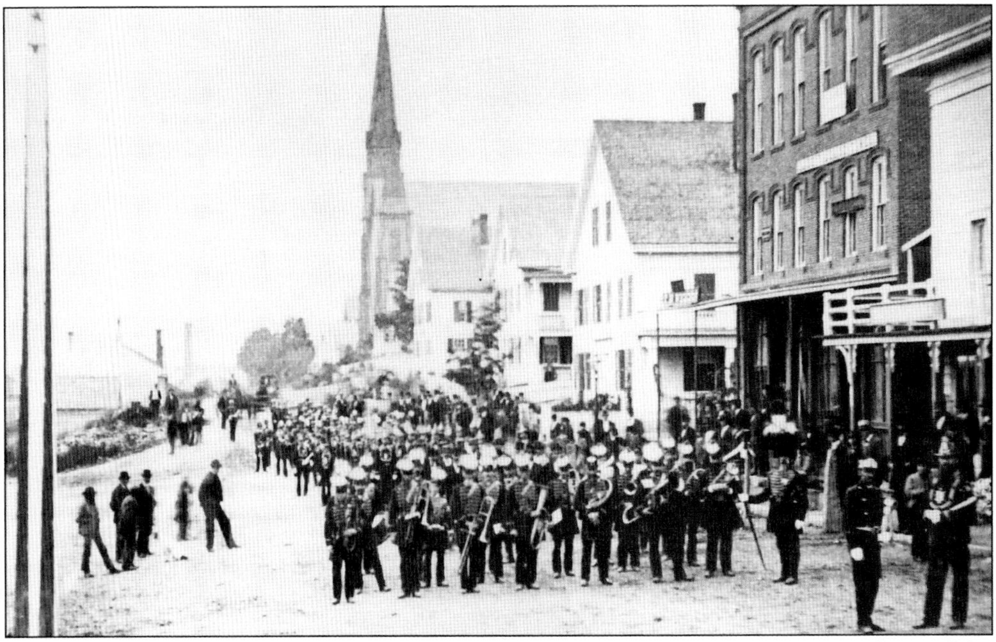

LAKEPORT SQUARE IN THE LATE 1870S. A parade, led by Rublee's Band, pauses in front of the Weeks Block, which burned in 1881. Train sheds of Boston, Concord & Montreal Railroad are visible at left.

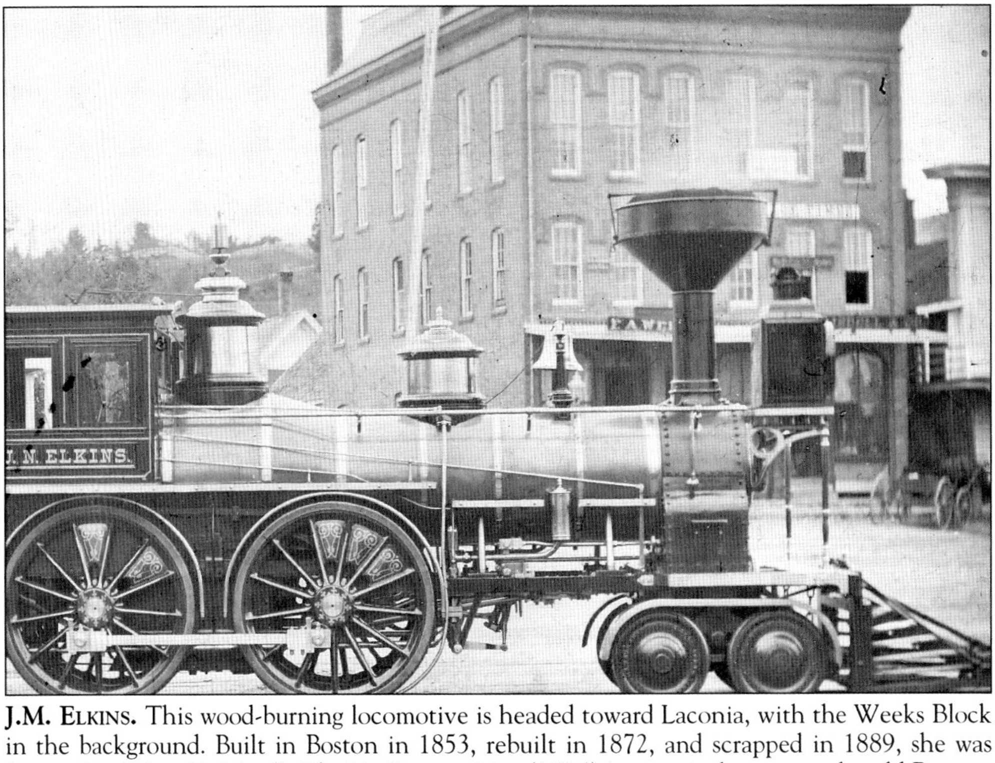

J.M. ELKINS. This wood-burning locomotive is headed toward Laconia, with the Weeks Block in the background. Built in Boston in 1853, rebuilt in 1872, and scrapped in 1889, she was featured in Edgar T. Mead's *The Up Country Line* (1975) in a typical run over the old Boston, Concord & Montreal Railroad. Elkins had been the first superintendent of the railroad.

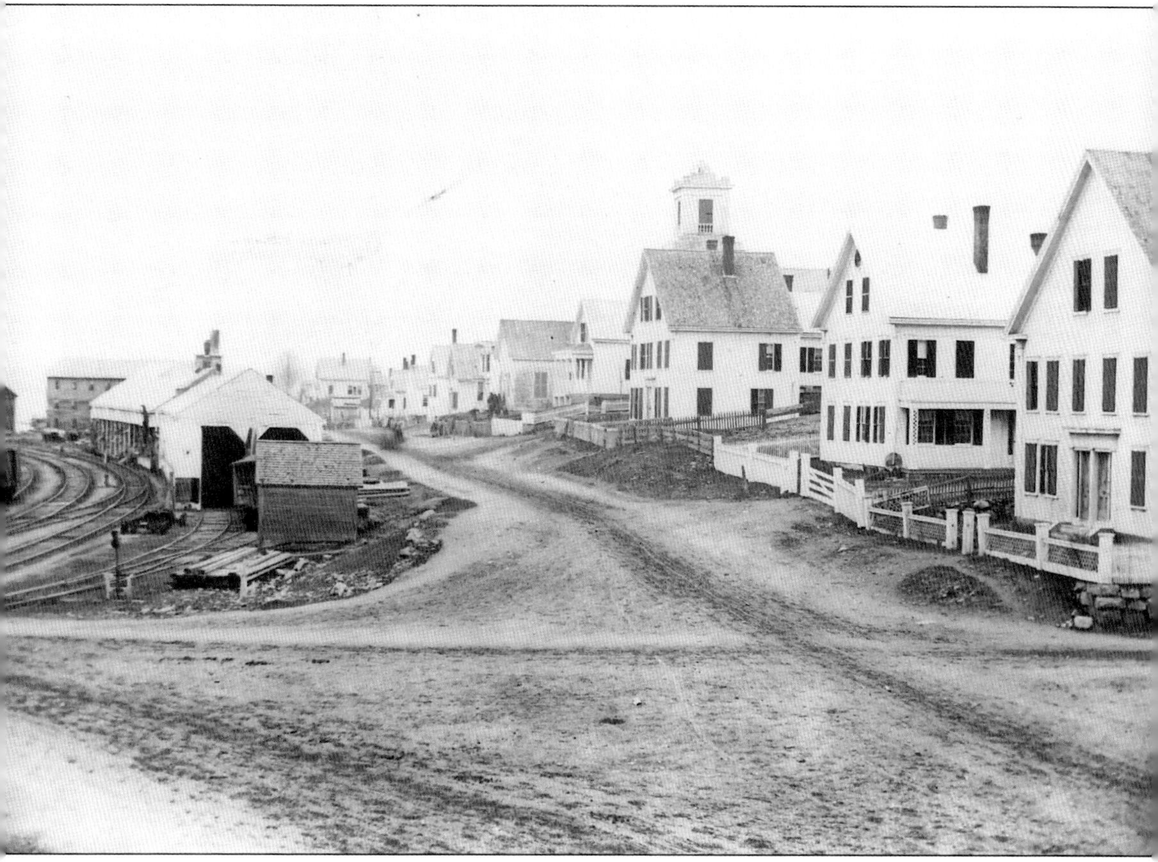

LAKEPORT SQUARE, C. 1865. The belfry of the Union Avenue Baptist Church is visible just beyond the dwelling later known as the Dr. Hodgdon House, center right. Today, much-modified architecturally, the old dwelling still remains at 831 Union Avenue. The other houses at right occupy the site of today's parking lot and Fratello's Restaurant. Train sheds of the Boston, Concord & Montreal Railroad are at left.

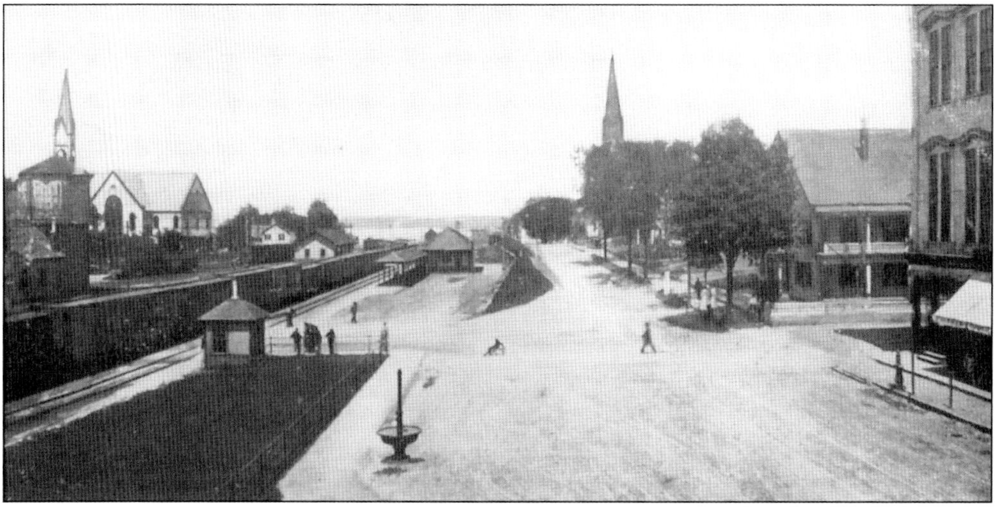

Lakeport Square, c. 1905. The Gothic Revival spire, added 1868–1871, of the Union Avenue Baptist Church appears at center right in the distance, and the new passenger depot (opened 1900) is at center, replacing earlier train sheds. The Park Street Church is visible at left.

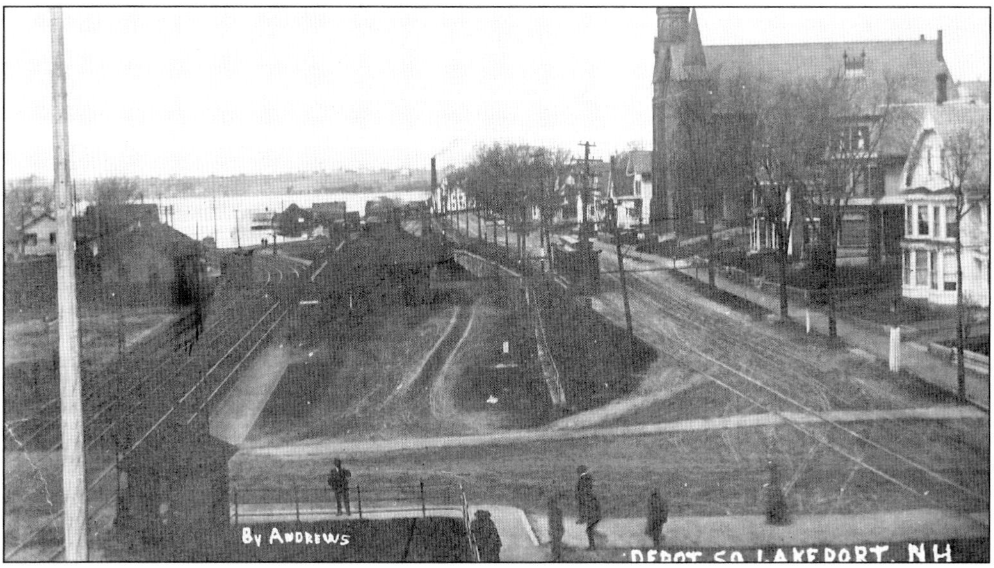

A Closer View, with a Trolley Car North of the Square.

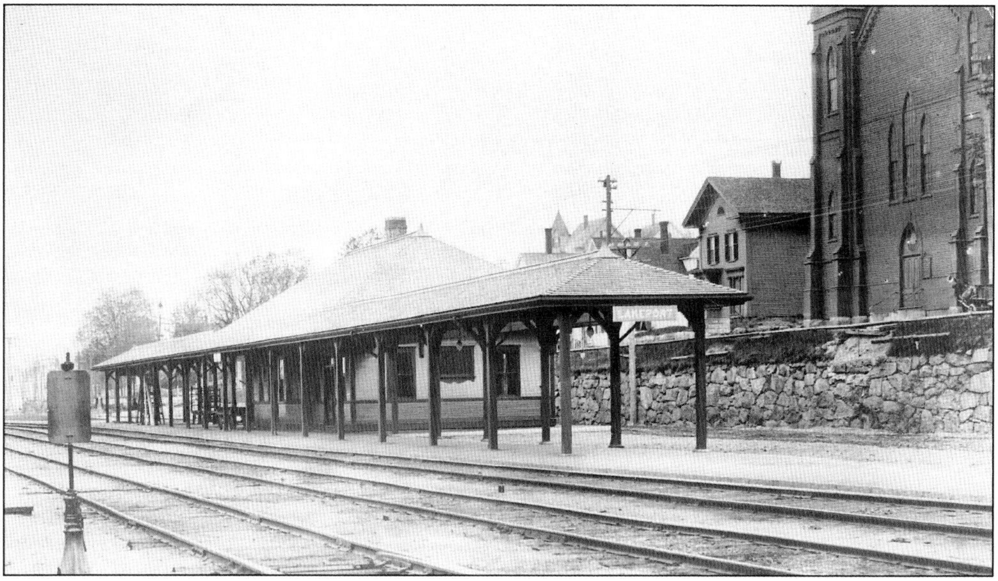

Railroad Station, early 1900s. The site of the Union Avenue Baptist Church (right) is now occupied by Case 'N' Keg convenience store.

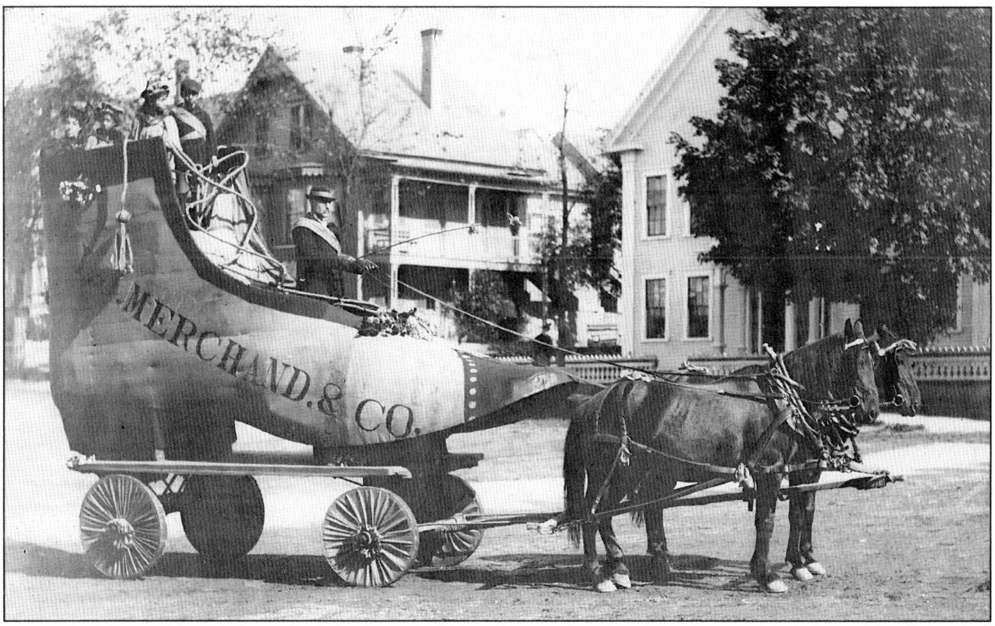

Fanciful Float of L.J. Merchand & Co., Shoe Dealer. Around the turn of the century, commerce and industry vied for the most imaginative floats in the frequent parades.

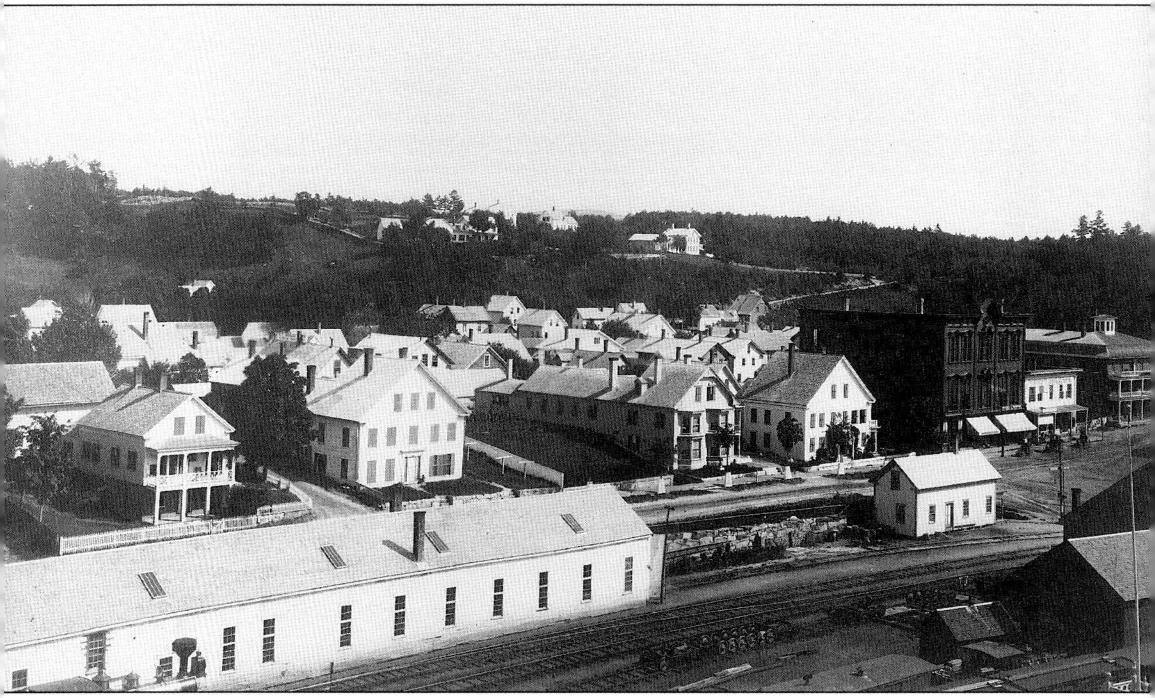

UNION AVENUE AND LAKEPORT SQUARE (RIGHT) FROM STEEPLE OF PARK STREET CHURCH, C. 1895. The Union Avenue Baptist Church is just off the photograph, at left. Cole's Hill looms above the village, with Benjamin J. Cole's first mansion, on Cole Street, just right of center. The switchback connecting with Cole Street at the top and running diagonally downward from right to left is aptly named Hill Street. The street running left to right at the top of the hill, from Clinton to Cole Streets, was, likewise, appropriately named Prospect Street. Except for the second house from the left (the Dr. Hodgdon House), the dwellings on Union Avenue are now long gone. The house at the corner of Clinton Street and Union Avenue (left of the Opera House) was razed for construction of Lakeport National Bank in 1916–1917. (The former bank building is now occupied by Fratello's Restaurant.) The site of the house (formerly the parsonage of the Union Avenue Baptist Church and later of the United Baptist Church) at extreme left, located at the northeast corner of Chestnut Street, is now part of the parking lot for Case 'N' Keg. Frame structures in the lower-right corner were part of the Boston, Concord & Montreal Railroad shops. The Osgood Block adjoins the Opera House; the Mount Belknap House is at right. See the photograph at the bottom of p. 30 for an earlier view of this area.

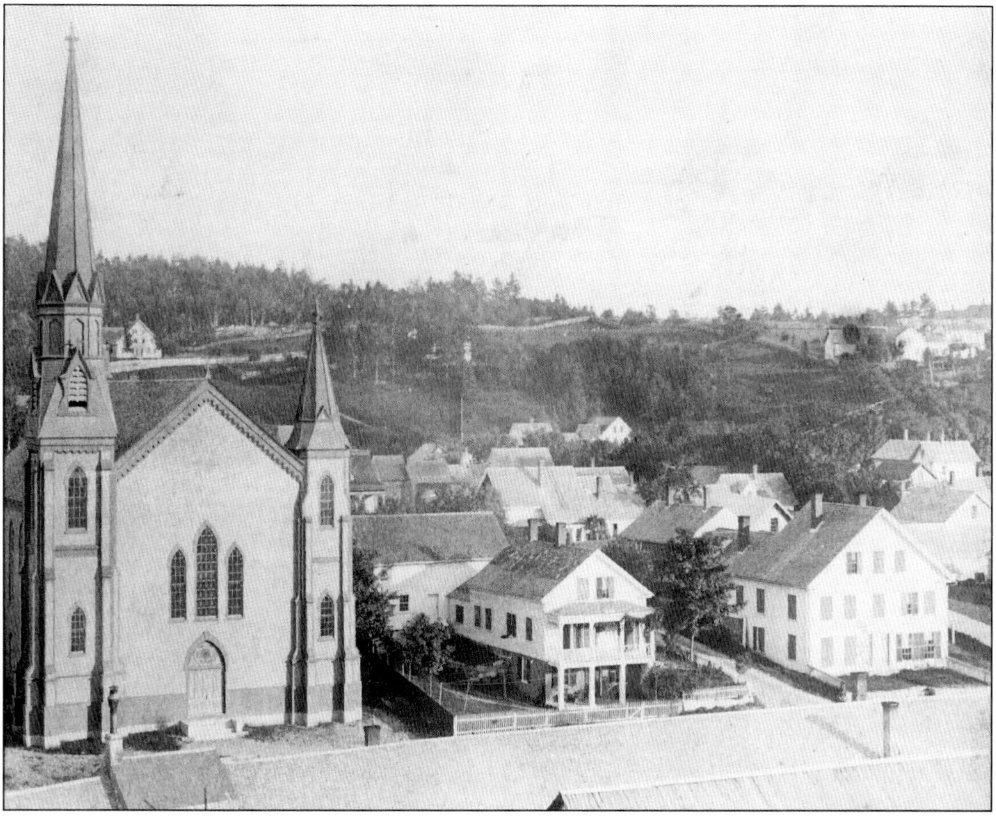

UNION AVENUE BAPTIST CHURCH FROM STEEPLE OF PARK STREET CHURCH.

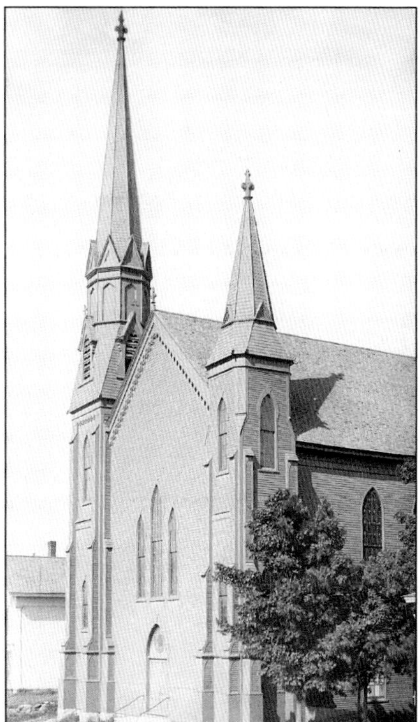

UNION AVENUE BAPTIST CHURCH. The new Gilford, Gilmanton, and Lake Village Baptist Church, with its soaring Gothic Revival towers, was dedicated, August 23, 1871, after three years of construction following demolition of the earlier structure. Its predecessor, with its plain belfry (see p. 25), had been dedicated on August 8, 1833. Known as the Union Avenue Baptist, "Brown" or "Gray" Church, its congregation joined with the Park Street Free Baptist Church in 1920 to form the United Baptist Church. In October 1940, the Union Avenue edifice was torn down. Today, the site is occupied by Case 'N' Keg.

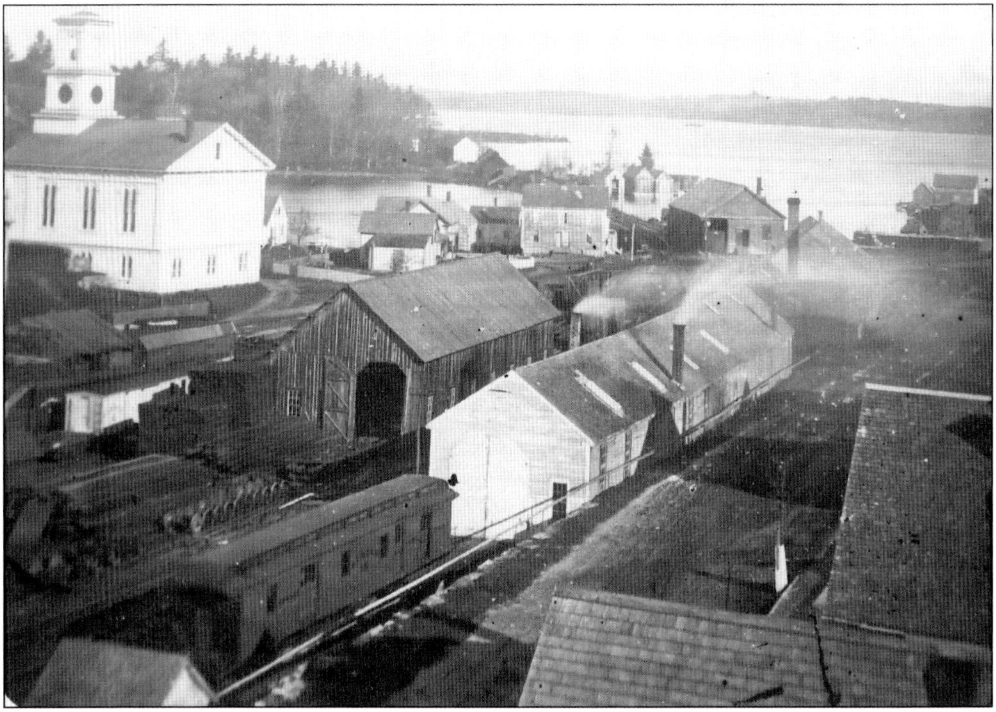

Main Line, Rail Yards, and Park Street Church, c. 1875, Looking Northwest. The railroad bridge is obscured by the buildings at top center.

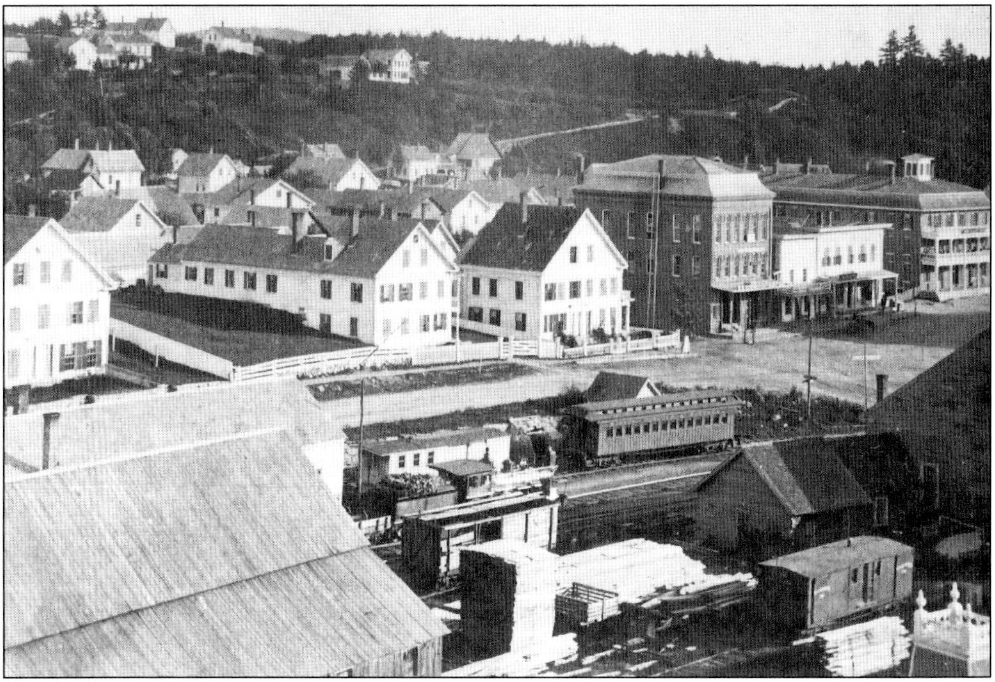

Another View of Lakeport Square, from Park Street Church, c. 1875. The tall brick building with mansard roof (center right) was the Weeks Block, built *c.* 1871 and burned in 1881. It was replaced in 1885 by the Opera House Block.

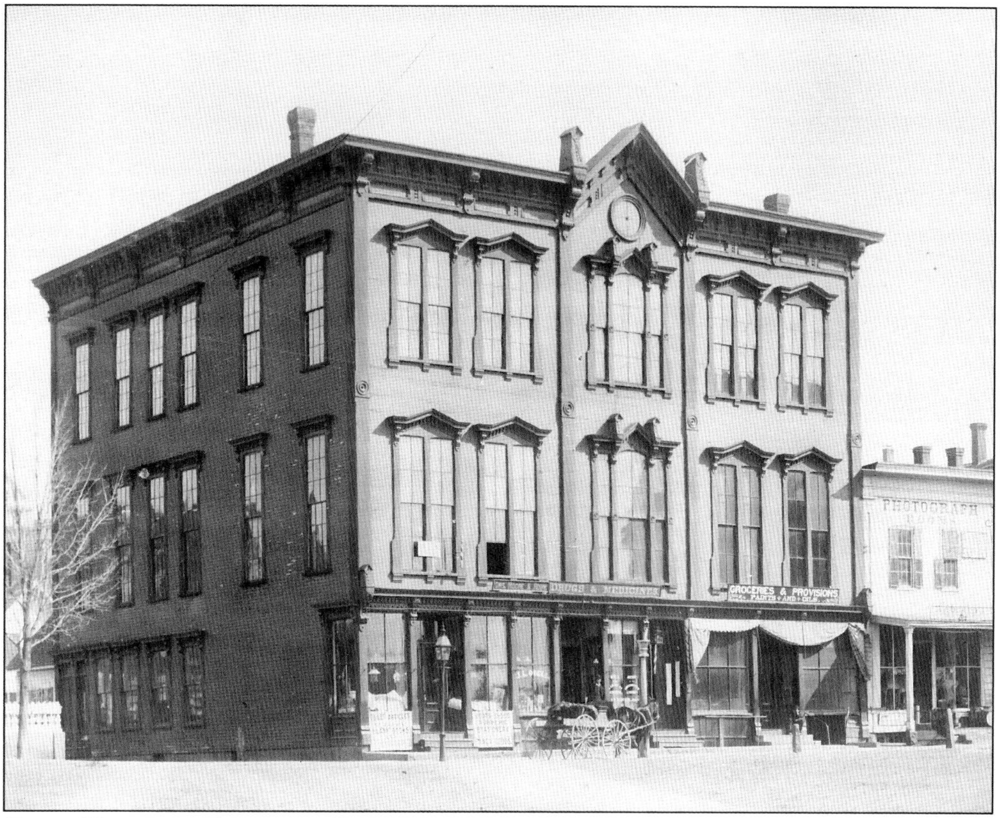

Opera House and Adjoining Osgood Block, c. 1895.

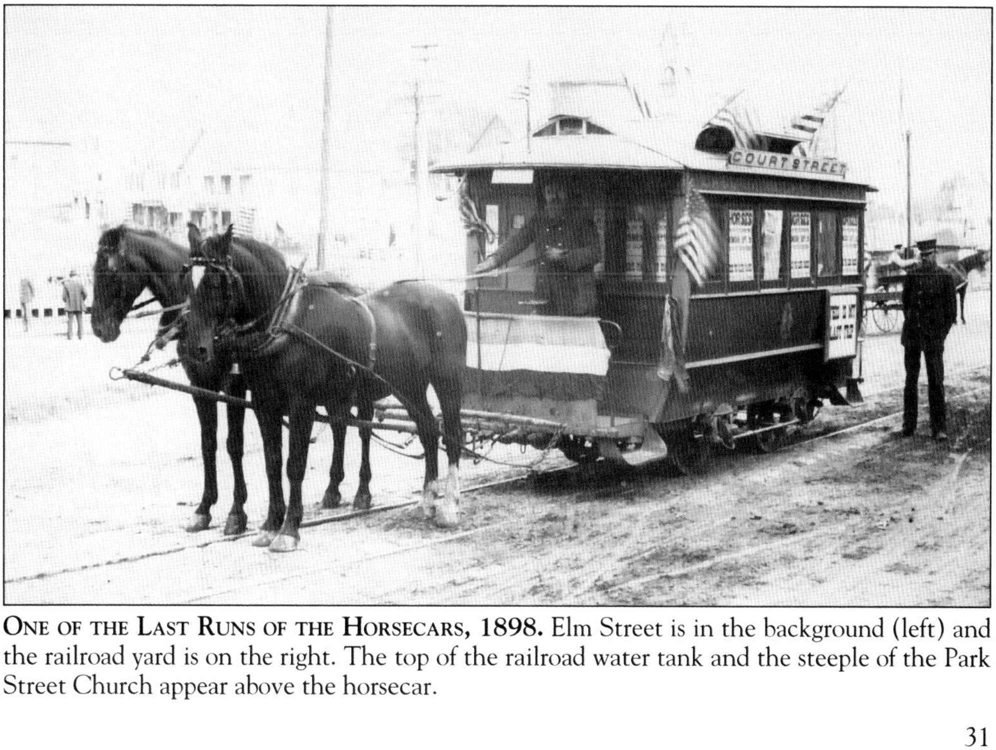

One of the Last Runs of the Horsecars, 1898. Elm Street is in the background (left) and the railroad yard is on the right. The top of the railroad water tank and the steeple of the Park Street Church appear above the horsecar.

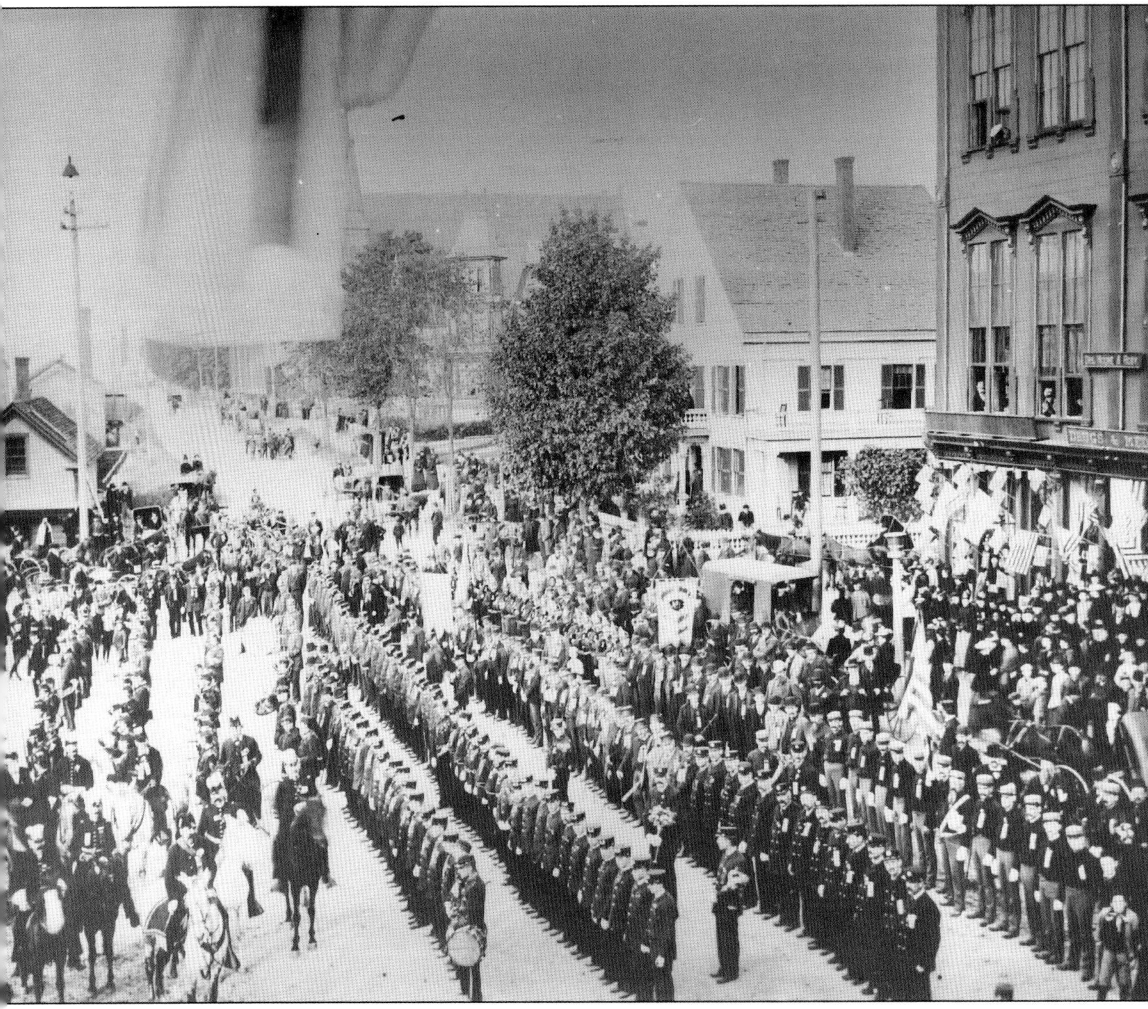

Fire Department Celebration, Autumn 1892. In this view of Lakeport Square, Rublee's Band and the Carroll County Band from Moultonboro are seen at left, in front of the firemen. Businesses occupying the Opera House Block include John M. Hubbard, dealer in boots and shoes, and a drugstore. Drs. Moore and Roby had offices on the second floor.

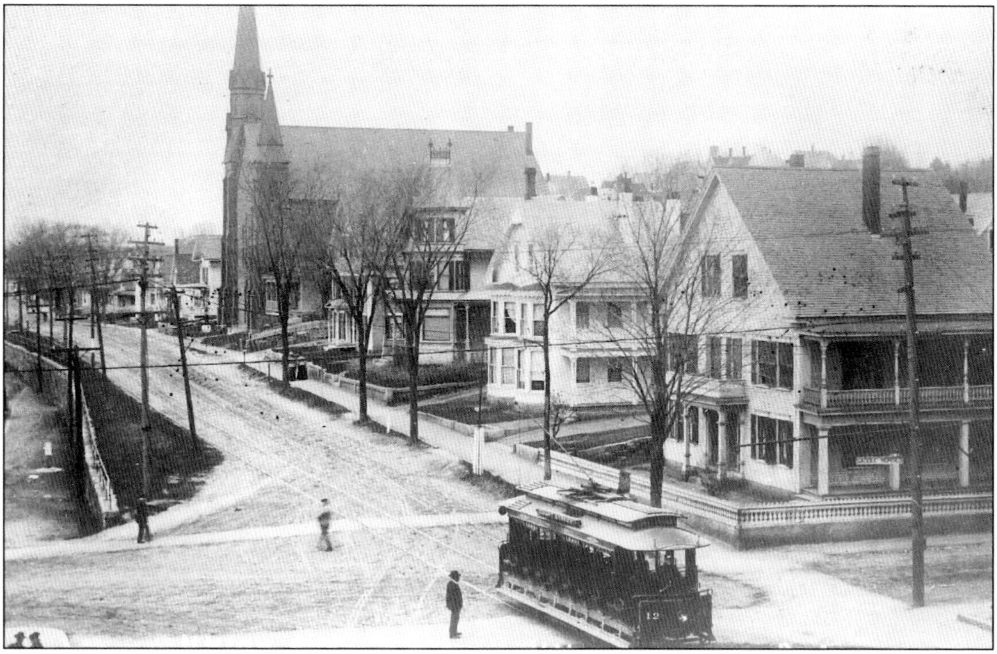

Trolley in Lakeport Square, c. 1900. The house at right was removed in 1916–1917 for construction of the Lakeport National Bank (today occupied by Fratello's Restaurant).

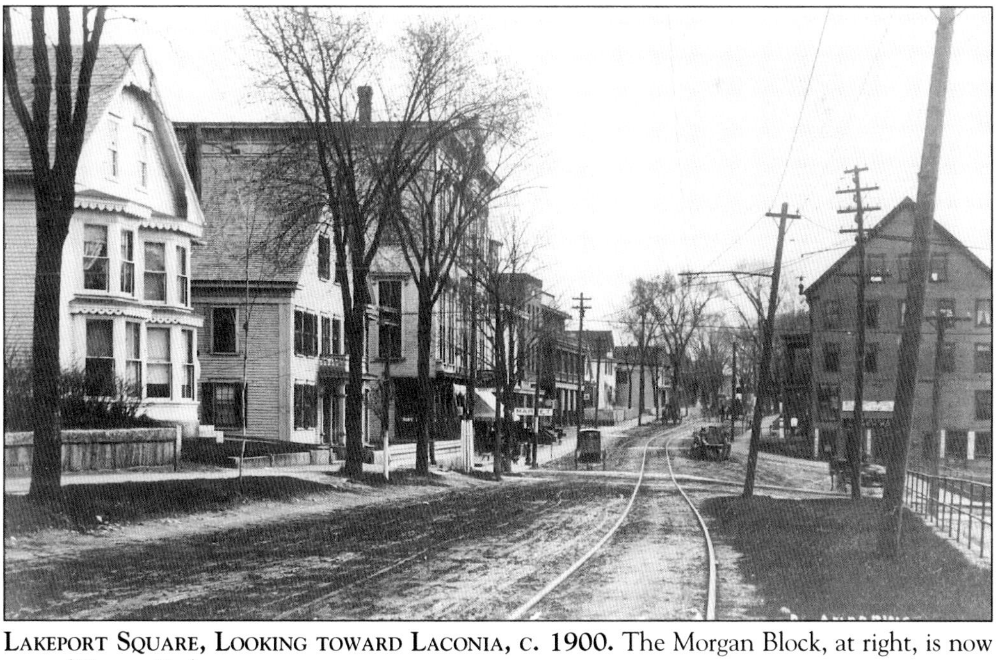

Lakeport Square, Looking toward Laconia, c. 1900. The Morgan Block, at right, is now part of Torrey Park.

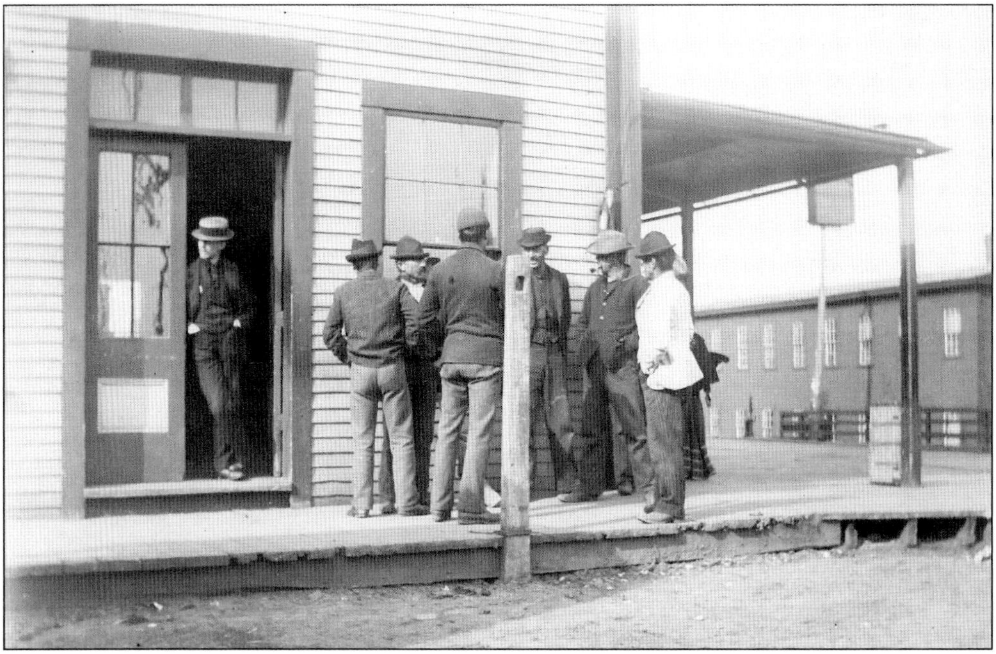

Basement of Morgan Block, c. 1894. Union Avenue is off the photograph at left and the tracks of the Boston & Maine Railroad run at right, just beyond the roof over the platform. The Cole Manufacturing Co. and Boston, Concord & Montreal Railroad shop buildings are at right, across the tracks.

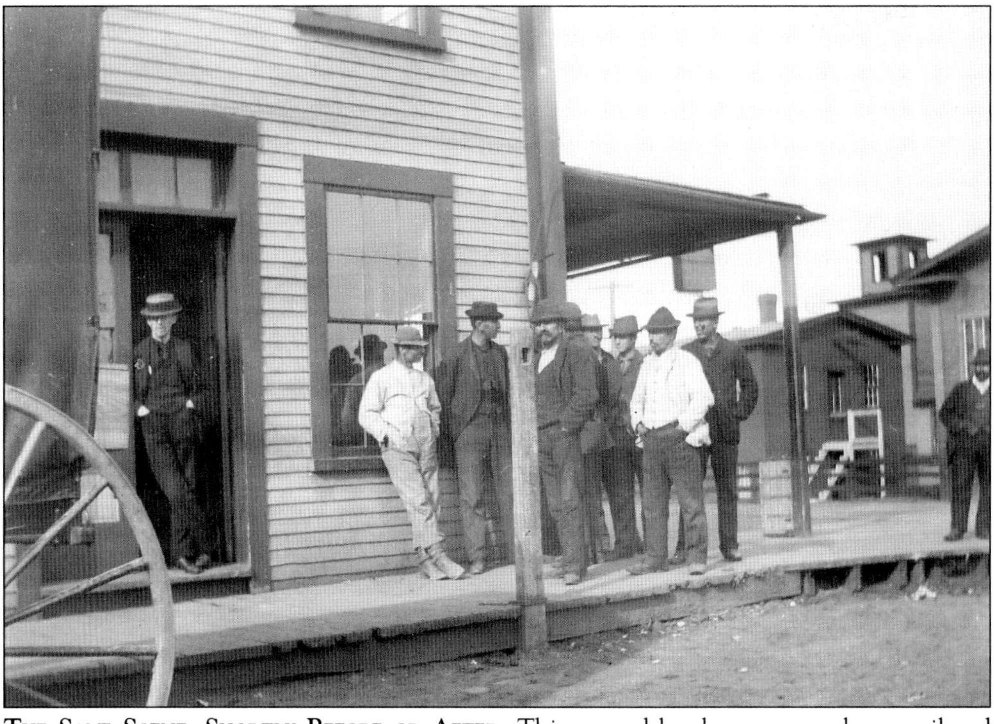

The Same Scene, Shortly Before or After. This ground-level space served as a railroad passenger station and waiting area before the new depot (see pp. 26–27) was opened in 1900.

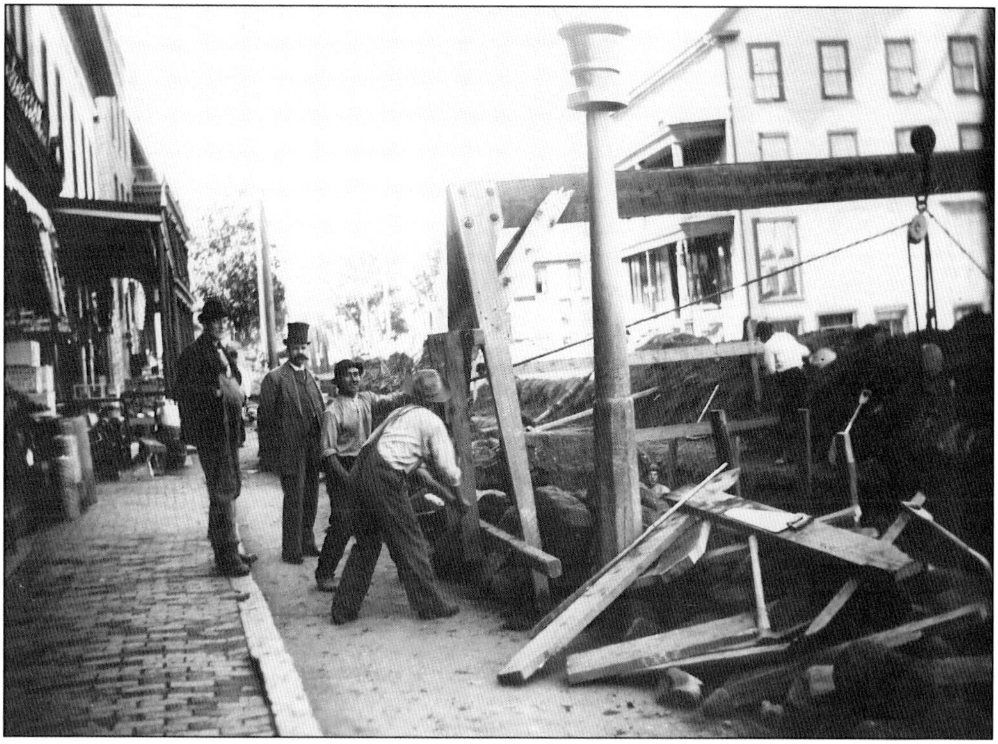

Sewer Construction in Lakeport Square, 1893–1894. The Opera House and other business blocks are at left, and the Morgan Block is at right.

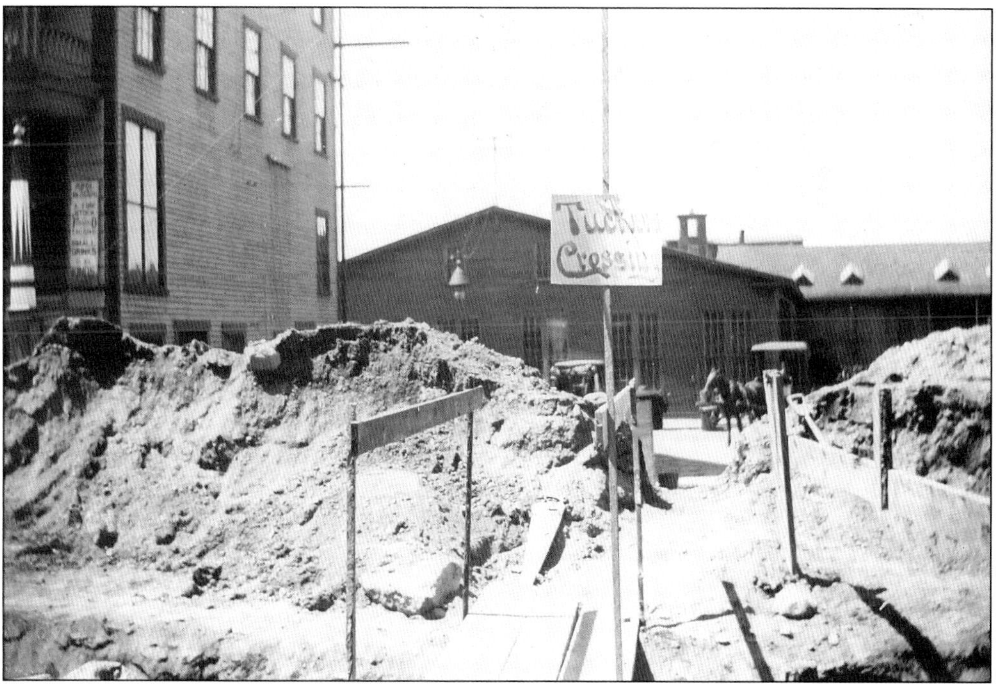

Another View of the Construction. The Morgan Block is at left, and the Boston, Concord & Montreal Railroad shops are at right, beyond the railroad tracks.

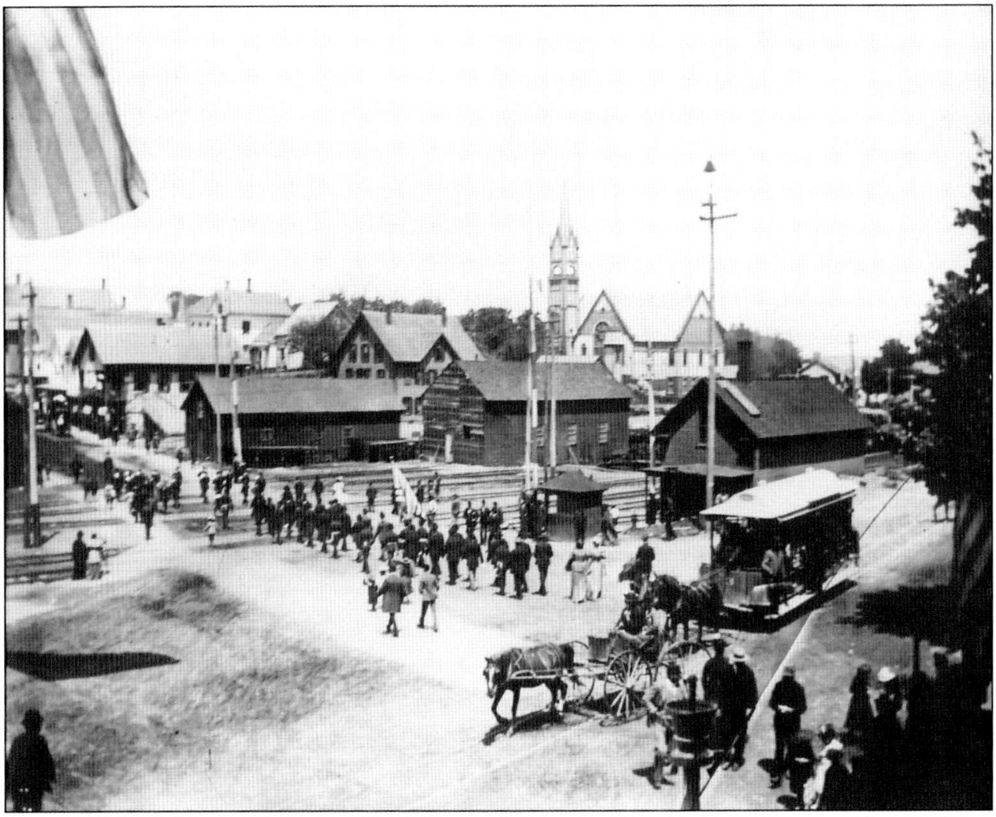

Parade Scene, Lakeport Square, early 1890s. A wagon and horsecar proceed down Union Avenue, while marchers head up Elm Street.

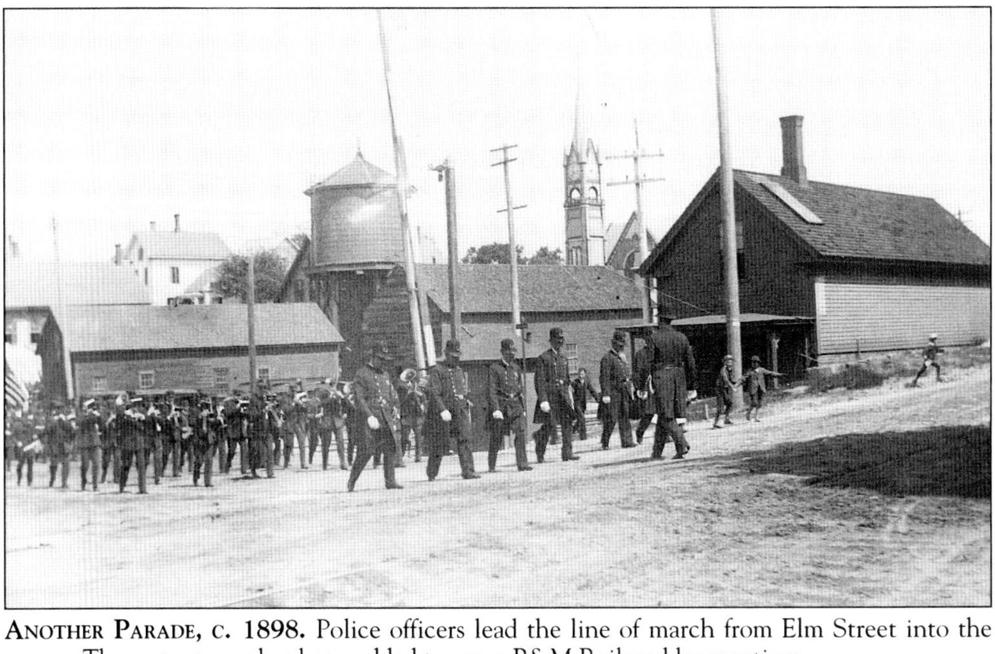

Another Parade, c. 1898. Police officers lead the line of march from Elm Street into the square. The water tower has been added to serve B&M Railroad locomotives.

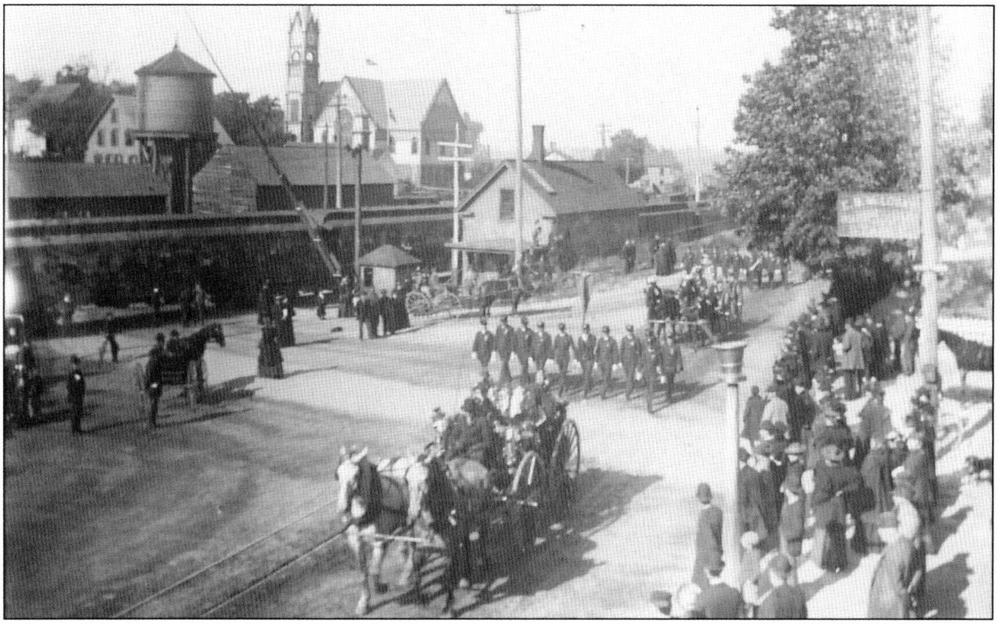

Parade Continues, c. 1898. A carriage bearing dignitaries is followed by members of the fire department.

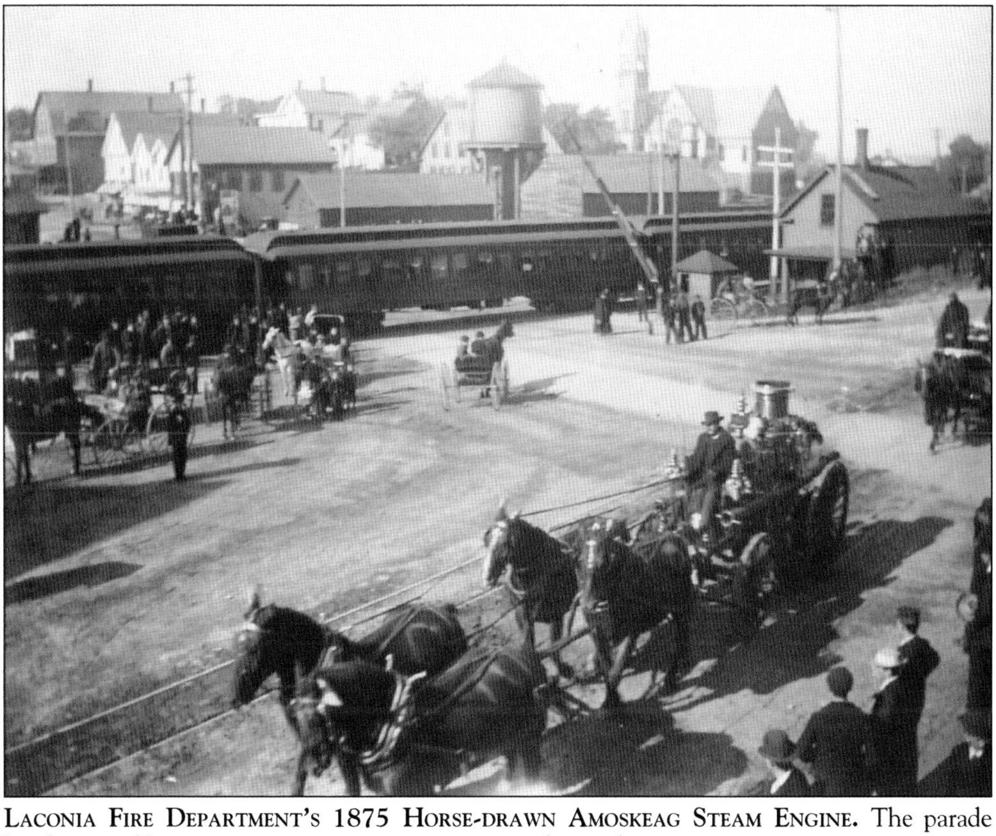

Laconia Fire Department's 1875 Horse-drawn Amoskeag Steam Engine. The parade heads toward Laconia as a passenger train stops on the tracks.

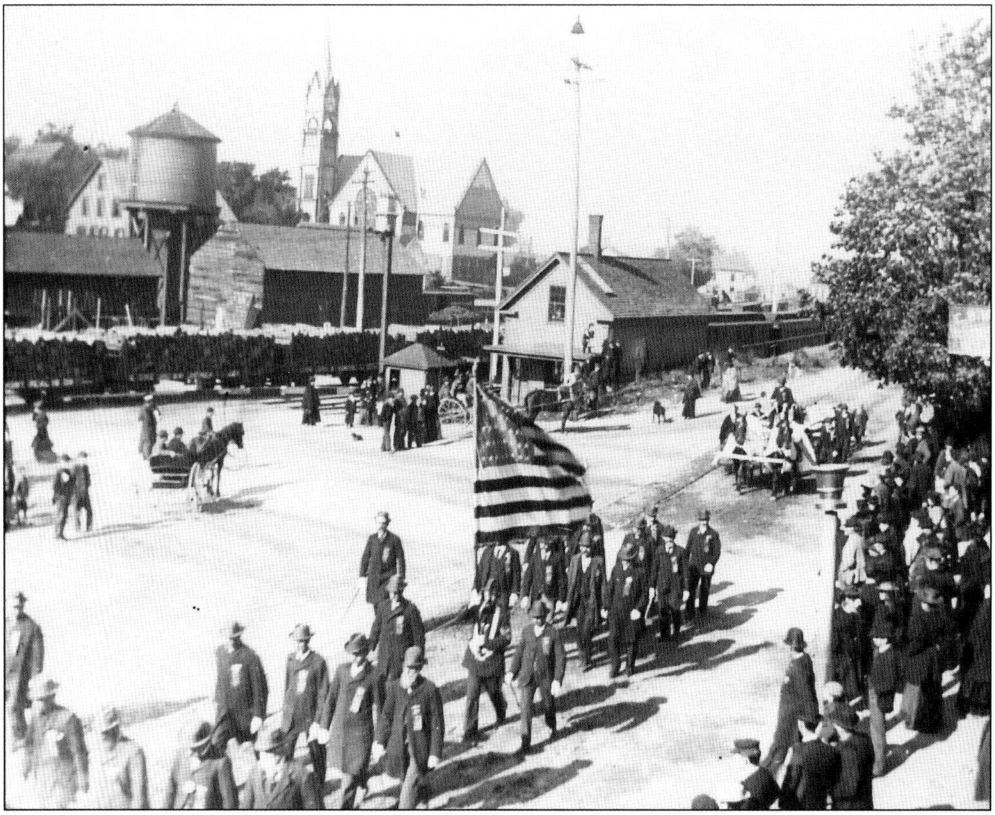

Civil War Veterans and Color Guard. At left, flatcars loaded with cordwood occupy the railroad tracks.

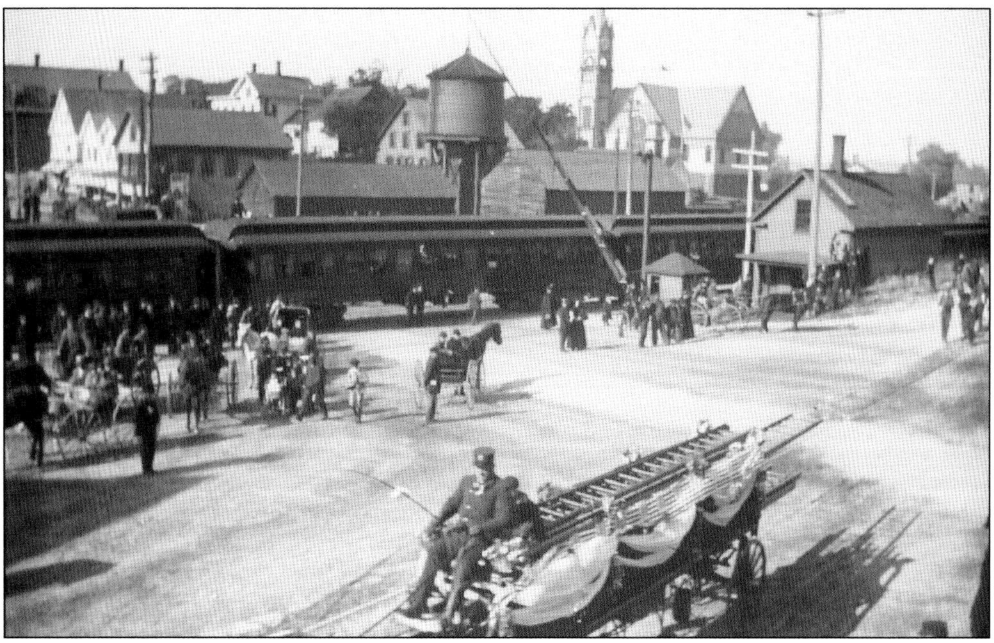

Hook and Ladder Wagon.

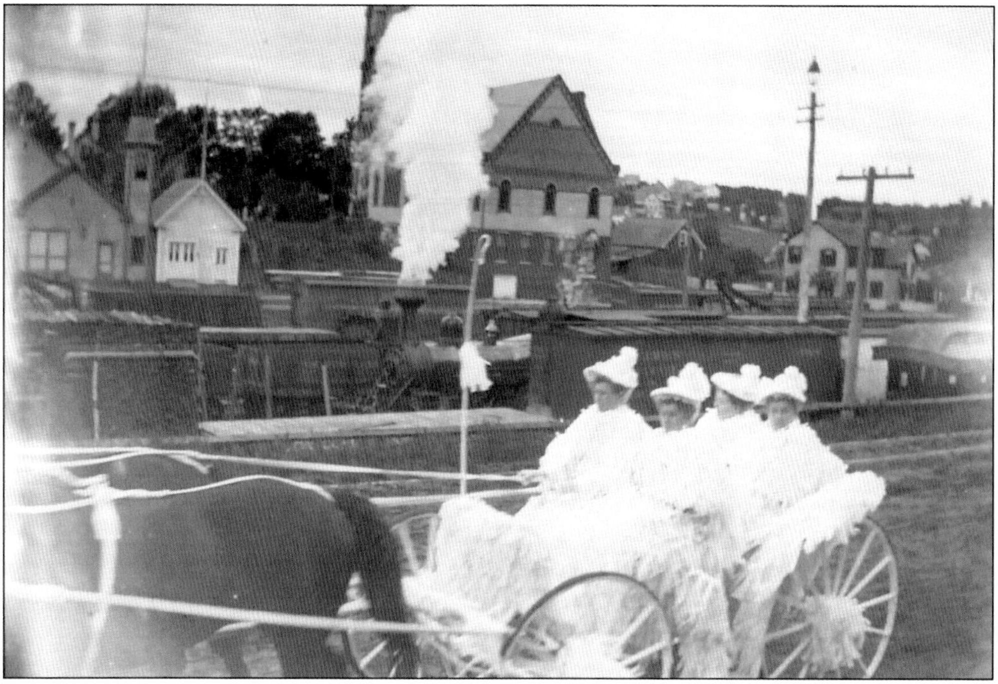

Mrs. Prescott's Fancifully Decorated Carriage. The ladies head south toward the square, with locomotive, freight, and passenger cars on the tracks beyond. The building of Hose Co. 4 (see p. 57) is visible at upper left.

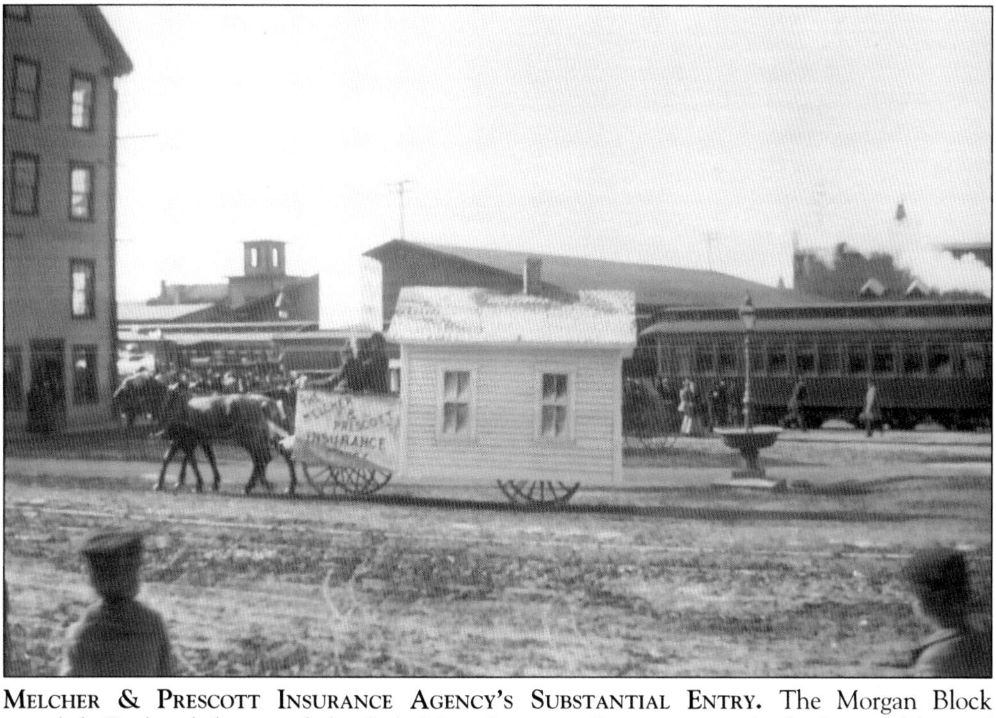

Melcher & Prescott Insurance Agency's Substantial Entry. The Morgan Block is at left. Railroad shops and the Cole Manufacturing Co. appear in the background beyond the train.

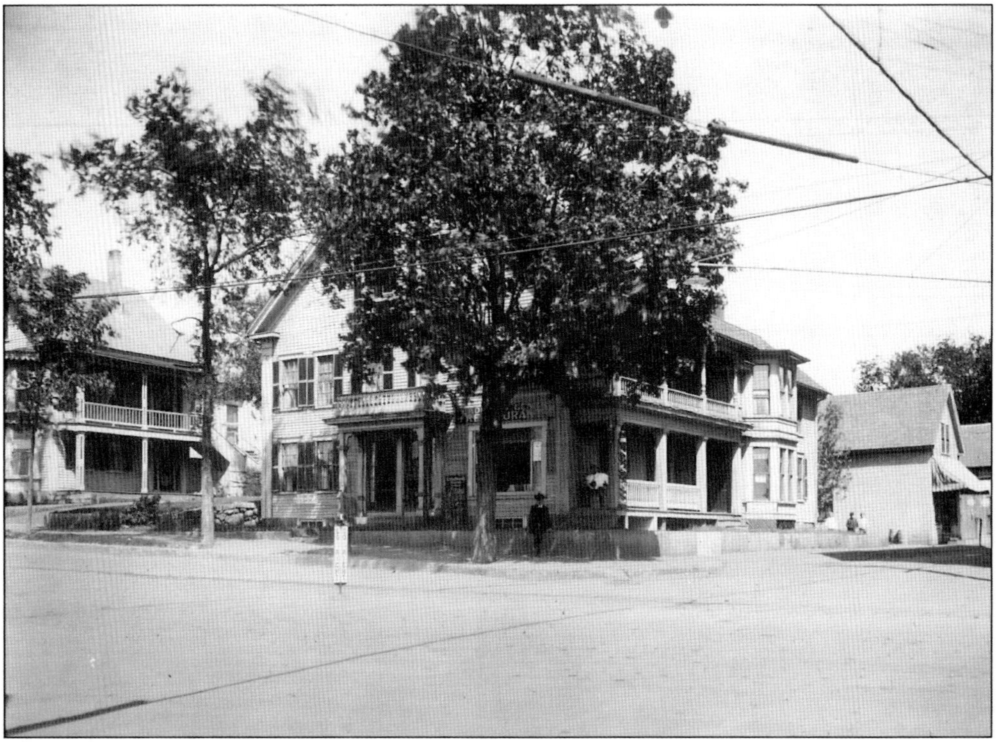

HOUSE AT THE CORNER OF UNION AVENUE AND CLINTON STREET. Chapman's Restaurant occupies part of the ground floor. The structure was removed for construction of the Lakeport National Bank Building in 1916–1917.

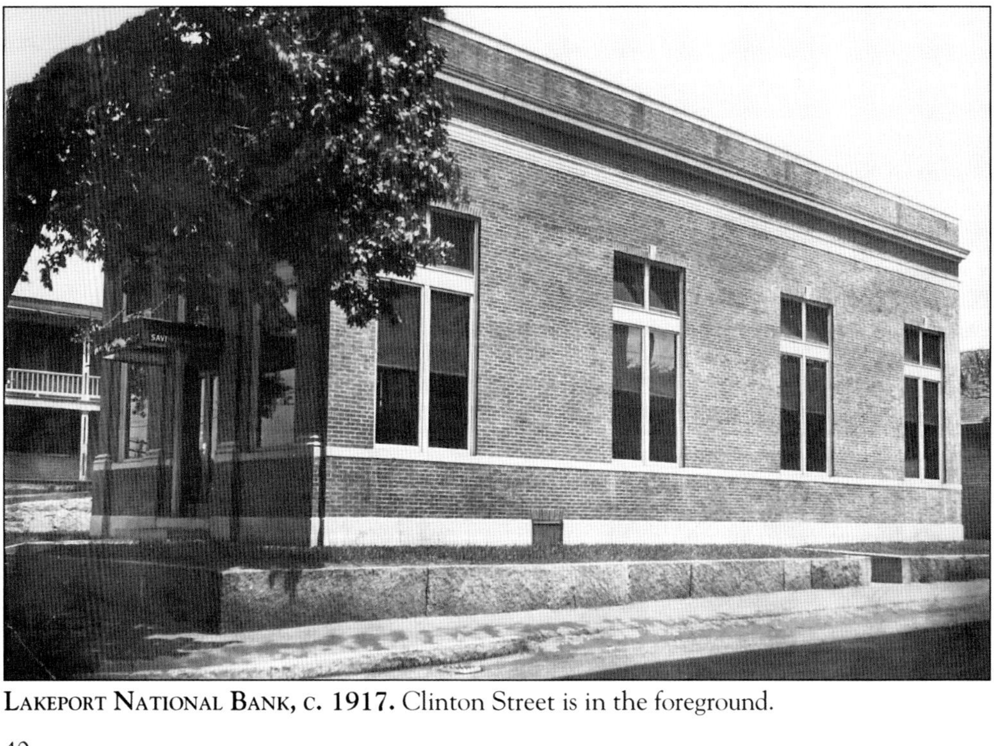

LAKEPORT NATIONAL BANK, C. 1917. Clinton Street is in the foreground.

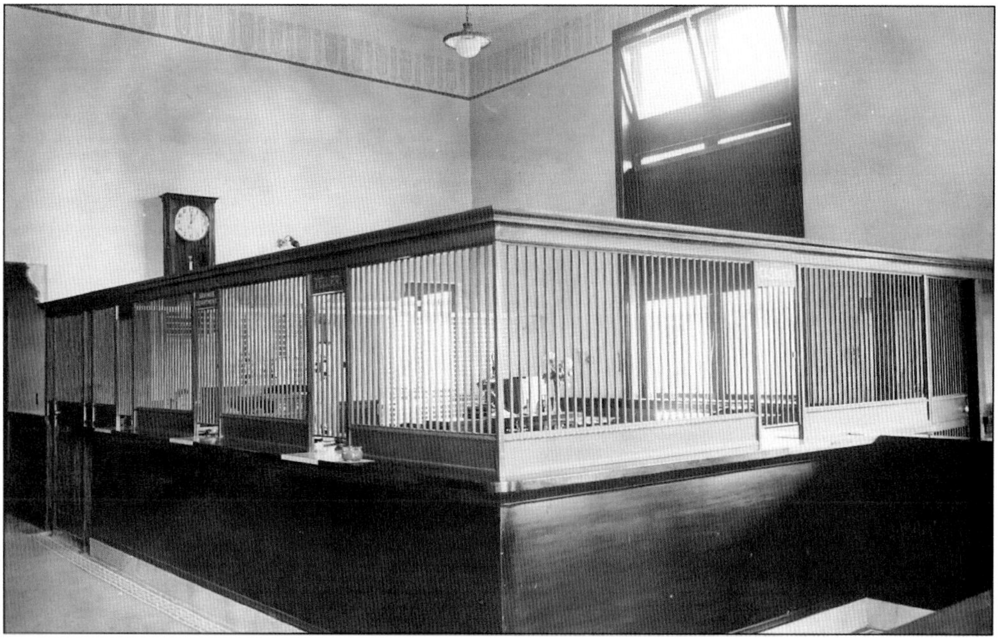

TELLERS' CAGE, LAKEPORT NATIONAL BANK, C. 1917.

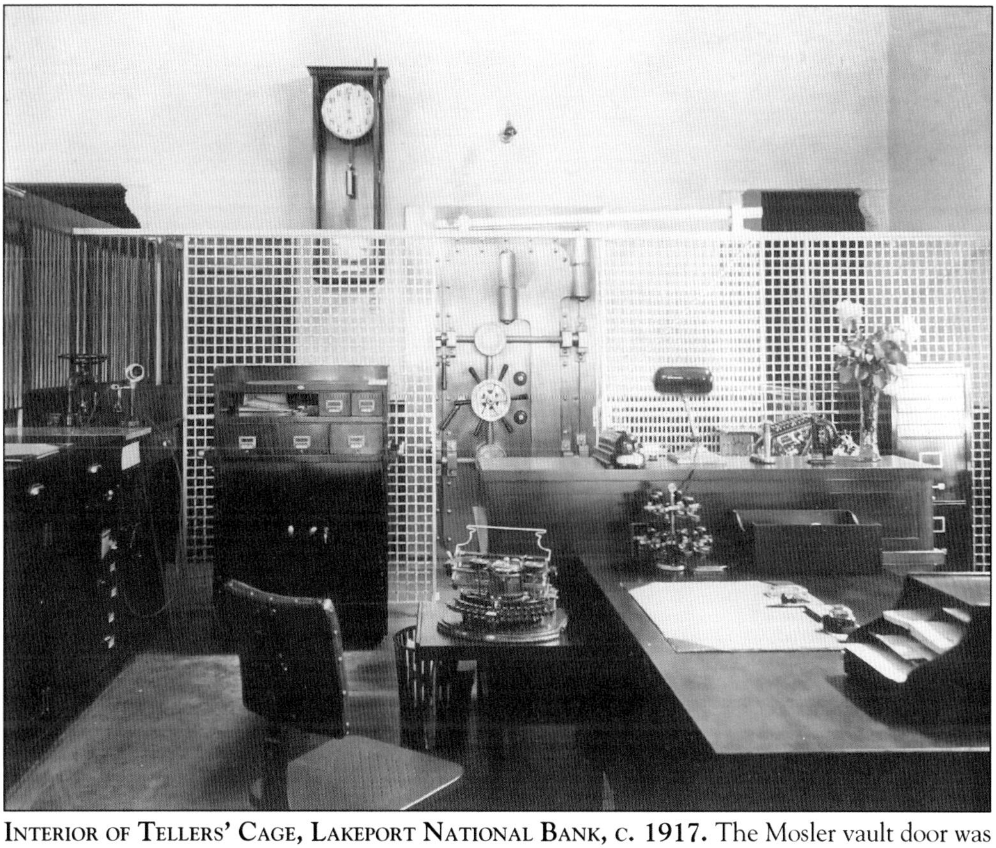

INTERIOR OF TELLERS' CAGE, LAKEPORT NATIONAL BANK, C. 1917. The Mosler vault door was 12 inches thick and weighed 8 tons.

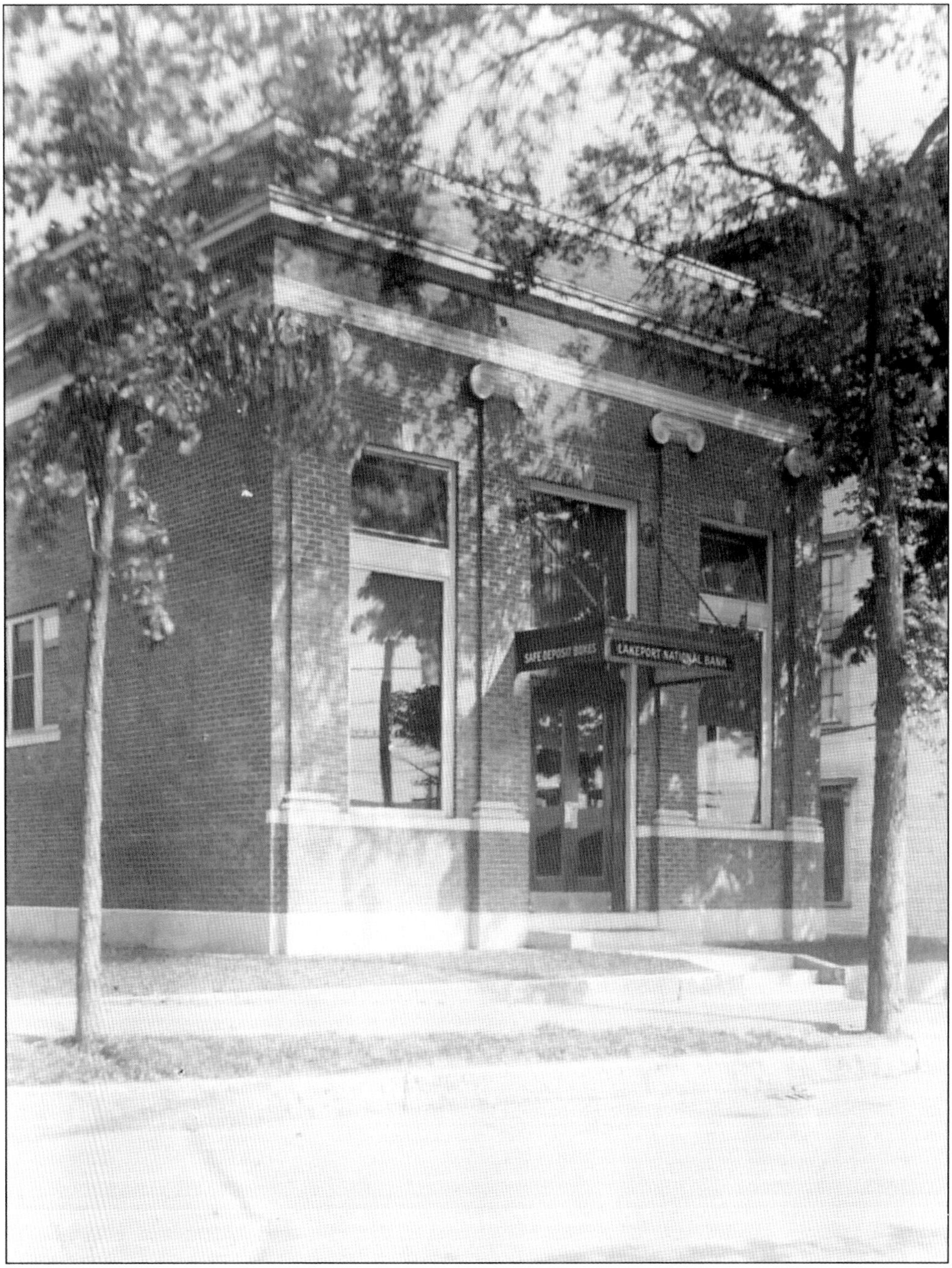

UNION AVENUE ENTRANCE, LAKEPORT NATIONAL BANK, C. 1917.

Three

Between Rails and River

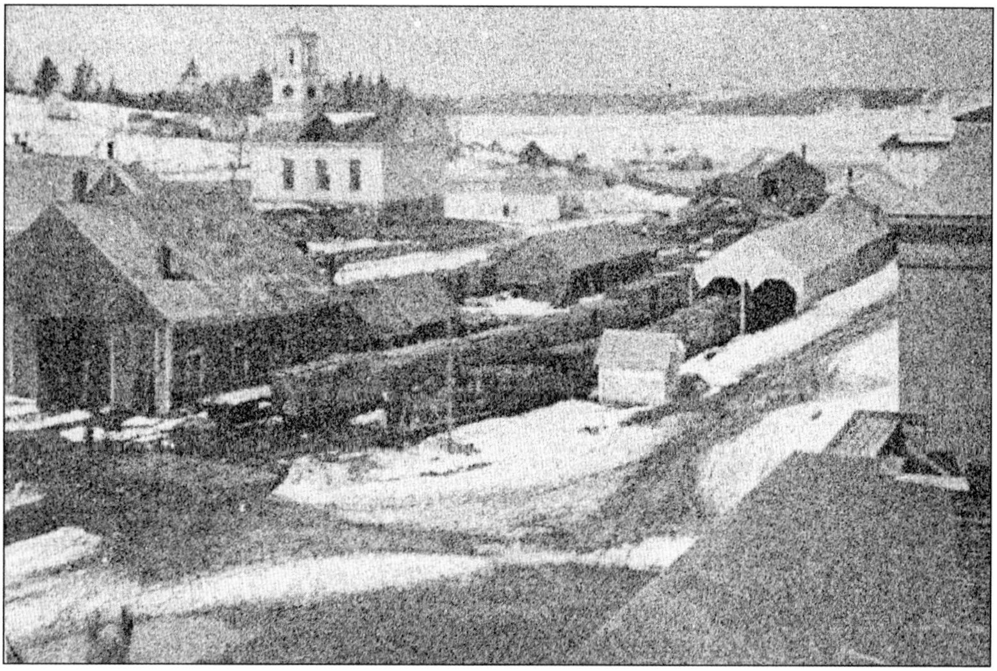

Railyards and Park Street Church, c. 1875. In this view from the Mount Belknap House with part of the Weeks Block visible at right and Lake Paugus in the distance, the Belvidere Hill area (upper left) is still open pasture. The large wooden structure at left is part of the Boston, Concord & Montreal Railroad shops. The residential area that extended southward toward Laconia between Union Avenue and Lake Opechee (off the photograph at left) was popularly known as "the island" after 1848, because it was isolated, save for the Bridge Street overpass, by the deep railroad cut.

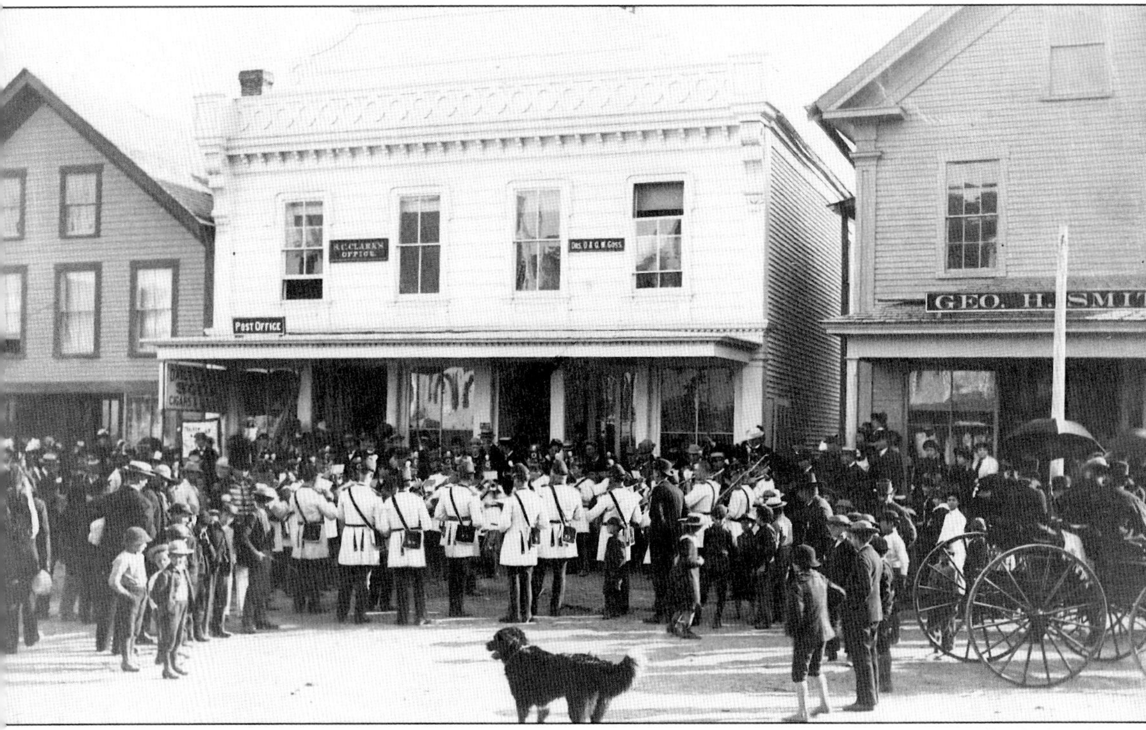

SOUTH SIDE OF ELM STREET, EARLY 1880S. This was one of many occasions at which local bands played. These buildings occupied the strip of land opposite Park Street (see next page). Drs. Oliver and Ossian Wilbur Goss had offices on the second floor of the center building, which also housed the post office. At one time, the *Belknap Republican* printing plant was also located in this building.

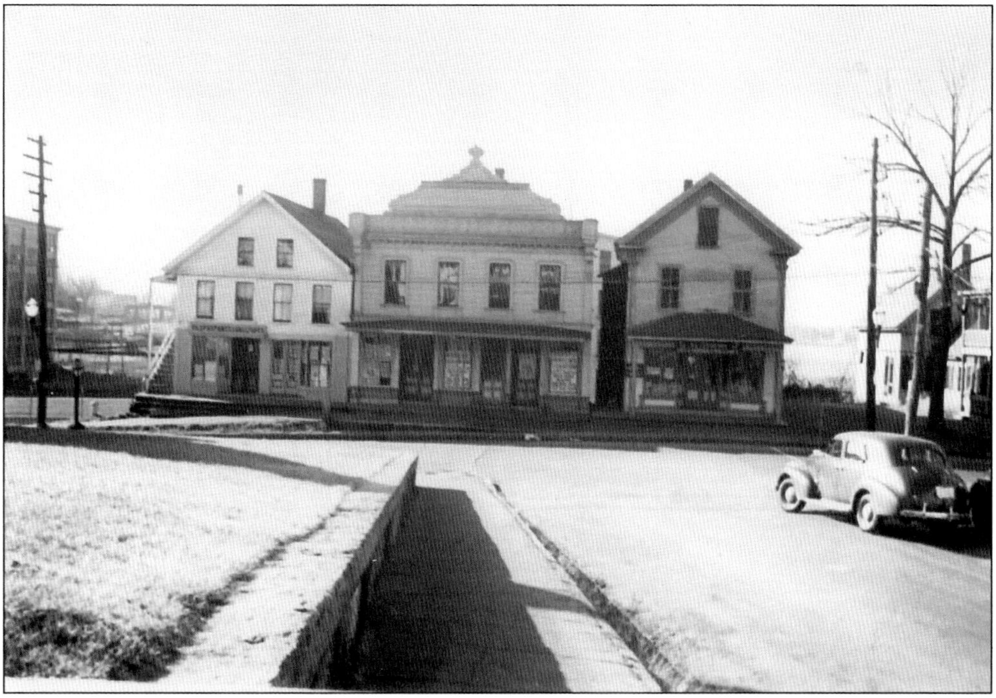

ELM STREET, LOOKING SOUTH FROM PARK STREET, NOVEMBER 16, 1941. The building visible at the extreme right appears again in photo below.

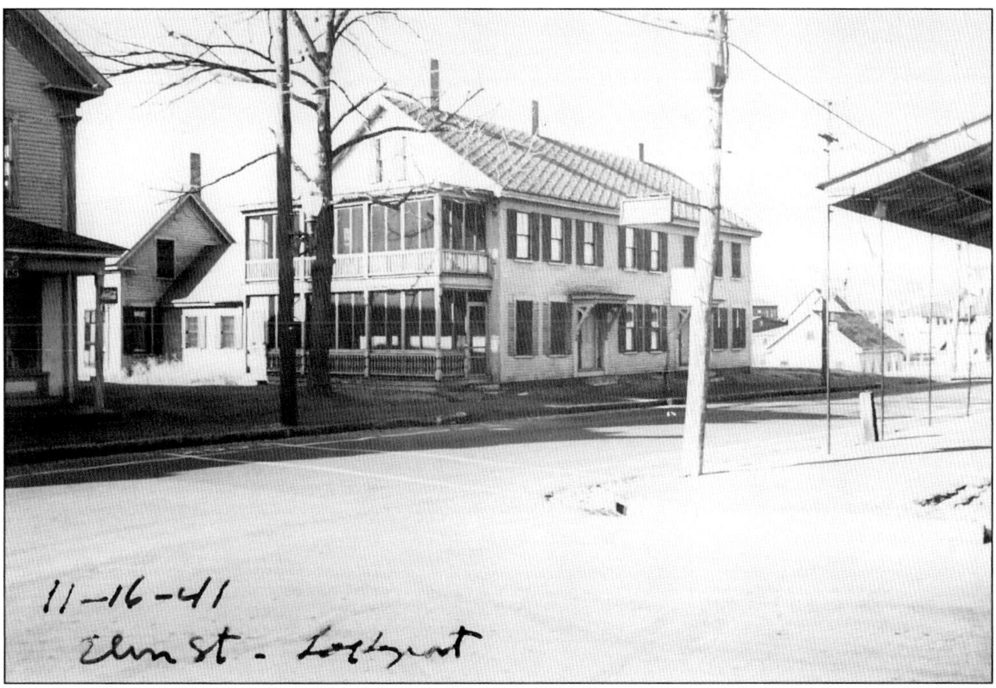

ELM STREET TENEMENT, NOVEMBER 16, 1941. Part of the canopy over the sidewalk in front of the Brawn Block is visible at right.

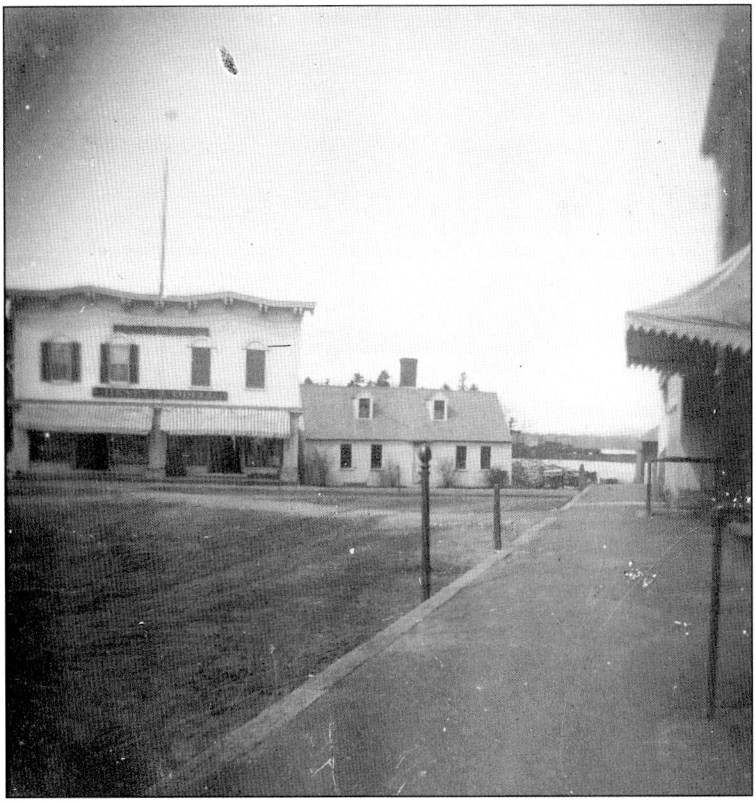

GOLD STREET, LOOKING NORTH TOWARD LAKE PAUGUS. The Daniel M. Gale House is visible at center, with Henry Odell's store at left.

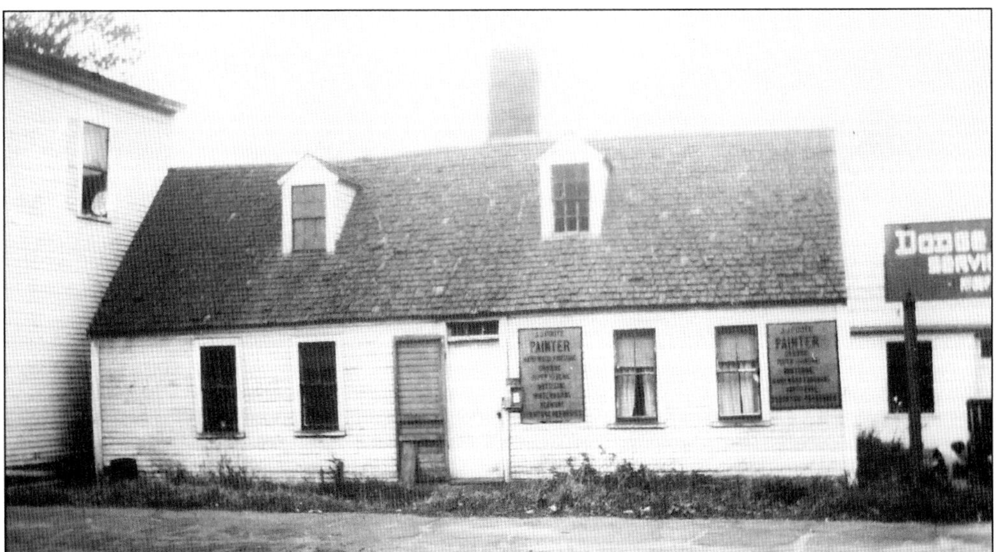

DANIEL M. GALE HOUSE, 95 GOLD STREET. This house is said to be the first one built on the east side of the river, c. 1800.

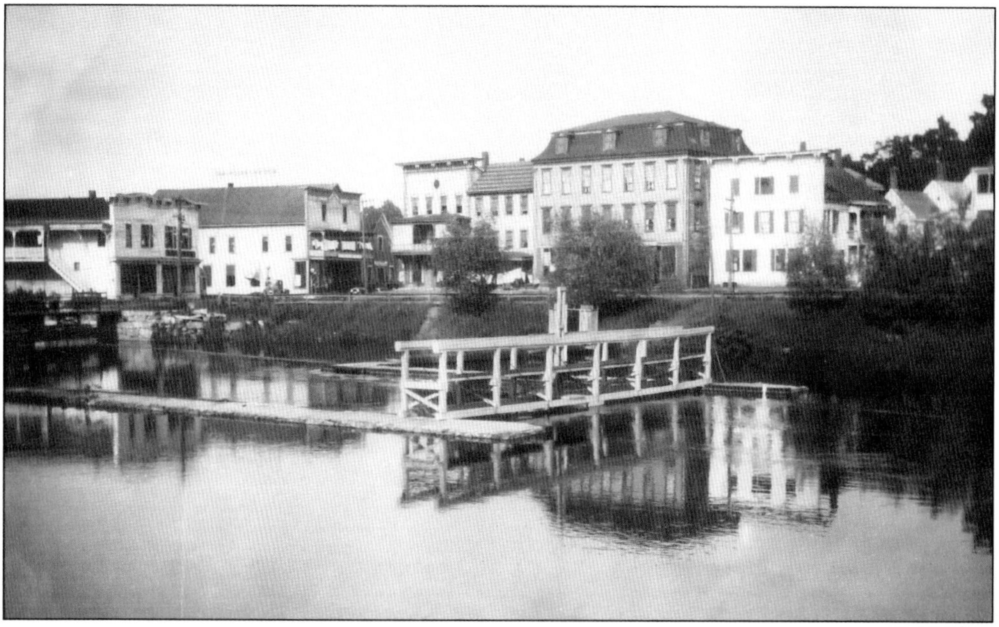

A PORTION OF GOLD STREET (LEFT) AND FORE STREET (RIGHT), FROM ELM STREET BRIDGE, JUNE 22, 1928. The building with the mansard roof was the Piper Block, built 1868–1869 and torn down in the early 1930s. The three-story building with a roundel was the Bugbee Block.

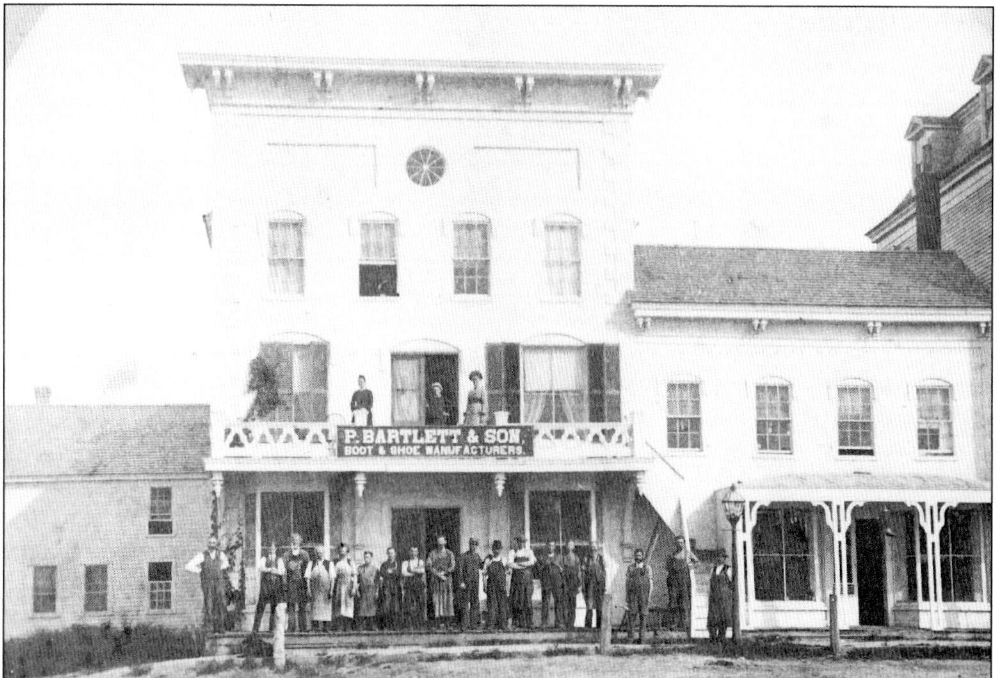

FORE STREET, C. 1879. The Bugbee Block was then occupied by P. Bartlett & Son. These two buildings appear at center in the photograph at the top of the page (in which the two-story building, above right, has gained a third story). Both structures were destroyed in a spectacular blaze on April 16, 1960.

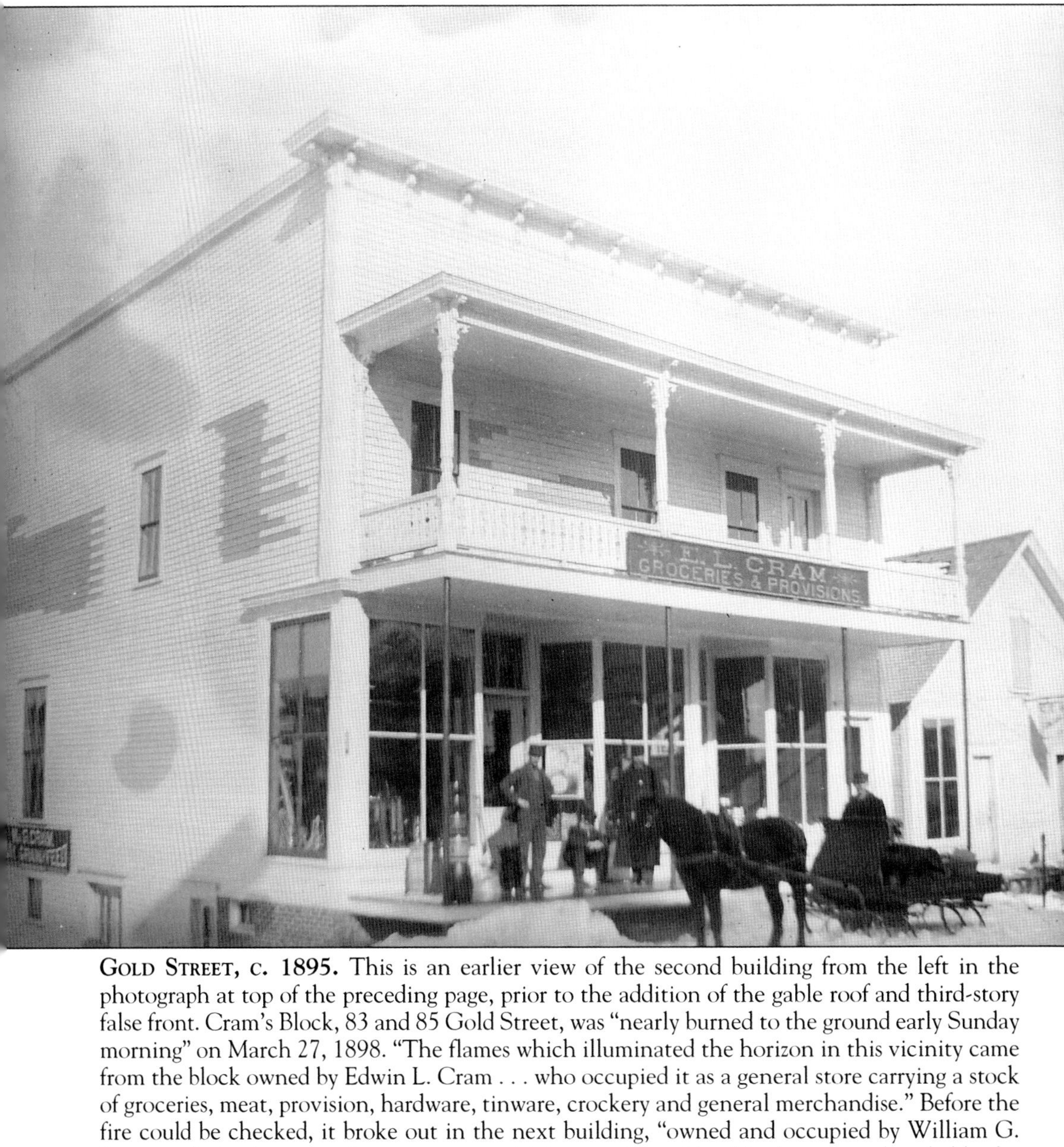

Gold Street, c. 1895. This is an earlier view of the second building from the left in the photograph at top of the preceding page, prior to the addition of the gable roof and third-story false front. Cram's Block, 83 and 85 Gold Street, was "nearly burned to the ground early Sunday morning" on March 27, 1898. "The flames which illuminated the horizon in this vicinity came from the block owned by Edwin L. Cram . . . who occupied it as a general store carrying a stock of groceries, meat, provision, hardware, tinware, crockery and general merchandise." Before the fire could be checked, it broke out in the next building, "owned and occupied by William G. Cram, a dealer in grains, hay, etc., etc., which caused considerable damage and probably the stock is a total loss." The hall above E.L. Cram's store was occupied by several fraternal bodies, which lost books, regalia, and paraphernalia, "and also two pianos." The building, rebuilt after the fire, still exists. For several decades after 1902, it was home to the McDuff Machine Co.

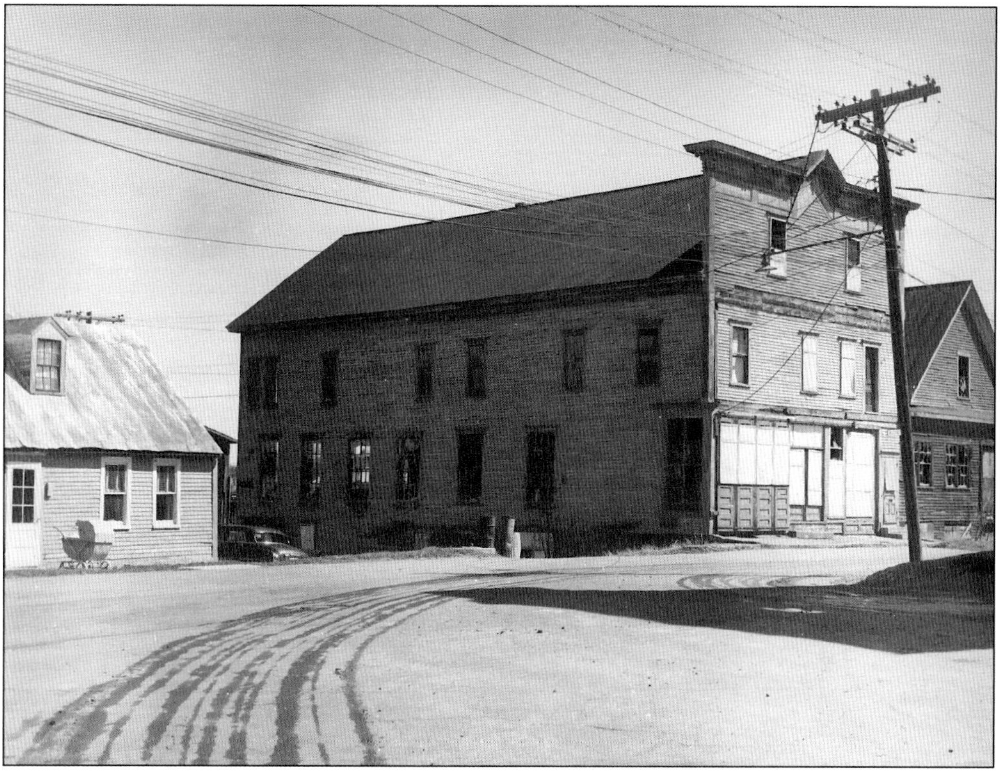

Same Buildings, 1950s. In the photograph above, part of the Daniel M. Gale House is visible at left.

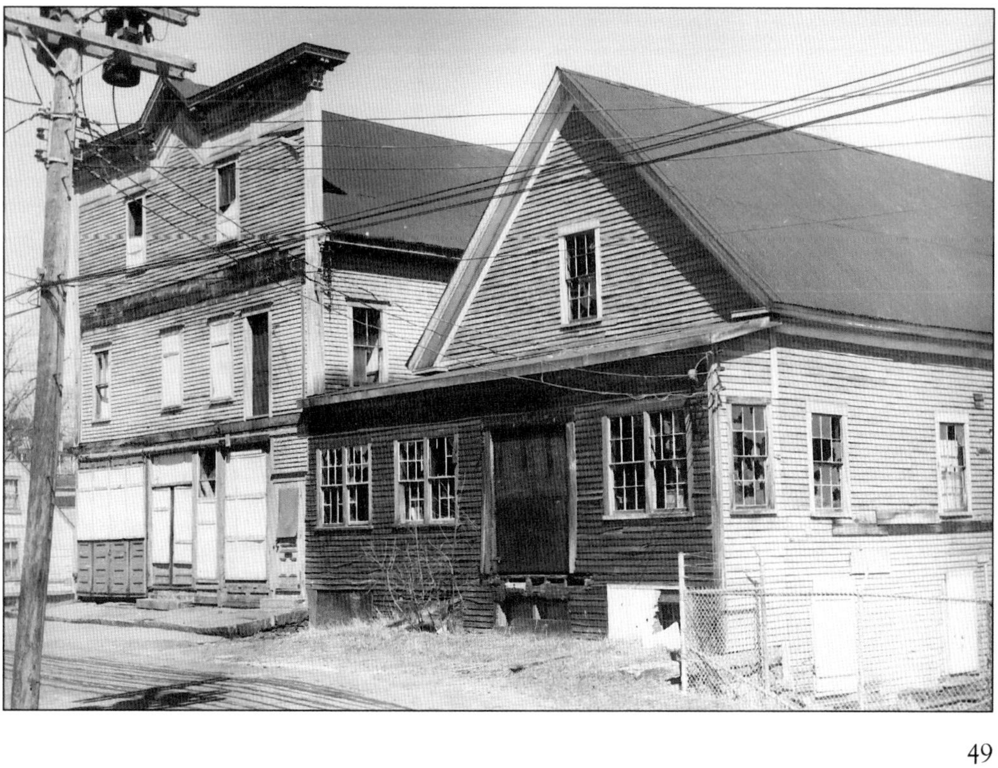

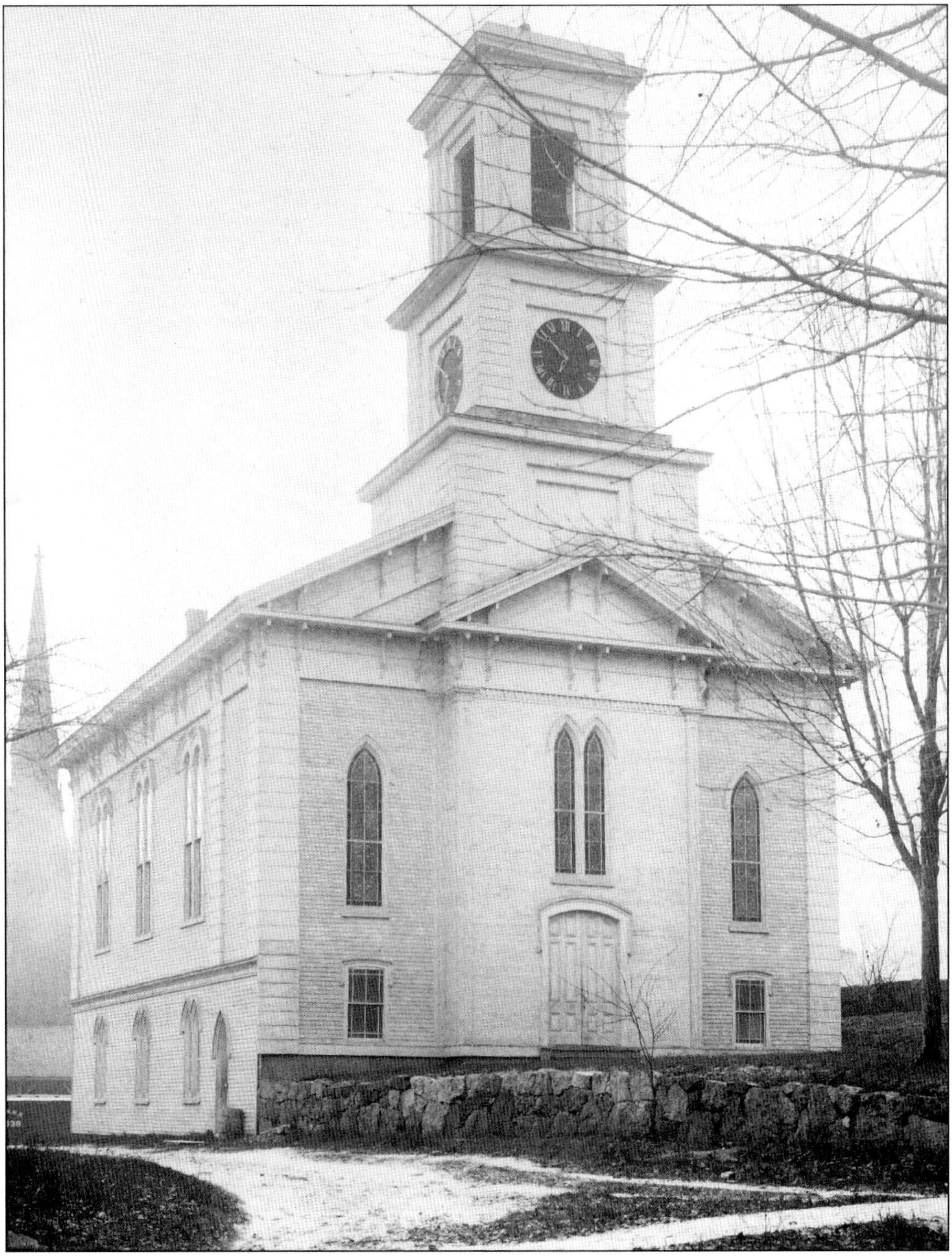

FREE WILL BAPTIST (PARK STREET) CHURCH IN THE 1880S. The Union Avenue Baptist Church is visible in the distance at left. Organized July 13, 1838, at the home of Isaac Cole, with nine members, the Free Will Baptists met for a time in private homes and in the Old School House at 38 Gold Street (see bottom of p. 52). From c. 1843 to 1852, the congregation worshipped in a chapel at 879 Union Avenue (see top of p. 119); in the fall of 1852, they built a large meetinghouse on Park Street, remodeling the structure c. 1877. When this building (above) was destroyed by fire, December 15, 1890, the church immediately rebuilt (see p. 53) on the site.

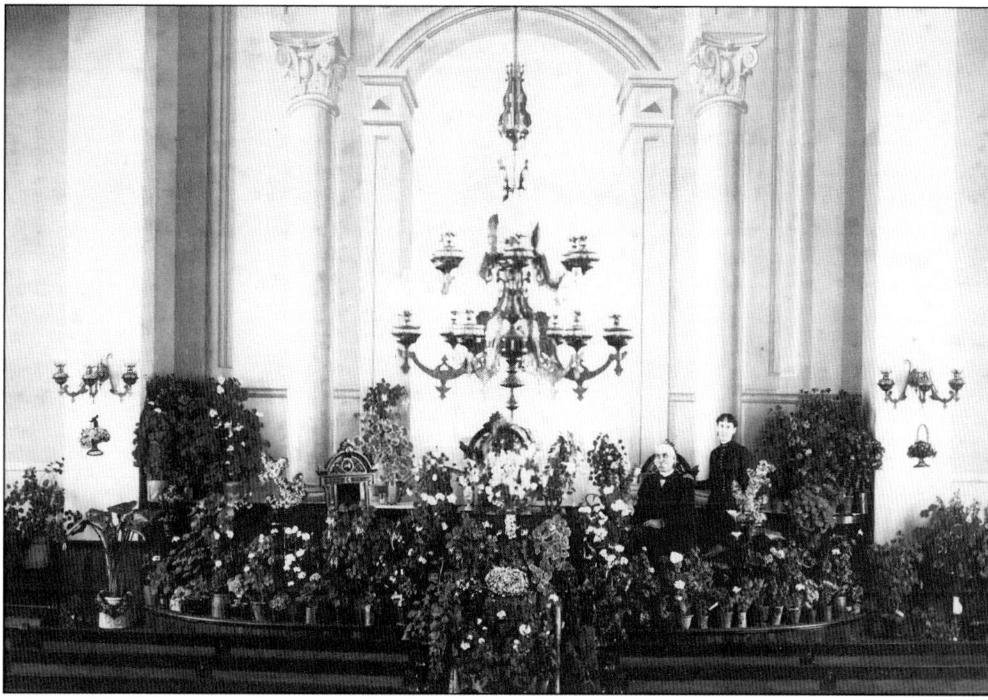

INTERIOR OF PARK STREET CHURCH, 1880S. Elder Porter and his wife are surrounded by Easter decorations.

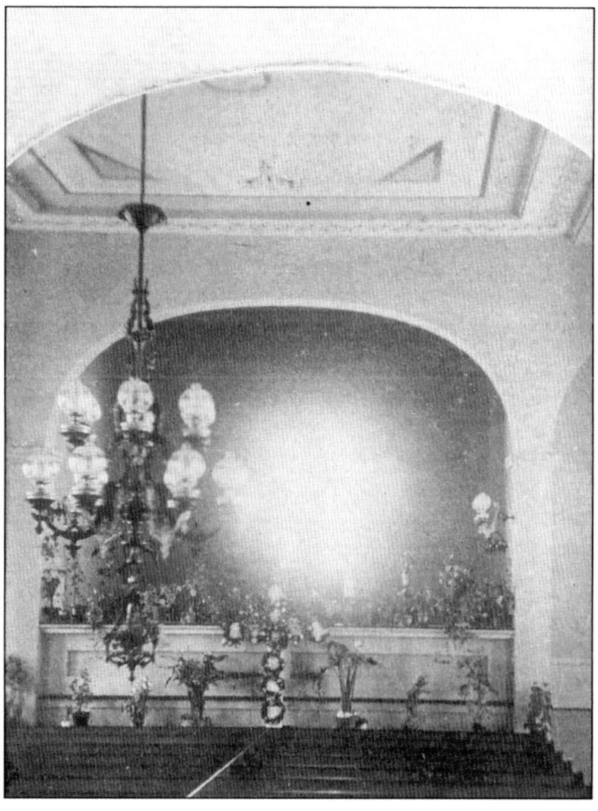

"SINGING ALCOVE" AT REAR OF PARK STREET CHURCH. A pipe organ was installed c. 1886, replacing a reed organ. "It was the custom to stand facing the choir and back to the minister during the singing."

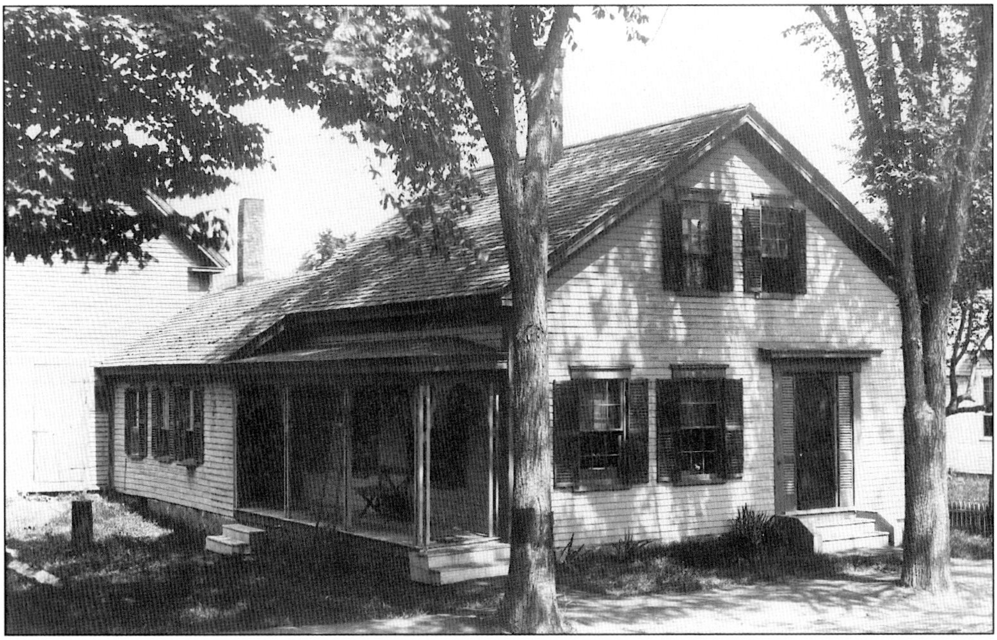

Deacon Isaac Cole House. Built in 1827 between the sites of the later Governor Quinby House at 713 Union Avenue and the Moulton-Adams House (*c.* 1830) at 743 Union Avenue, the Deacon Isaac Cole House was moved back on the lot, before the Civil War, to 130 Mechanic Street. It remains there today. The Free Will (Park Street) Baptist Church was organized in the front room here on July 13, 1838.

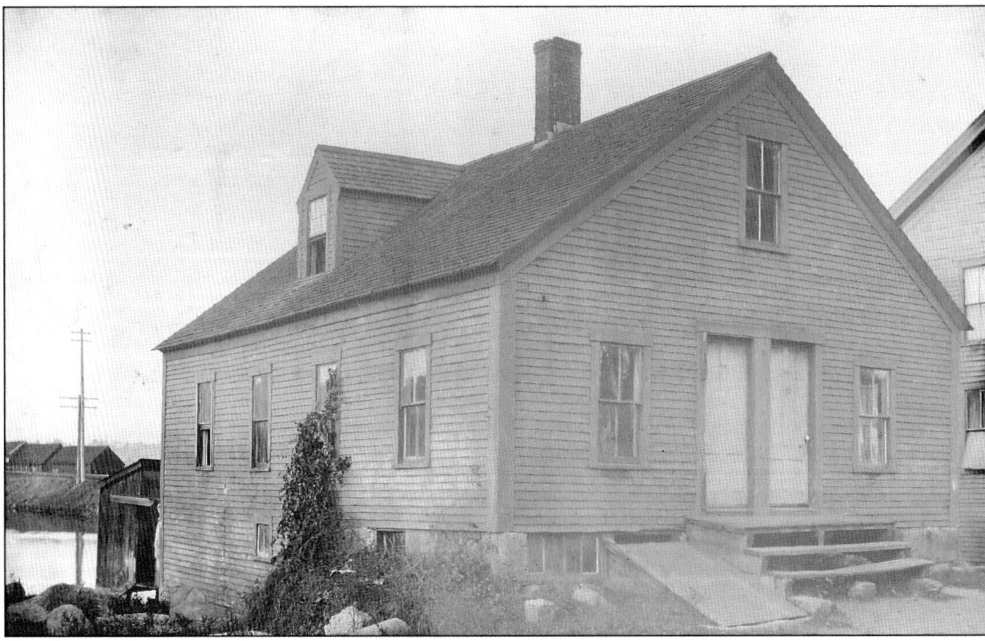

Old School House. For a time, the congregation met in private homes and here in the Old School House, which was then located across the street at 38 Gold Street. By the time of this photograph, the building had been moved across the street and converted into a double-tenement house at 37–39 Gold Street.

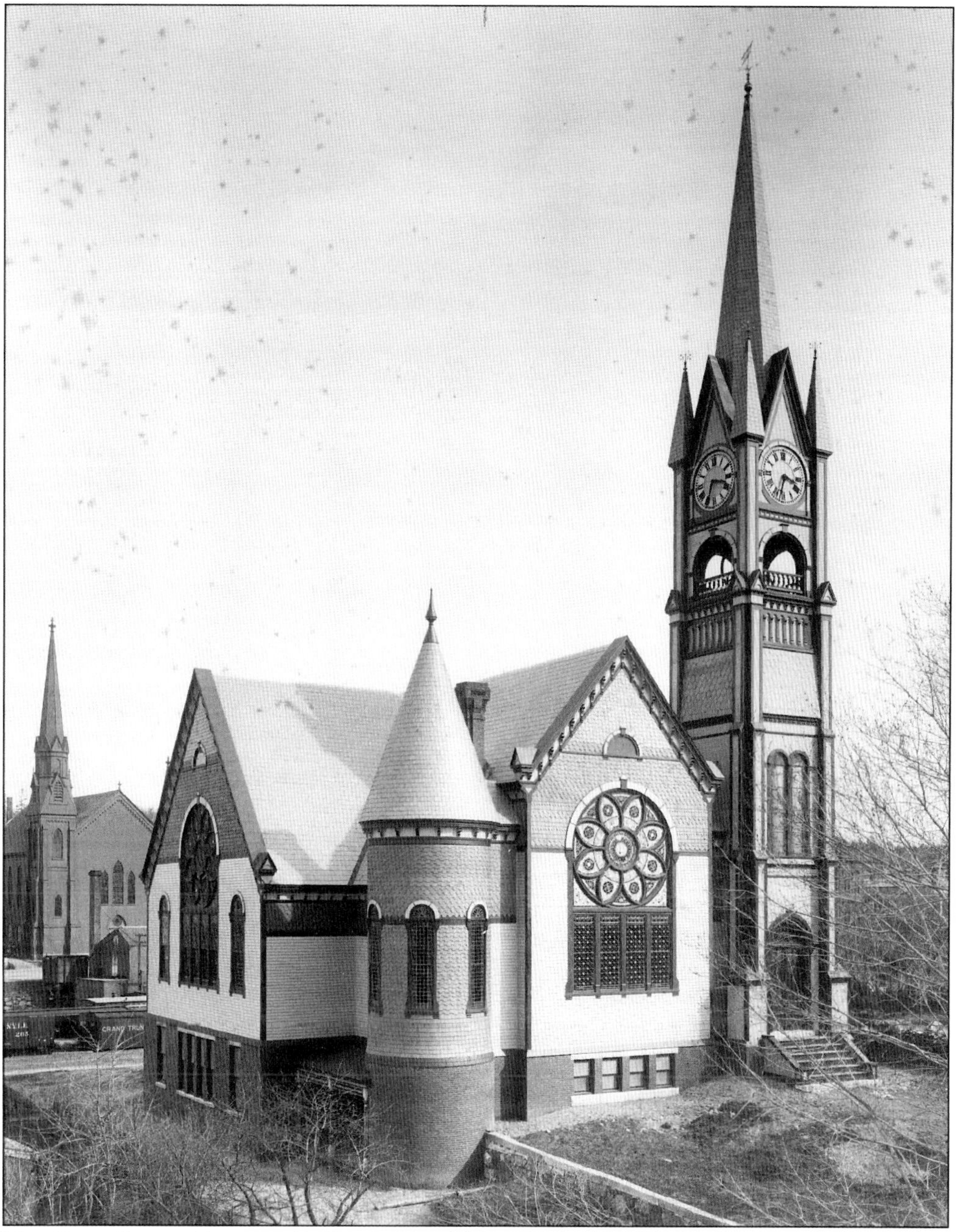

New Park Street Church. Built at a cost of $19,427.68, the new structure was dedicated, free of debt, on May 27, 1892. The Union Avenue Baptist Church is visible in the distance (at left) beyond the railroad tracks.

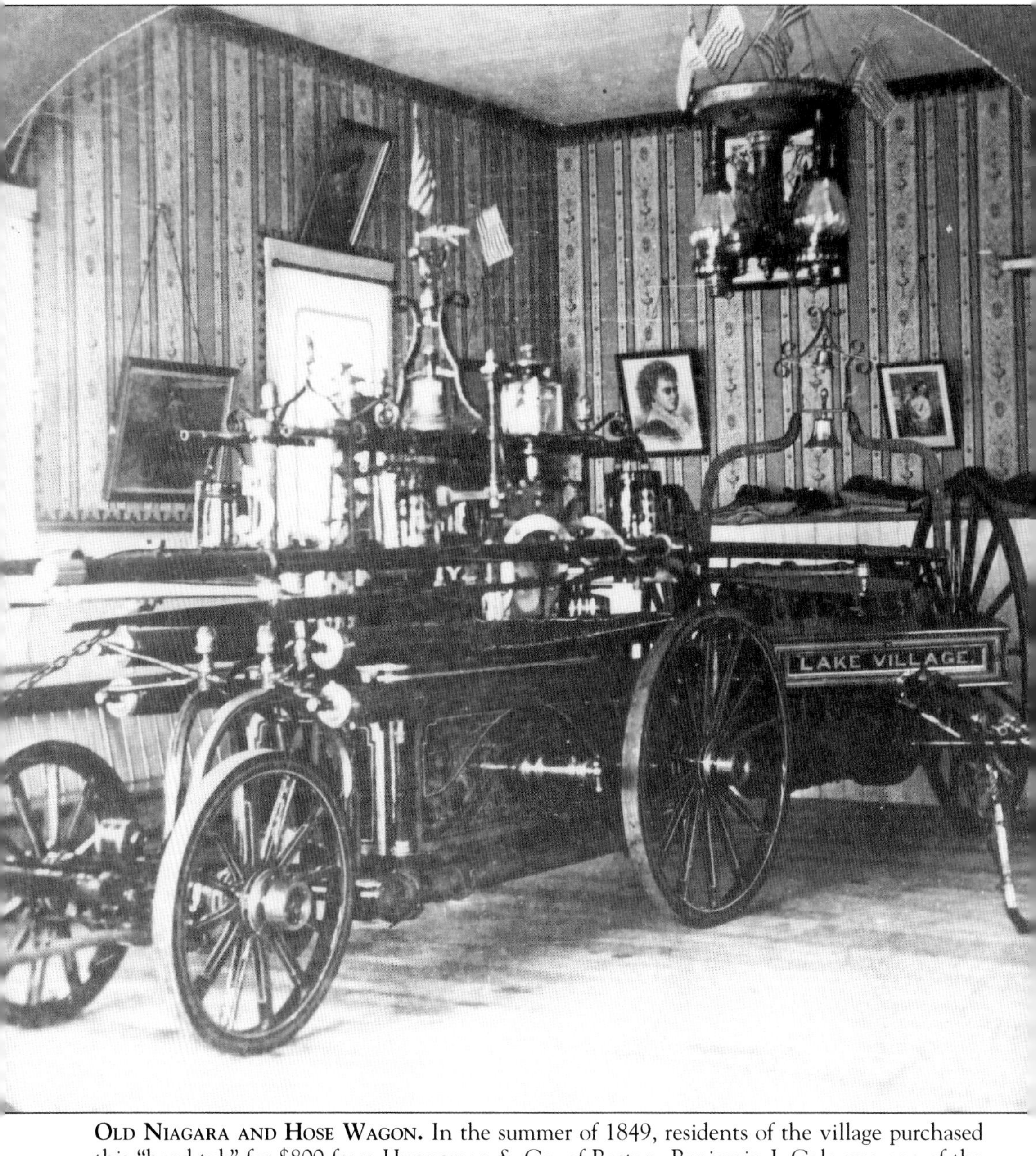

OLD NIAGARA AND HOSE WAGON. In the summer of 1849, residents of the village purchased this "hand tub" for $800 from Hunneman & Co. of Boston. Benjamin J. Cole was one of the leaders in the acquisition of the engine and provided the first engine house on the property of the Cole Manufacturing Co. off Elm Street, opposite Park Street. That engine house stood on the hill where the buildings occupied by the *Belknap Republican* and George H. Smith were later located (see pp. 44–45). It was "just large enough to hold company meetings in if they crowded the engine a little." In the spring of 1861, a more spacious engine house (see next page) was constructed on Gold Street, on the east side of the river, adjoining the Henry Odell clothing store. The Niagara was moved to the new house on July 6, 1861.

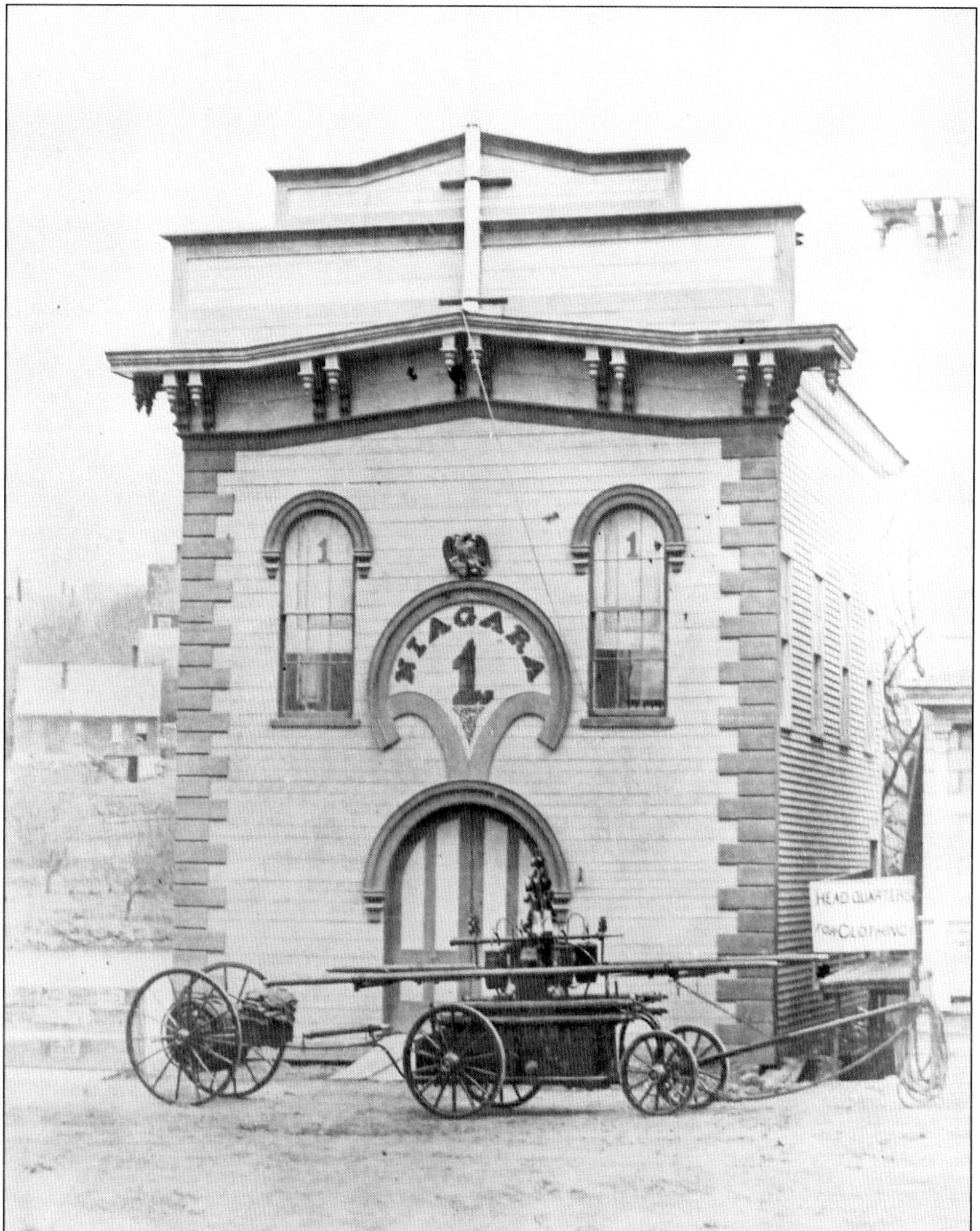

NIAGARA NO. 1 ENGINE HOUSE, GOLD STREET, NEXT TO THE WINNIPESAUKEE RIVER (LEFT). Old Niagara, with its hose carriage, is seen in front of the building. In 1908, the city conveyed the building to the Darius A. Drake Post No. 36 of the GAR, which moved it across the river in May of that year.

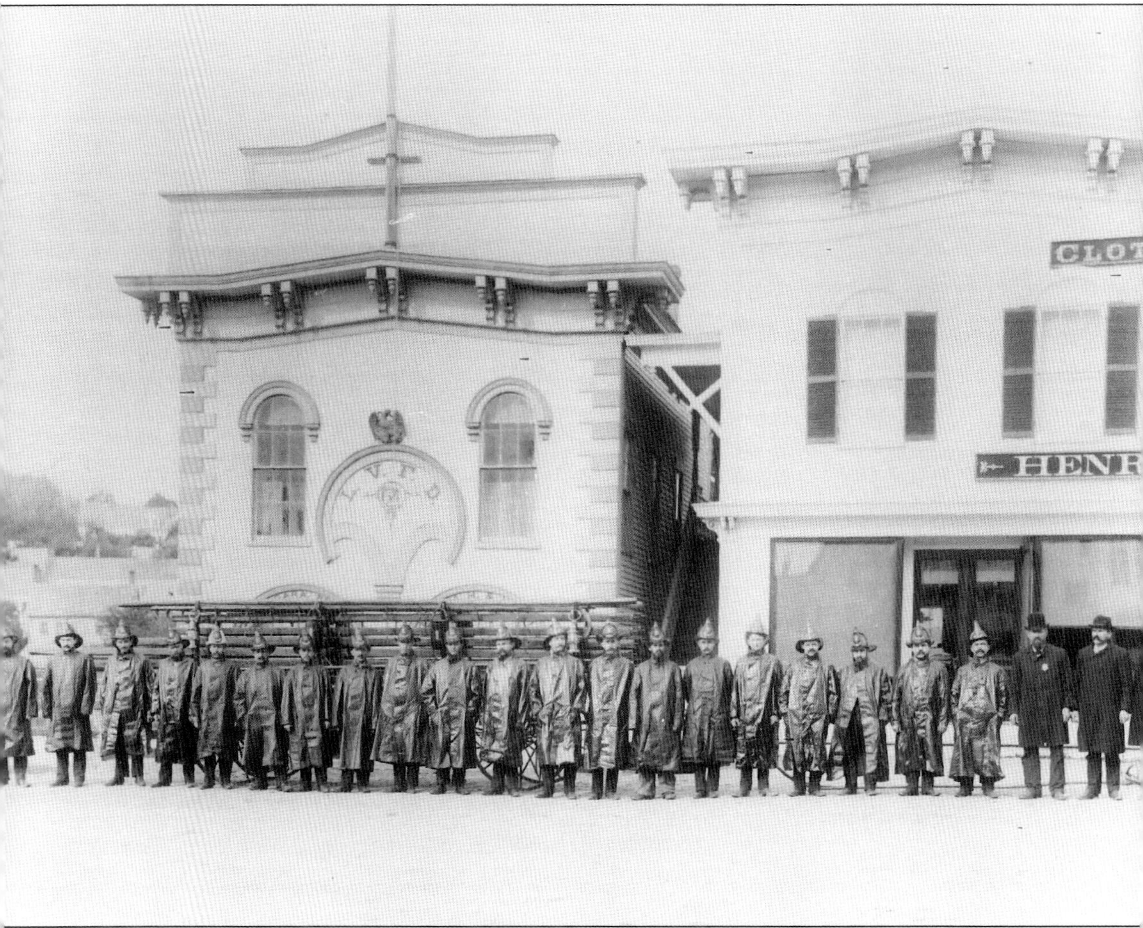

Another View of Niagara Engine House on Gold Street, with the River at Left. Here the structure is labeled LVFD, with two entrances—Niagara on the left and the Hook & Ladder Co. on the right. Henry Odell's Gold Street clothing store is at right. Firemen in full regalia and city officials pose in front of the hook & ladder wagon.

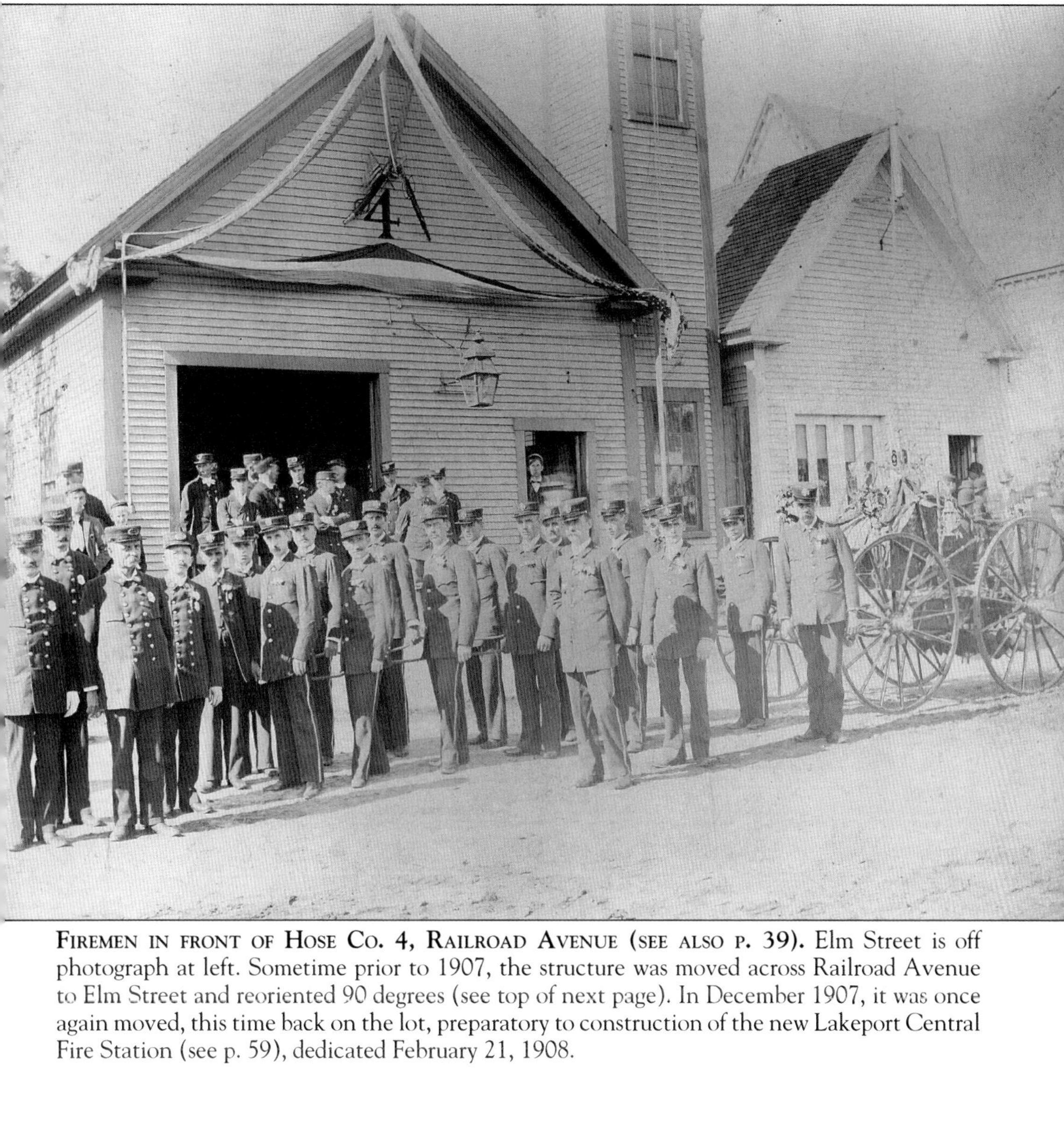

FIREMEN IN FRONT OF HOSE CO. 4, RAILROAD AVENUE (SEE ALSO P. 39). Elm Street is off photograph at left. Sometime prior to 1907, the structure was moved across Railroad Avenue to Elm Street and reoriented 90 degrees (see top of next page). In December 1907, it was once again moved, this time back on the lot, preparatory to construction of the new Lakeport Central Fire Station (see p. 59), dedicated February 21, 1908.

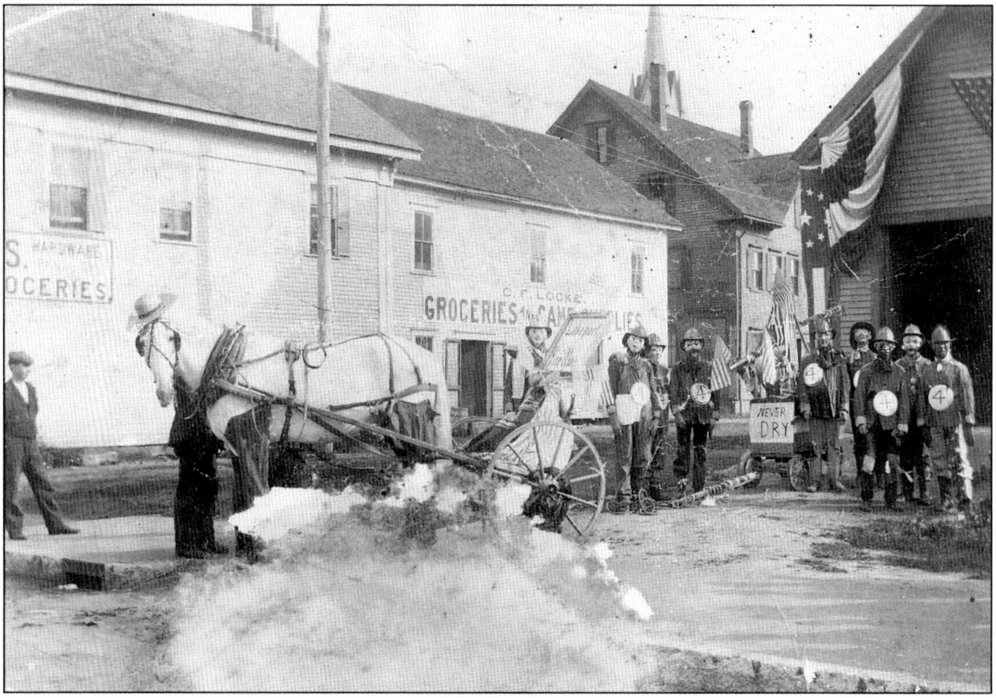

Firemen's Group in front of Hose Company No. 4. They appear to be preparing for a parade. Railroad Avenue runs from left to right, and the photographer is standing on Elm Street.

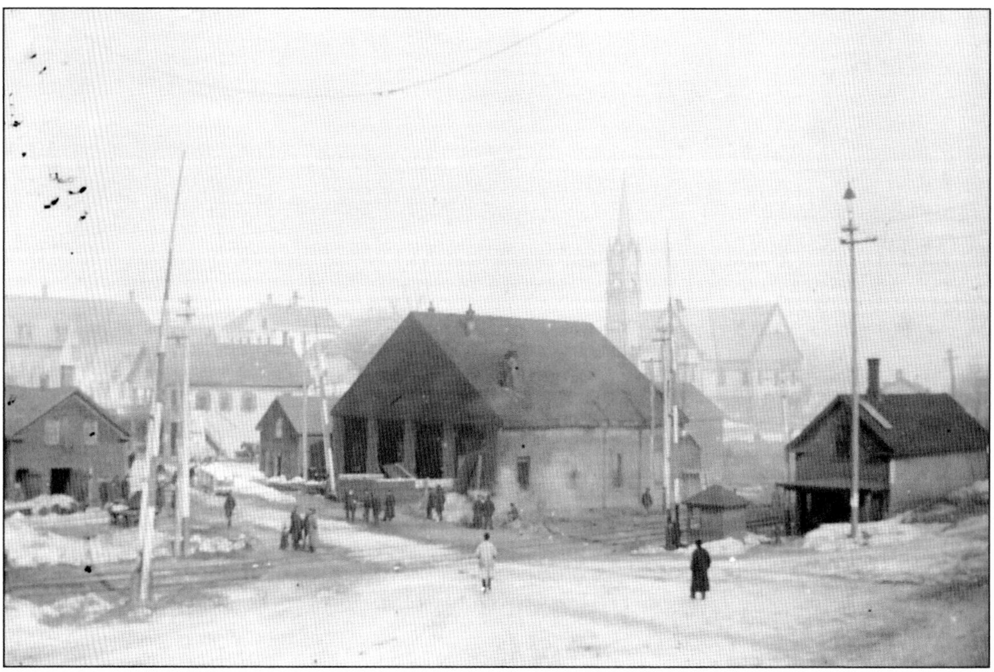

Elm Street Crossing, c. 1890. The large building at center and the smaller building across Elm Street were part of the railroad shops. In 1907–1908, the first Lakeport Central Fire Station occupied the site to the left of the large engine house building.

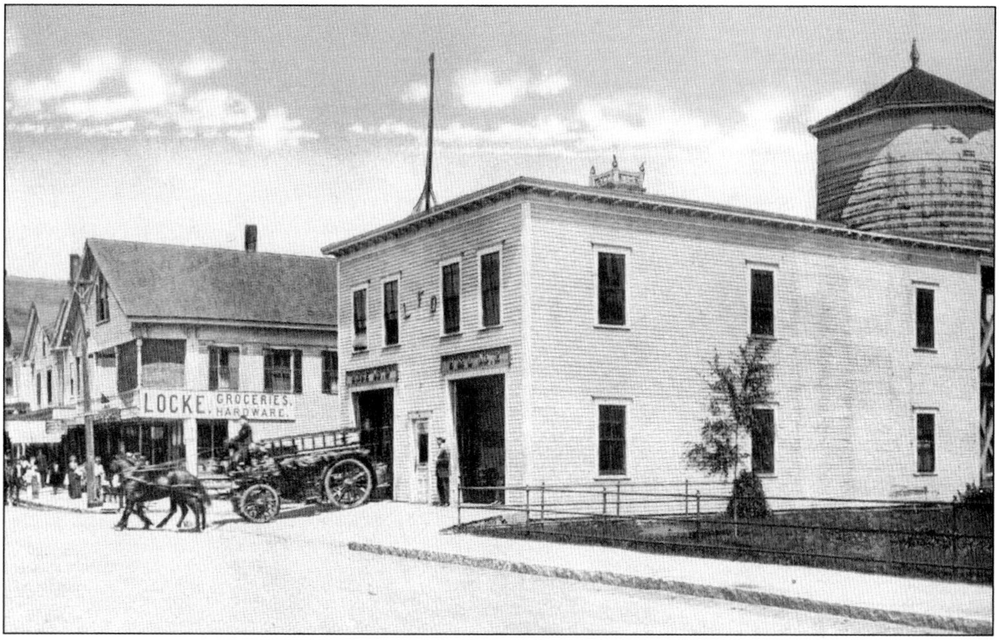

Lakeport Central Fire Station. The new, much larger, structure was built in 1907–1908, on the site of the Hose Co. No. 4 House (see pp. 57–58). A hose wagon is pulling out into Elm Street.

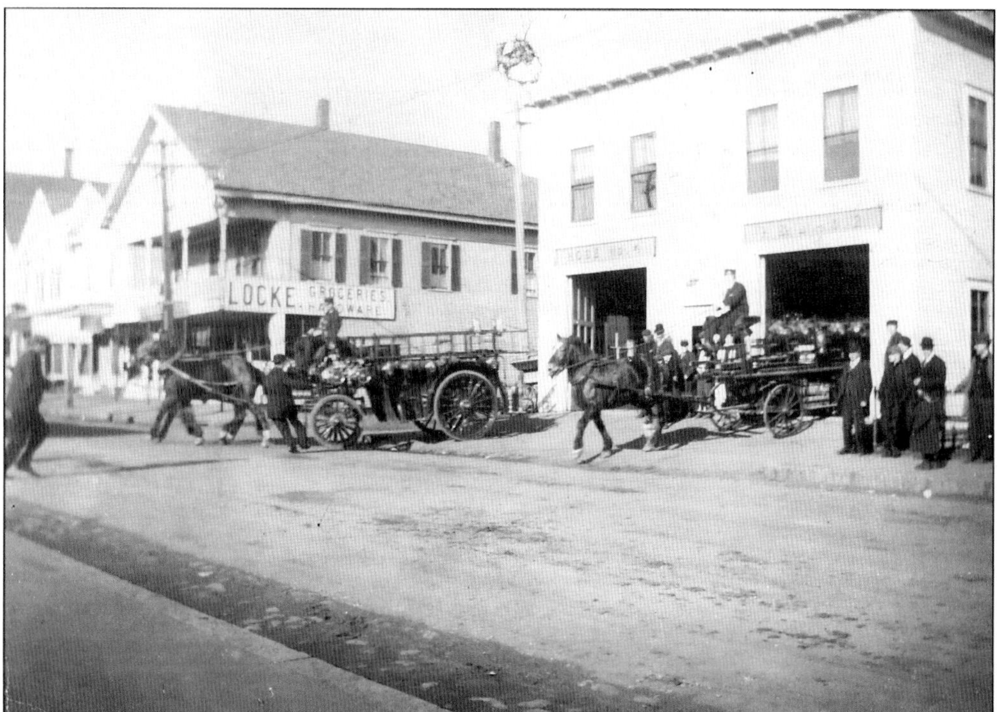

Responding to a Call. In this view of the new fire station, the horse-drawn hose wagon appears on the left and the hook and ladder on the right. The building served until 1955–1956, when a new brick facility was built at right and the old wooden building was torn down.

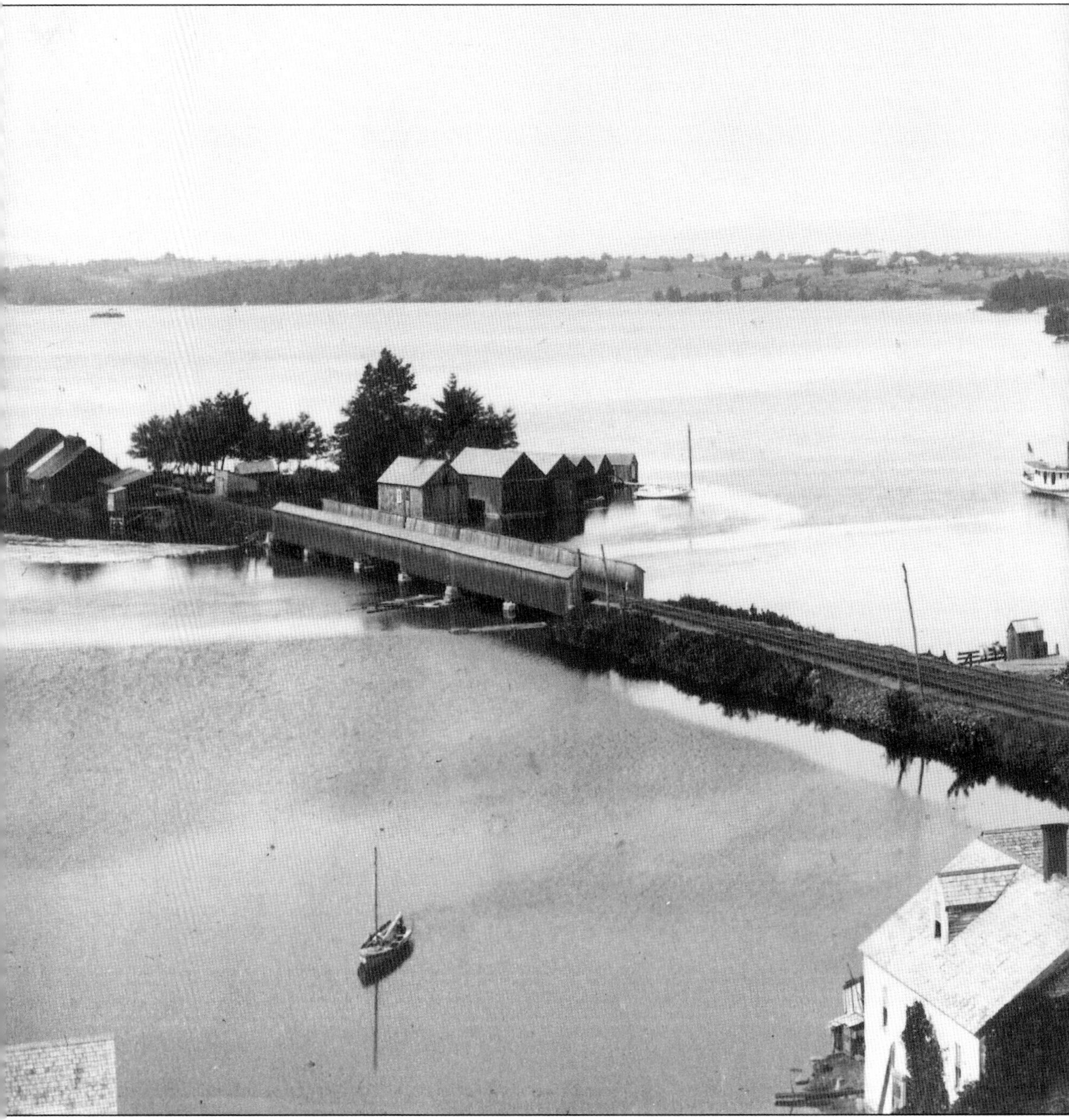

LAKE PAUGUS AND THE RAILROAD BRIDGE FROM BELFRY OF PARK STREET CHURCH, EARLY 1880S. The Old School House (see bottom of p. 52) is the one-and-a-half-story building seen just left of center. It was torn down around 1930 to make room for boathouses. The long building on the other side of the railroad tracks was the old freight depot, with the steamer *James Bell* seen at its left. The tall chimney at right was all that remained of the old sawmill, later Appleton's hosiery mill. In 1865, Thomas Appleton had purchased the "steam mill," equipping it with machinery for the manufacture of cotton hosiery. The mill burned January 20, 1870. "The lone tall chimney towered as a landmark for many years afterwards before being taken down." The photograph was probably taken prior to 1883, since there is no indication of the Laconia Water Works, built 1884–1885 at top center. Gold Street runs from left to right in the foreground. The area to the right of the small steamboat (center) is now occupied by Irwin Marine. Houses on

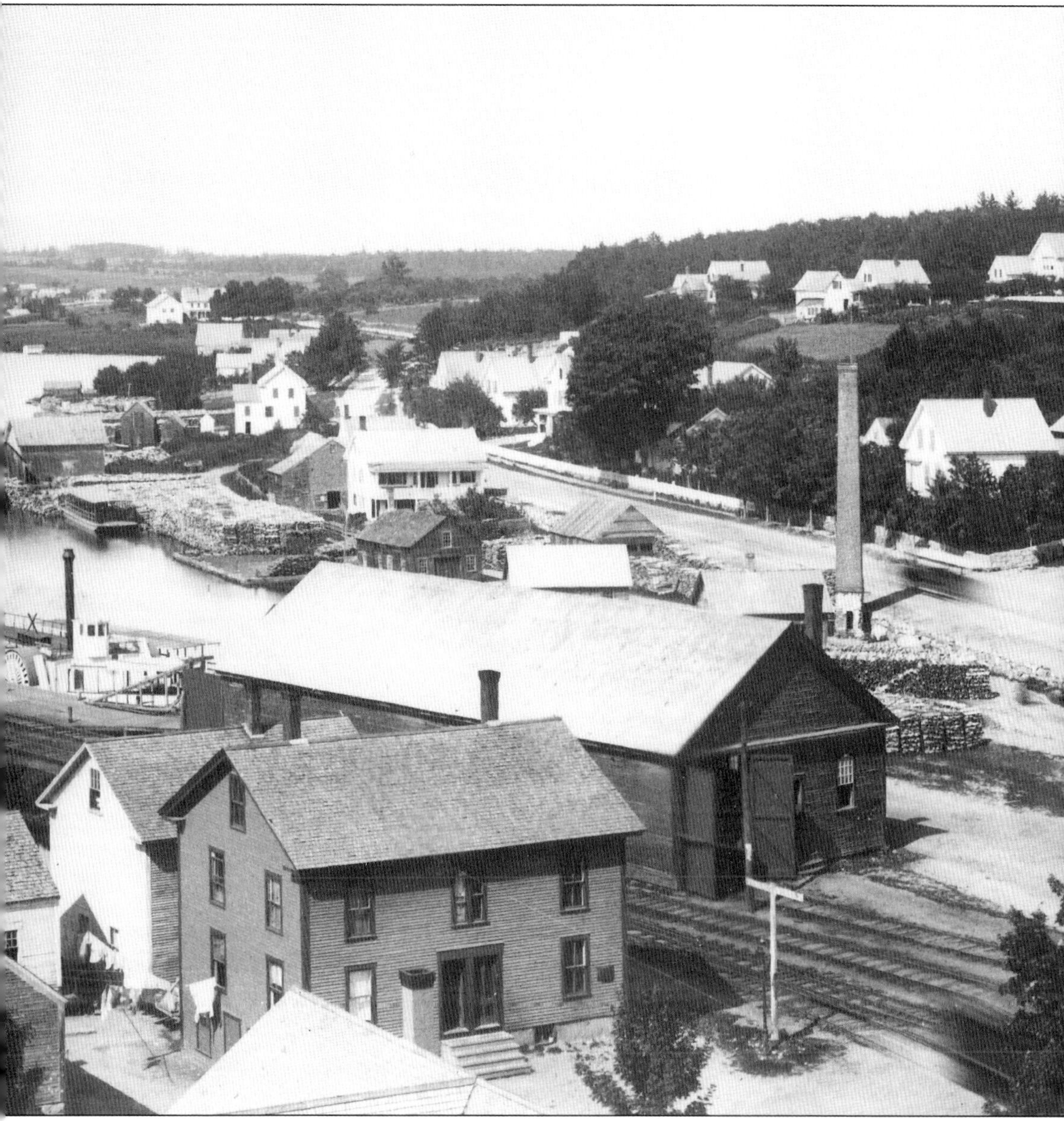

Mechanic Street appear on Locke's Hill at upper right (see p. 123 and bottom of p. 124). Until c. 1871, Lake Paugus was known as Long Bay. Around that year, Martin A. Haynes, publisher of the *Lake Village Times*, and Professor J. Warren Thyng, "in one of their frequent sanctum smoke-talks, decided that Long Bay and Round Bay were not worthy names for such beautiful sheets of water, and they proceeded to re-christen them, each choosing a name. Haynes selected Paugus as a suitable substitute for Long Bay, in honor of the old Indian chieftain who once ranged this region and the country to the north of it." In the local newspaper, thereafter, these lakes were always alluded to as Paugus and Opechee, "and the names met popular approval and have become firmly established." Thyng explained that robins used to be numerous in the vicinity of Round Bay, and meeting the word "Opechee" in Longfellow's *Hiawatha*, he "thought it would be an appropriate name for that little body of water."

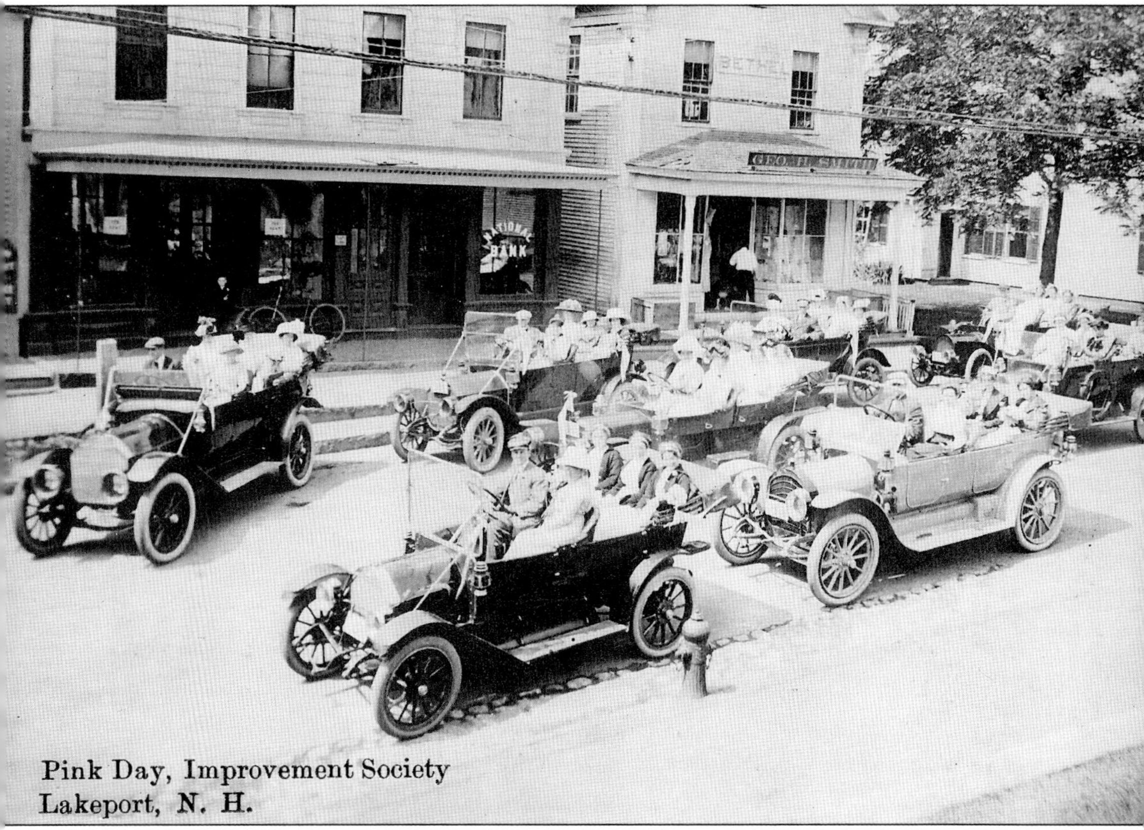

PINK DAY. "In the summer of 1912, the Village Improvement Society of Lakeport had a 'Pink Day' to raise money for a project they were promoting," recalled Harold H. Young, a former resident of Lakeport. "A small triangular piece of land at the junction of Union Avenue and Messer Street was to be used for a billboard and the VIS sought to buy the land and give it to the city for a park. The profit from the sale of the pinks was sufficient to achieve their end. This picture was taken before the volunteers fanned out to various sections of the city to make calls." Young "is standing in the doorway of a vacant store, next to the bicycle. Mother is in front seat of the last car in left hand lane. Note that most cars have right-hand drive." These are the same Elm Street buildings pictured on pp. 44–45. The vehicles are headed toward the railroad crossing and Union Avenue. The river and the Elm Street Bridge are off the photograph at right.

Four

Industry and Waterpower

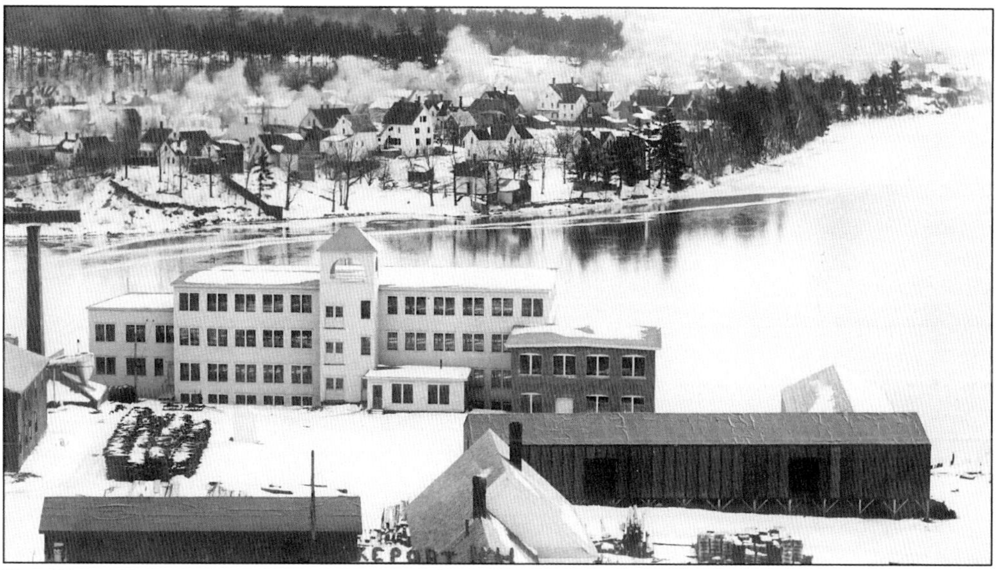

The New Wood's Mill, c. 1915. It was from this location that the Great Lakeport Fire of May 26, 1903, had started, destroying two c. 1828 mills built by Nathan Batchelder (see pp. 72–73). The new Wood's Mill was occupied by Sweaterville when it was destroyed by fire on December 25, 1968. Situated at the upper end of Lake Opechee, the early textile and hosiery mills drew waterpower from the Lakeport Dam (off the photograph at left). In this view, Union Avenue and the railroad run from left to right on the opposite shore, with Laconia off the photograph at right. Horace Hanson Wood (1842–1909) began his manufacturing career here in 1865, starting his own woolen and hosiery mill in 1880. After the fire of 1903, he immediately rebuilt. His widow, Jennie, and Charles G. St. Clair, manager and treasurer, continued the business, which ultimately closed in 1938.

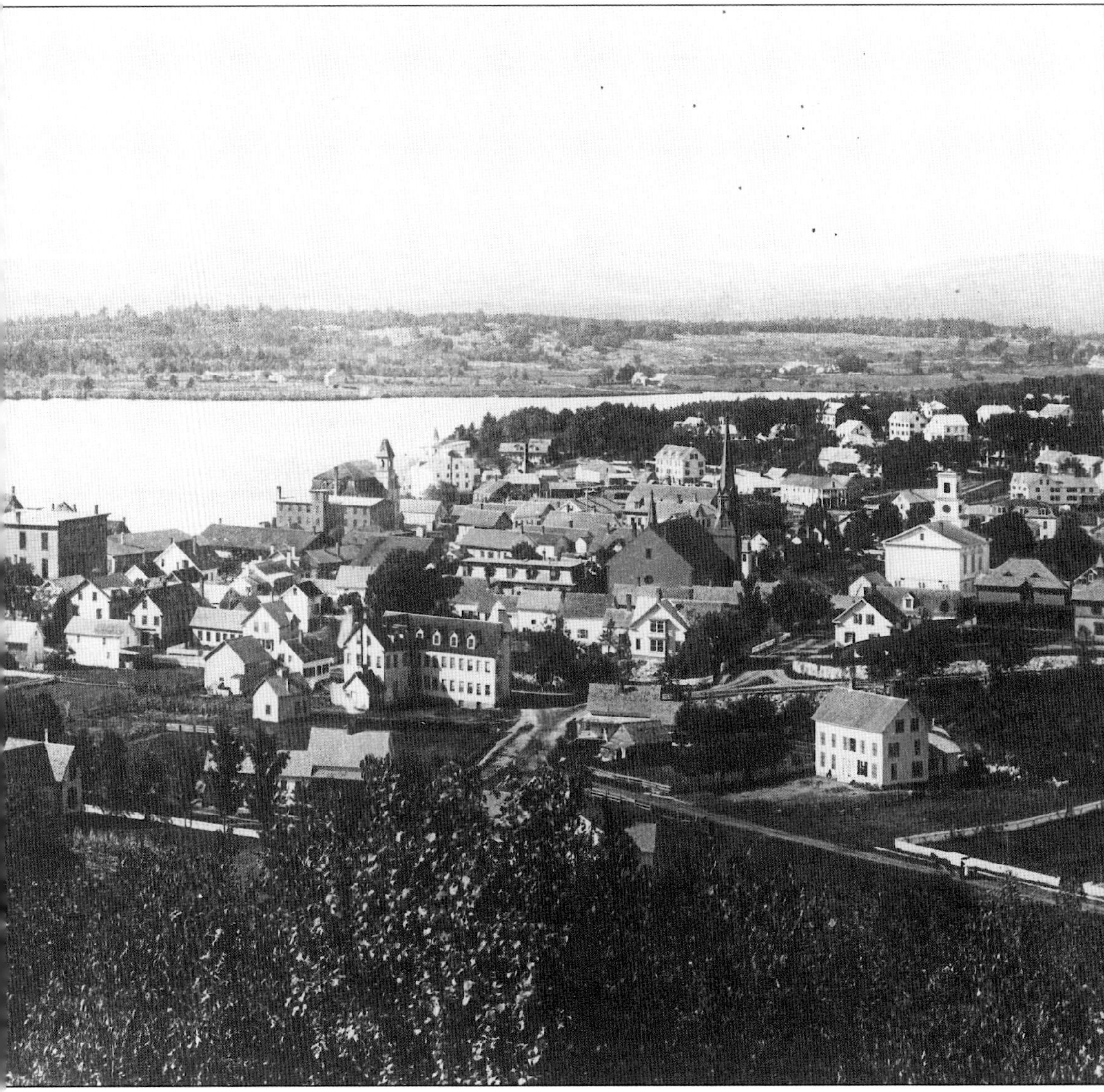

LAKEPORT FROM COLE'S HILL, 1888. The Opera House Block is at left. To the right, along the shore of Lake Opechee beyond the buildings of the Cole Manufacturing Co., are the Halifax and Bayside Mills with their distinctive stair towers. Here, the early-19th-century mills still line the west bank of the Winnipesaukee River. The spires of the Union Avenue Baptist Church and the belfry of the Free Will Baptist Church appear at right. The building with dormer windows piercing the roof, at center foreground, is the Wardwell (later Torrington) Needle Co., on the site of today's Sanborn Park at the corner of Mechanic and Manchester Streets. The John L. Sanborn Park was dedicated November 11, 1973. Private Sanborn was the first soldier from this city to give his life in the Korean War. In 1889, the Crane Manufacturing Co. would build on the property to the left of the Wardwell plant. Also to the left of the Wardwell Building, across Mechanic Street, on the site of today's drive-in post office, is the Rublee Carriage Shop (see p. 119). Though barely discernible, Union Avenue and the tracks of the Boston, Concord & Montreal Railroad run from left to right at the center of this photograph. Portions of Mechanic and Manchester Streets are visible in the lower right corner.

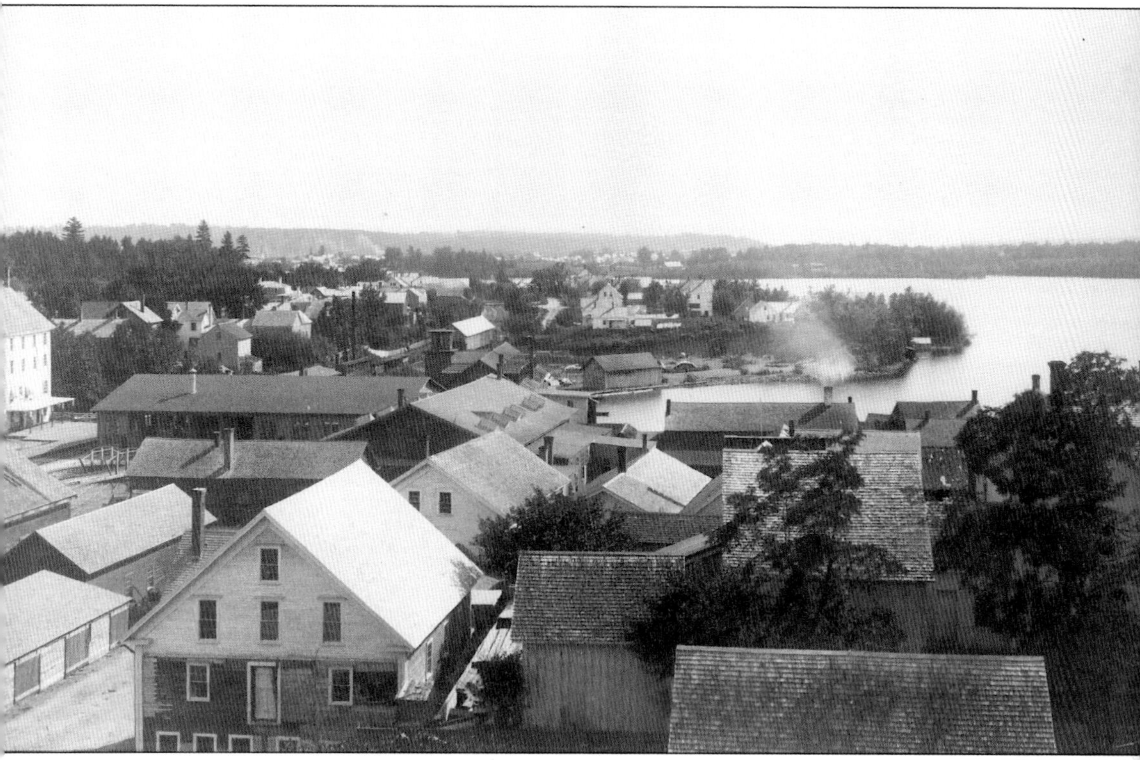

INDUSTRY AND COMMERCE, C. 1890. Looking south, the Morgan Block is at left, with the former Boston, Concord & Montreal Railroad shops and the buildings of the Cole Manufacturing Co. between it and Lake Opechee (upper right). Part of the railroad shops also appears at the extreme center left. Elm Street runs left to right in the center of the photograph. The Brawn Block is just off the photograph at right. Part of the railroad shop's turntable (see p. 68) is visible at center left.

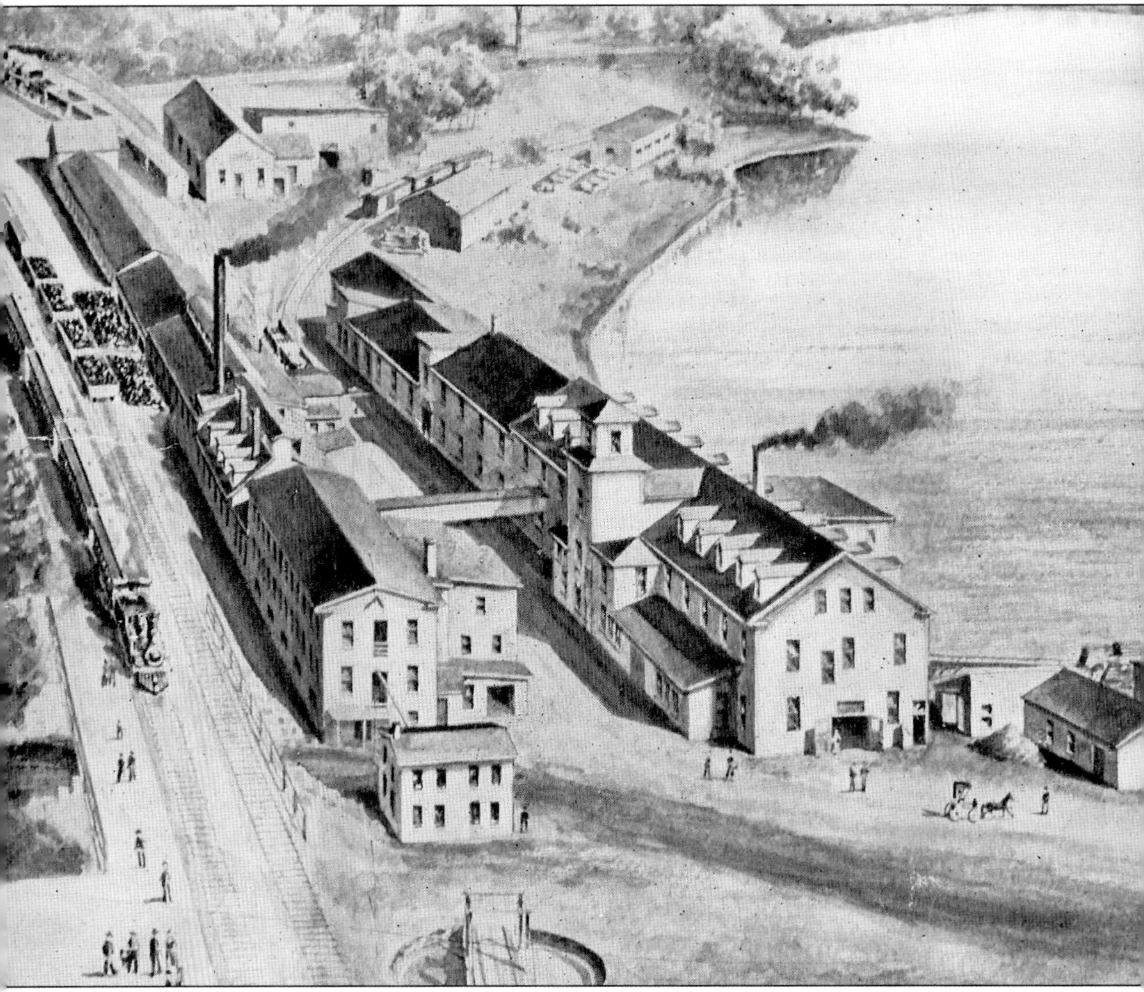

Cole Manufacturing Company. In this idealized 1892 conception, artistic license has been taken—omitting the Boston, Concord & Montreal Railroad shop complex, lower left, except for the turntable. Cole buildings appear at left, between the main line of the railroad and Lake Opechee. Union Avenue would be off drawing at left. Beginning with a small foundry built by his father, Isaac Cole, in 1827, Benjamin J. Cole expanded the business, becoming widely known throughout northern New Hampshire for the manufacture of parlor and cooking stoves and agricultural implements. By 1873, having constructed a steam forge, the company began the manufacture of car axles for steam railroads, also making hosiery, needle, bobbin, and sawmill machinery, forgings, castings of all kinds, and iron work generally, including friction clutches, shafting, pulleys, and hangers. In the early 1900s, the company went out of business and the property was acquired by the Scott & Williams Co., which cleared away the old buildings and constructed its Building 25 (see p. 11, bottom) in 1919–1920. The Halifax Mill is at right, along with other Cole Manufacturing Co. structures. The original Niagara Engine House was located on high ground, either at extreme right or just off the drawing. Throughout the 80-year existence of the Cole Manufacturing Co., the physical layout of the plant was in continual flux as new buildings were erected and old ones torn down, to say nothing of the frequent fires that removed prominent landmarks with some regularity. The Bayside Mill, for example, occupied the site to the right of the Halifax Mill from 1879–1880 to February 16, 1905, when it fell victim to flames.

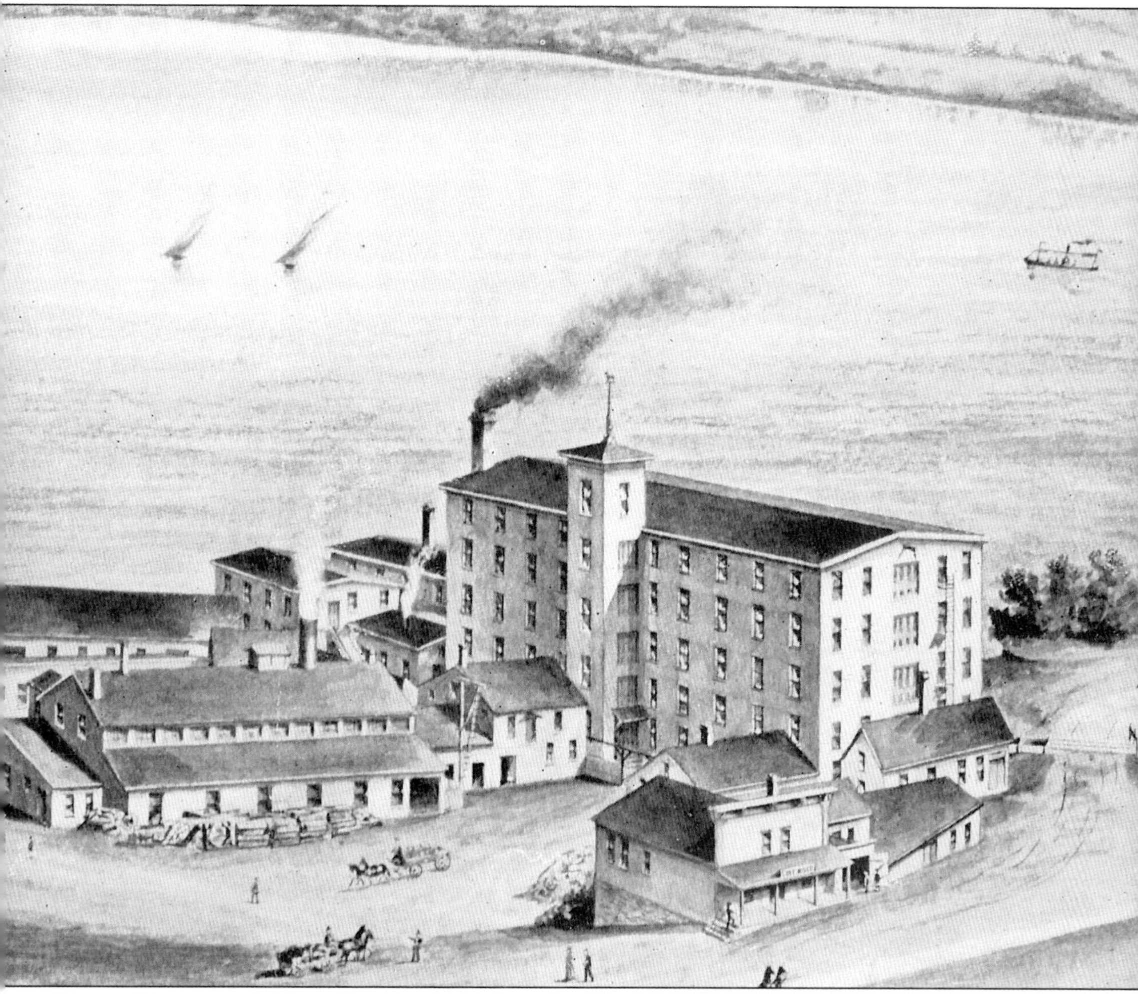

***RIGHT*: BENJAMIN J. COLE (1814–1899).** In addition to his industrial activities, Benjamin J. Cole was president of the Winnipesogee Steamboat Co. for more than 40 years, having built the *Lady of the Lake* in 1848–1849. During his 72 years in Lakeport, he built more than 60 buildings. He donated land for a church and a schoolhouse, as well as the first house for the Niagara 1 engine. Although he was obliged to go through bankruptcy in 1876, "subsequently when prosperity smiled upon him, he paid with interest every debt, in full, from which he had been legally released; and that he was able to do this afforded him more pleasure than any other act of his business career."

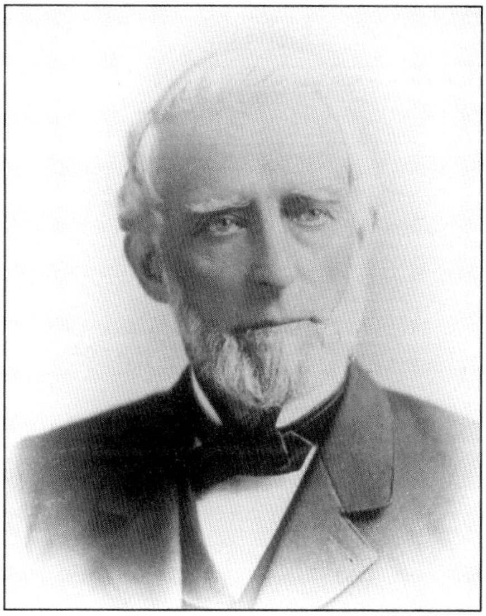

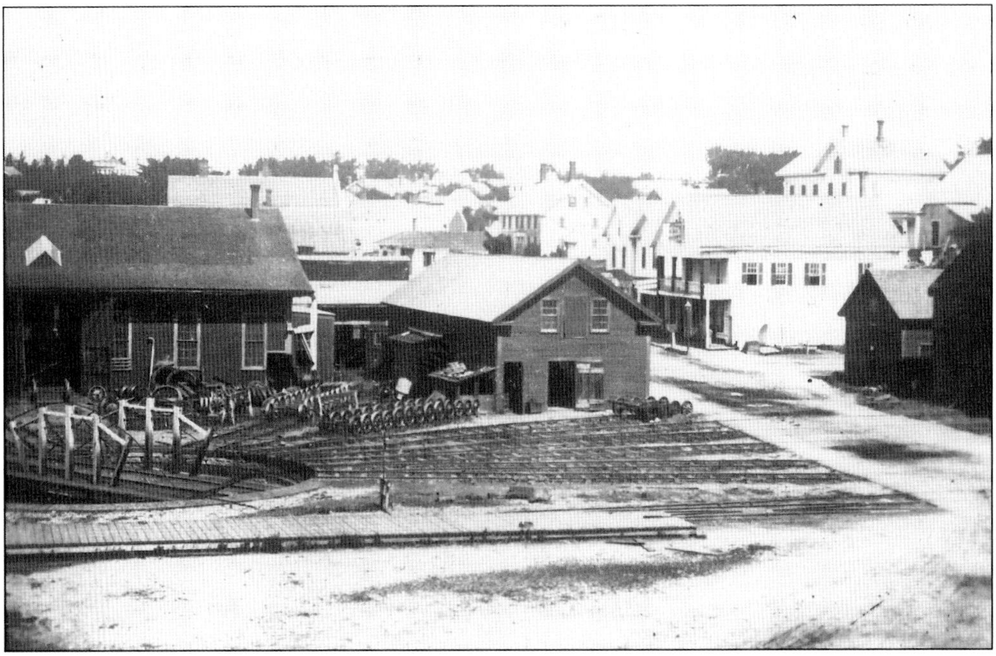

RAILROAD SHOPS, C. 1890. The turntable, with tracks leading to the Engine House, across Elm Street (which runs diagonally from center right to upper left), served the Boston, Concord & Montreal, later the Concord & Montreal and Boston & Maine Railroads, from *c.* 1849 to around the end of the century.

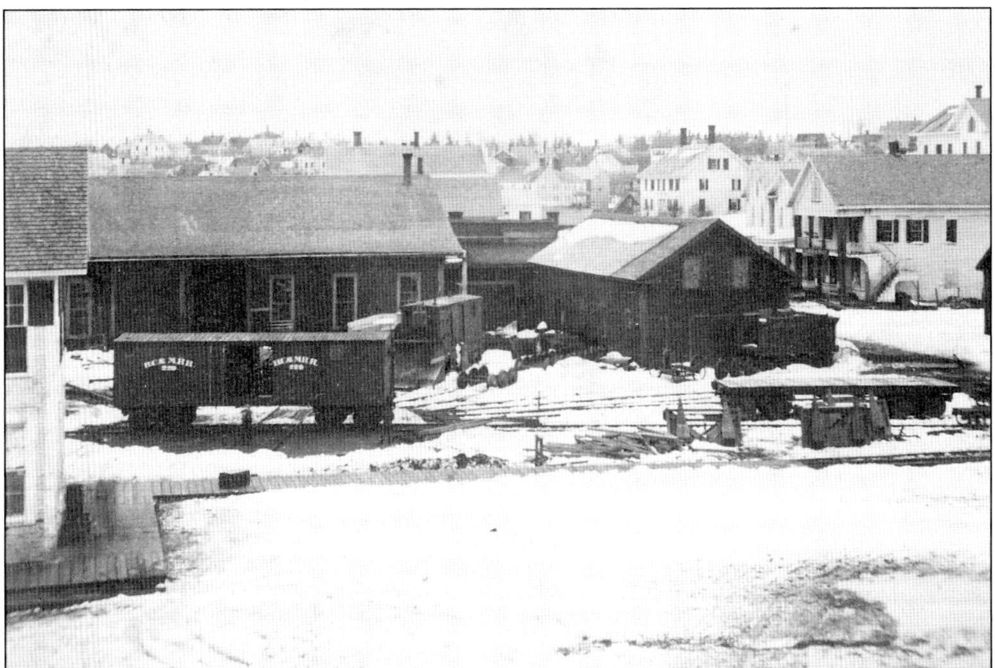

ANOTHER VIEW OF TURNTABLE. The low building beyond the freight car was part of the Boston, Concord & Montreal Railroad shops. The Cole Manufacturing Co. complex is at left, off the photograph.

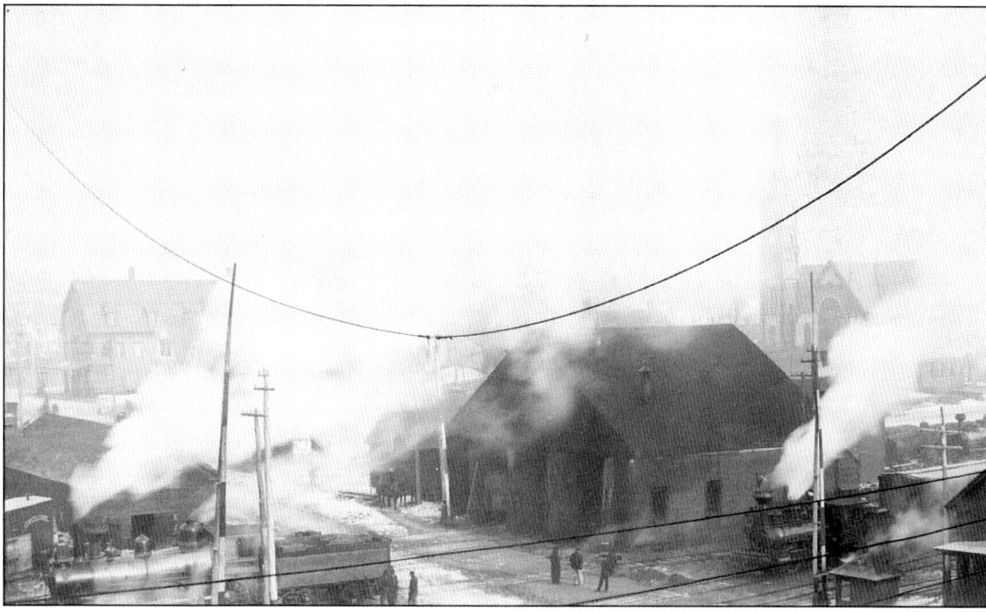

Elm Street Crossing. The Engine House, which dominates the photograph, was part of the railroad repair shops.

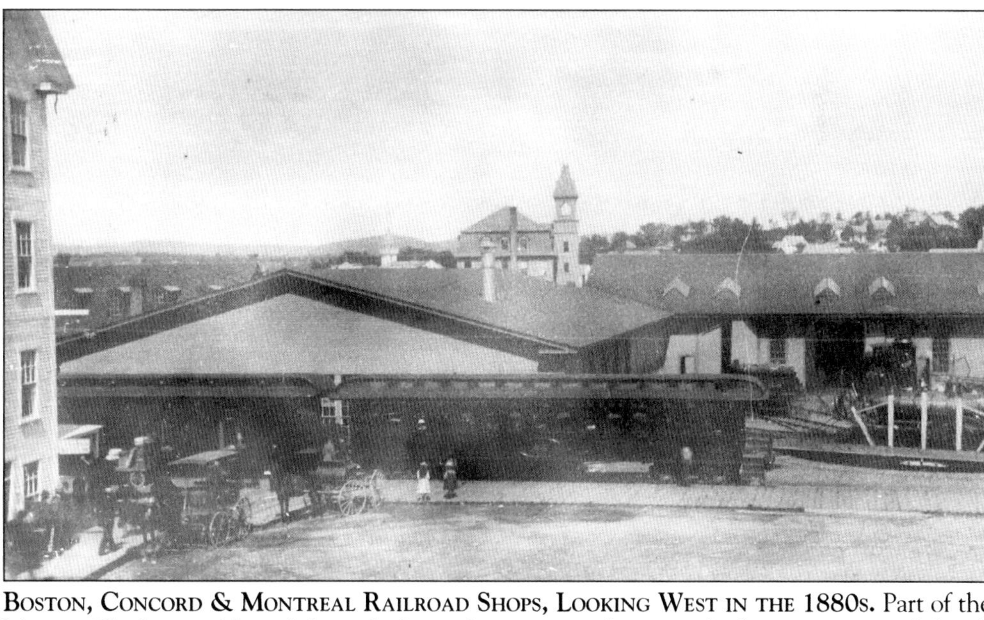

Boston, Concord & Montreal Railroad Shops, Looking West in the 1880s. Part of the Morgan Block is visible at left, with the early passenger depot in the basement at track level. The Bayside Mill, with the stair tower, is at center in the distance.

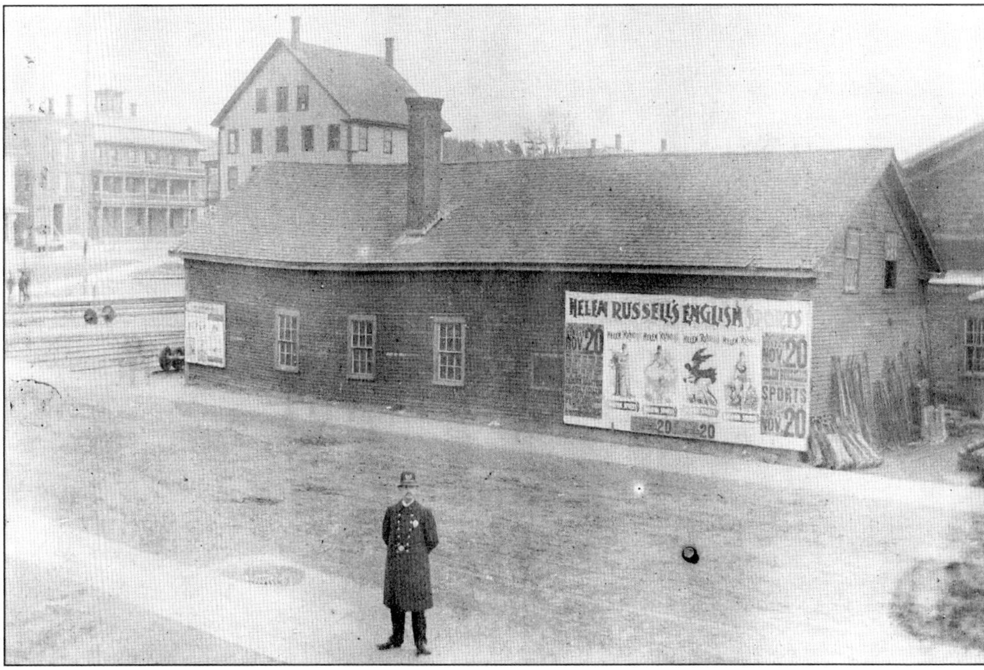

Railroad Wheel Shop, Looking Southeast toward Mount Belknap House and Morgan Block from Elm Street. Police Officer Frank Bailey stands in front of the shop building.

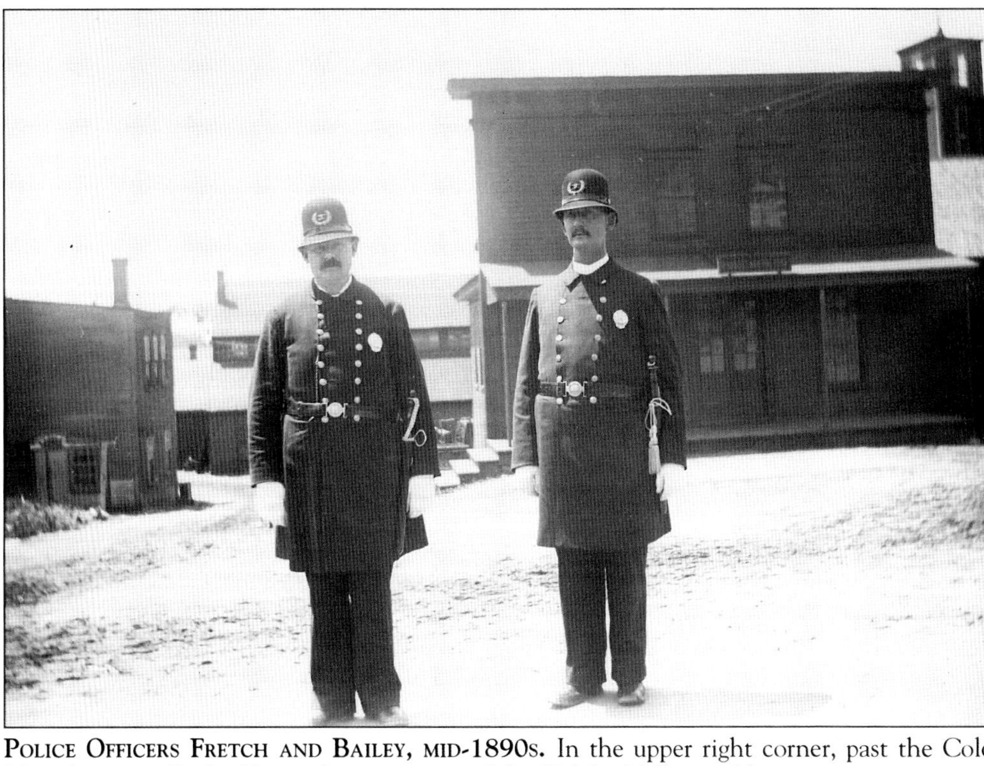

Police Officers Fretch and Bailey, mid-1890s. In the upper right corner, past the Cole Manufacturing Co. buildings, the stair tower of the Halifax Mill is visible.

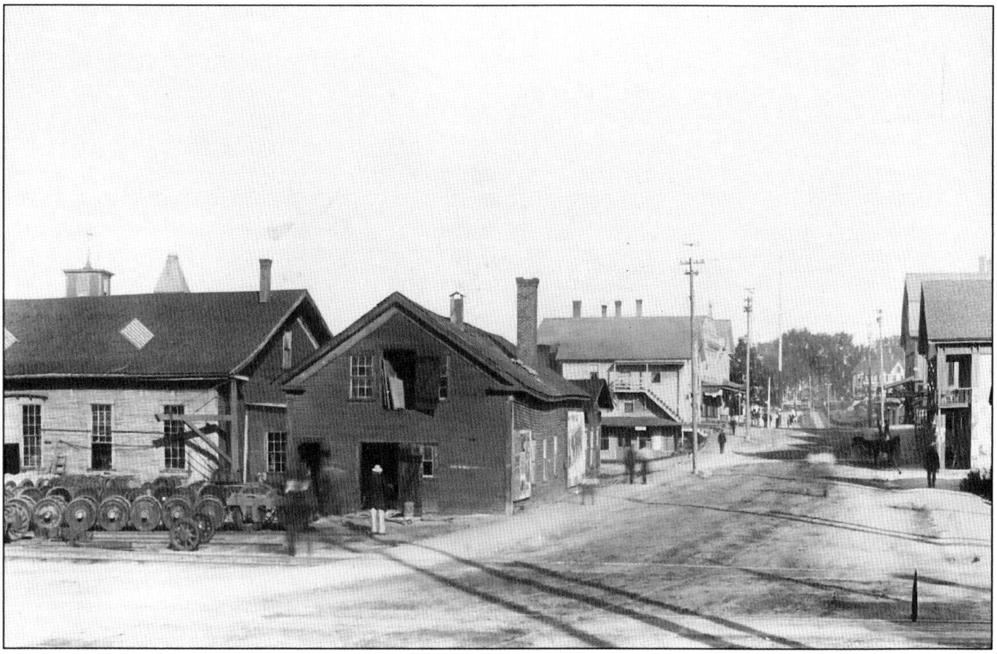

Elm Street from the Railroad Tracks. The turntable is off the photograph at left. Railway wheels and axles are arrayed in front of the railroad wheel shop. The Elm Street Bridge is in the distance.

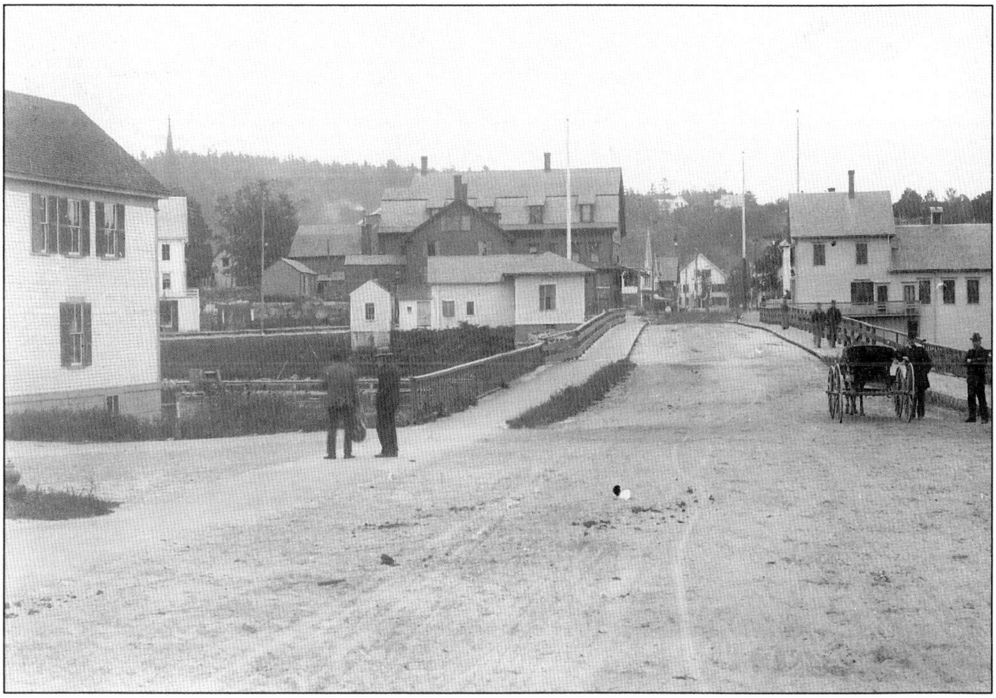

Elm Street Bridge (Built in 1870), Looking East toward Union Avenue from Franklin (now McGrath) Square. The office of the Lake Co. can be seen at center, beyond the bridge. The dam is off the photograph at right.

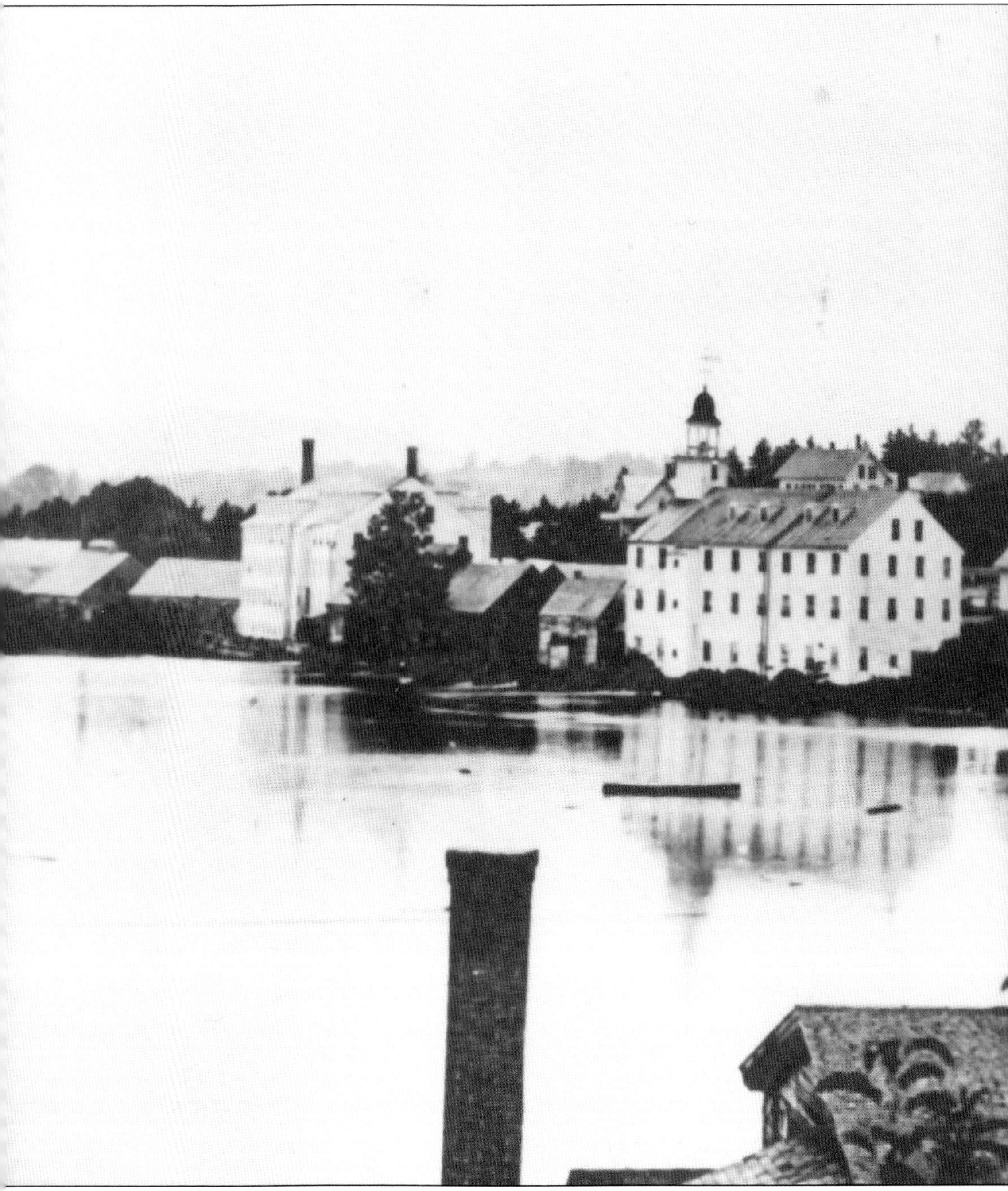

EARLY VIEW OF LAKEPORT MILLS, C. 1868. The building with the bell tower (left of center), known as "the old cotton mill," or the Howard Mill, was later occupied by Horace H. Wood. At center was the "old woolen mill," or Old Pulcifer Mill, and obscured by foliage at right are various other structures associated with manufacturing. The large clerestory building at left was at one time occupied by the Belknap Mills and at another by the Union Lace Co., which made shoelaces. The Pulcifer Mill burned in 1885 and was not rebuilt. The other two mills were casualties of the Great Fire of 1903 (see Chapter Six). The wooden Elm Street Bridge (built in

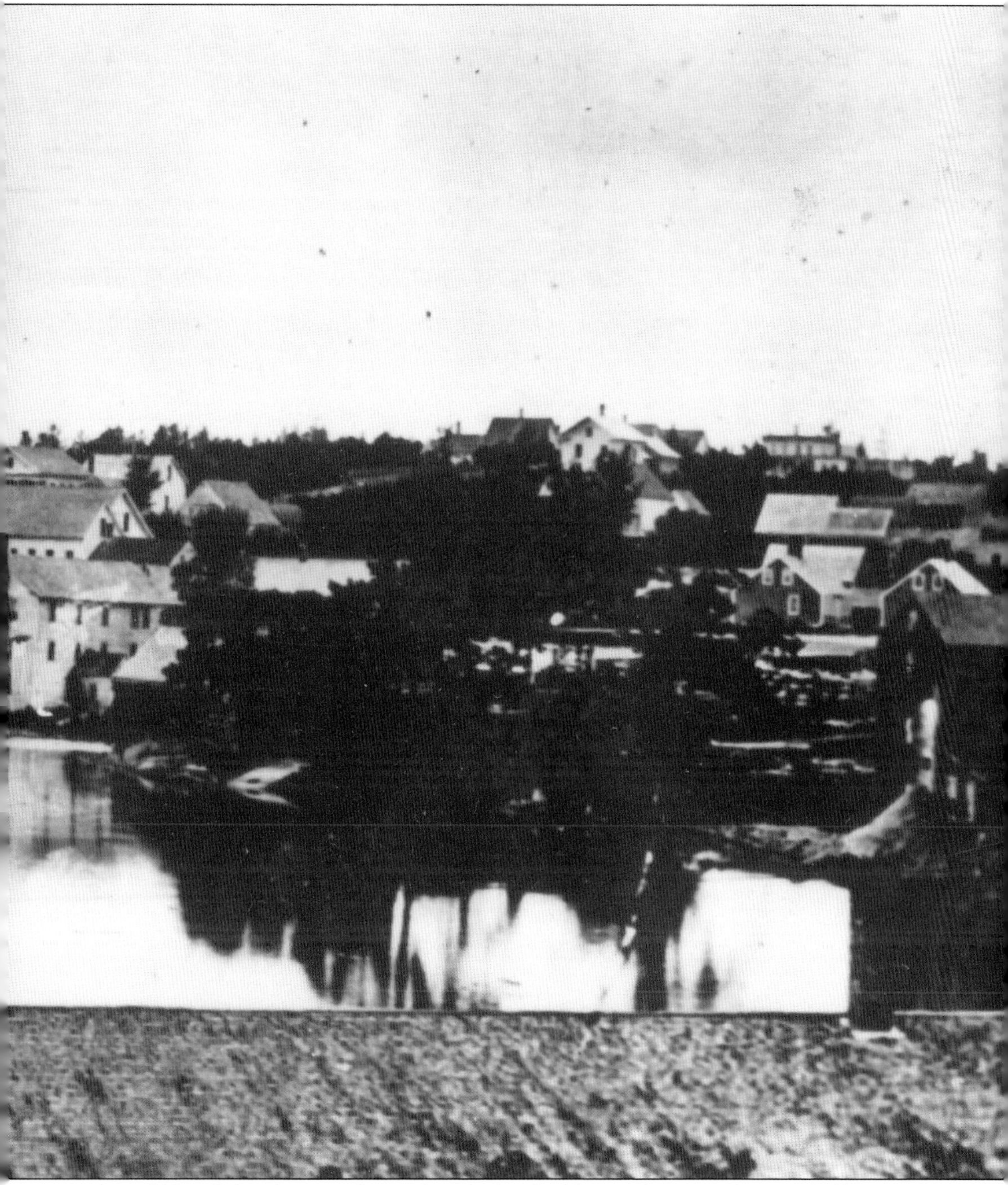

1870) would be off the photograph at right. The low building in foreground was probably part of the Cole Manufacturing Co. plant. The Union Lace, Howard, and Pulcifer Mills had been built around 1828 by Nathan Batchelder to take advantage of the waterpower generated by the new Lakeport Dam. These buildings were occupied sporadically by various manufacturers until the Great Fire of 1903, although the longest occupancy was in the middle structure, later known as Wood's Mill. After the fire of 1903, this was the only one of the mills rebuilt (see p. 63). Waterpower was provided by a long flume on the west side of the river, serving all of the mills.

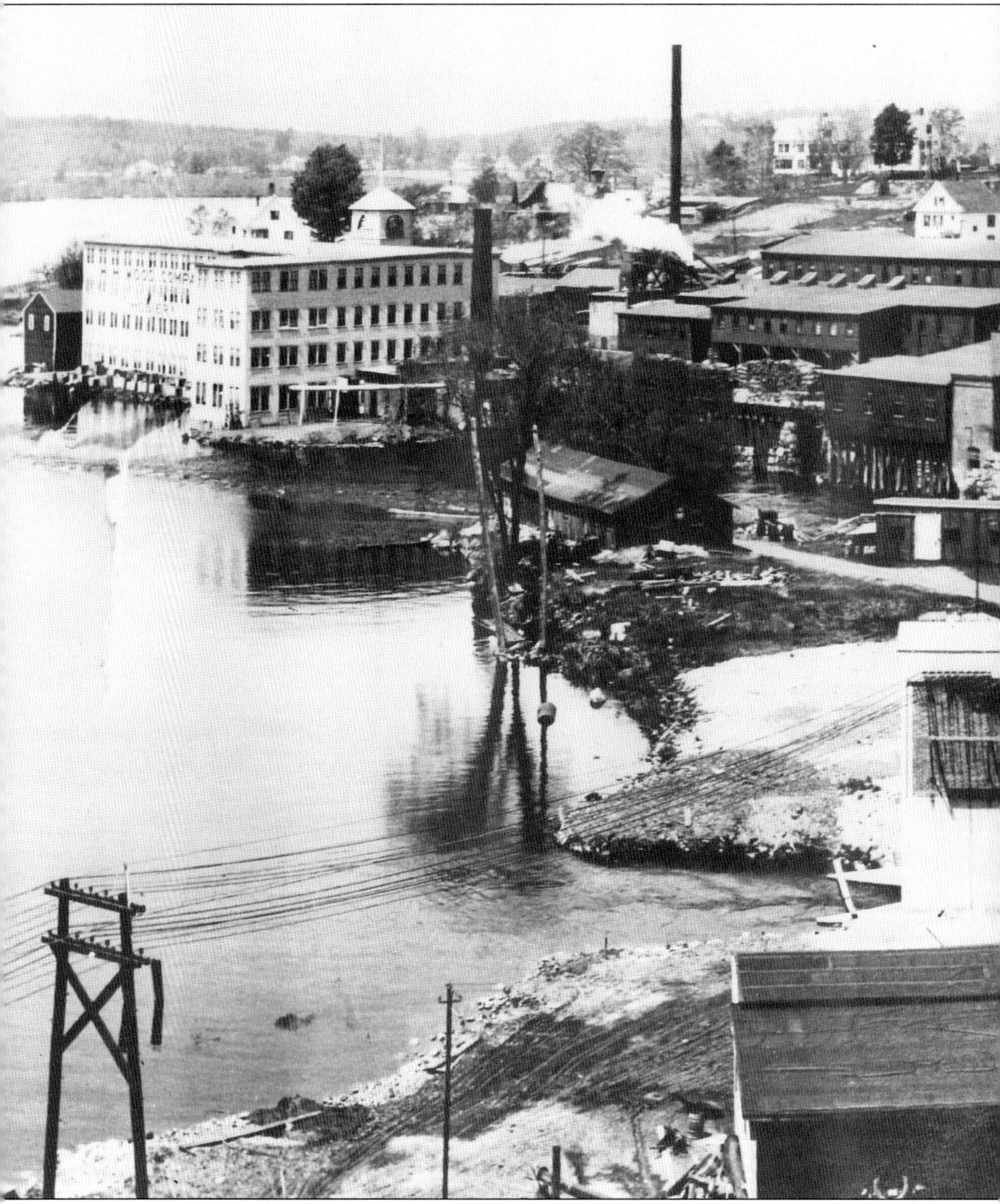

LATER VIEW OF LAKEPORT MILLS, C. 1918. The 1904 Wood's Mill is at left, with the Boulia-Gorrell Lumber Co. at center. Our Lady of the Lakes Church, dedicated 1905, is at top center. The Halifax Mill, built 1886–1887 and expanded by one story in December 1891, is at right. By the time of this photograph, the Elm and Franklin Streets area had begun to be rebuilt after the Great Fire of 1903. The Boulia-Gorrell plant was again destroyed by fire on August 30, 1918 (see bottom of p. 80) but

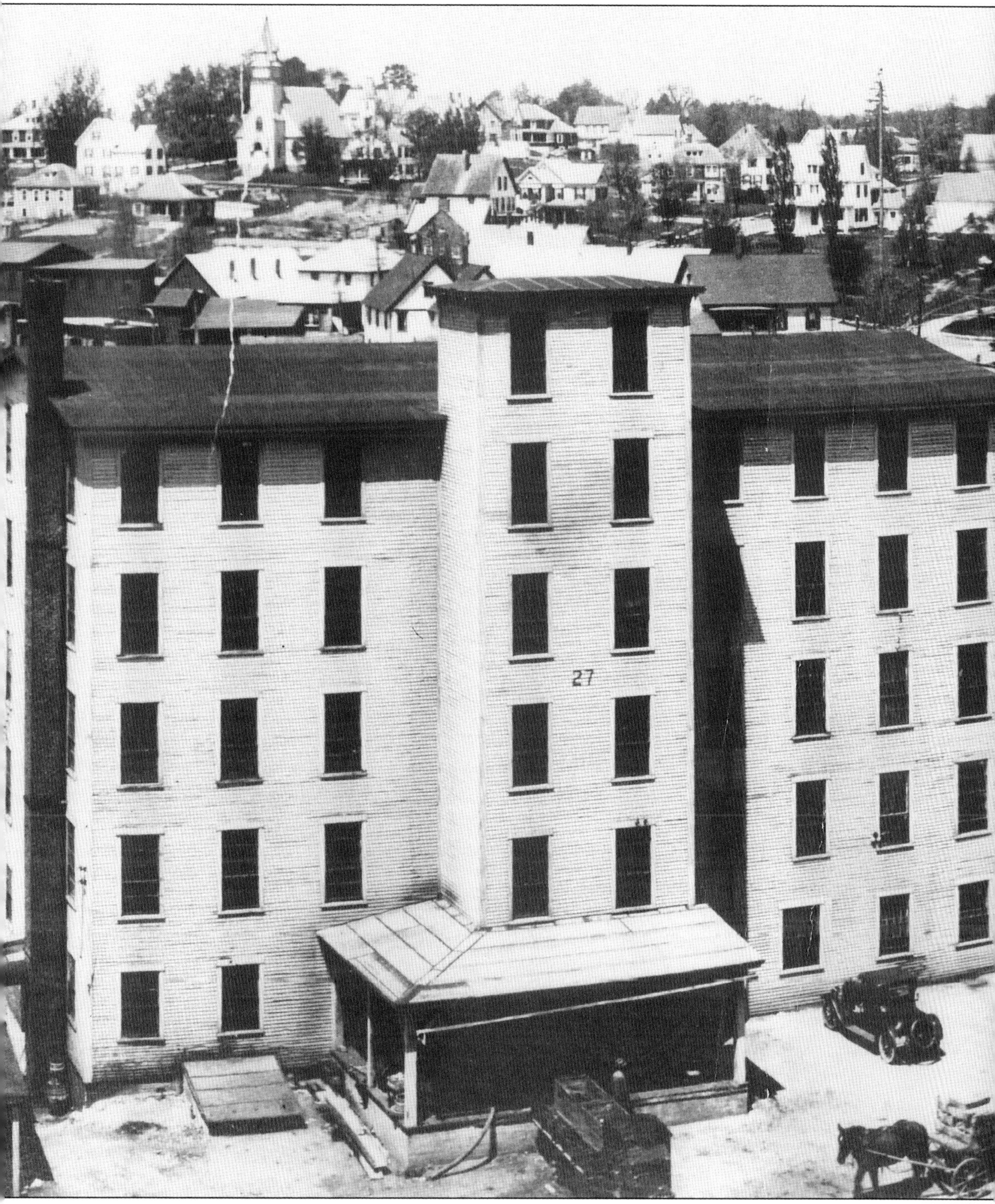

was rebuilt. The Halifax Mill was torn down in 1966, the same year a new Our Lady of the Lakes Church was built. Engineers preparing the foundations for Scott & Williams Building 25 in 1919, "discovered that the entire property was practically resting on a foundation of sawdust. The early settlers at Lakeport had a sawmill located at about this point and down under the dirt is a big stratum of ancient sawdust varying in depth from eight or ten feet to over forty feet."

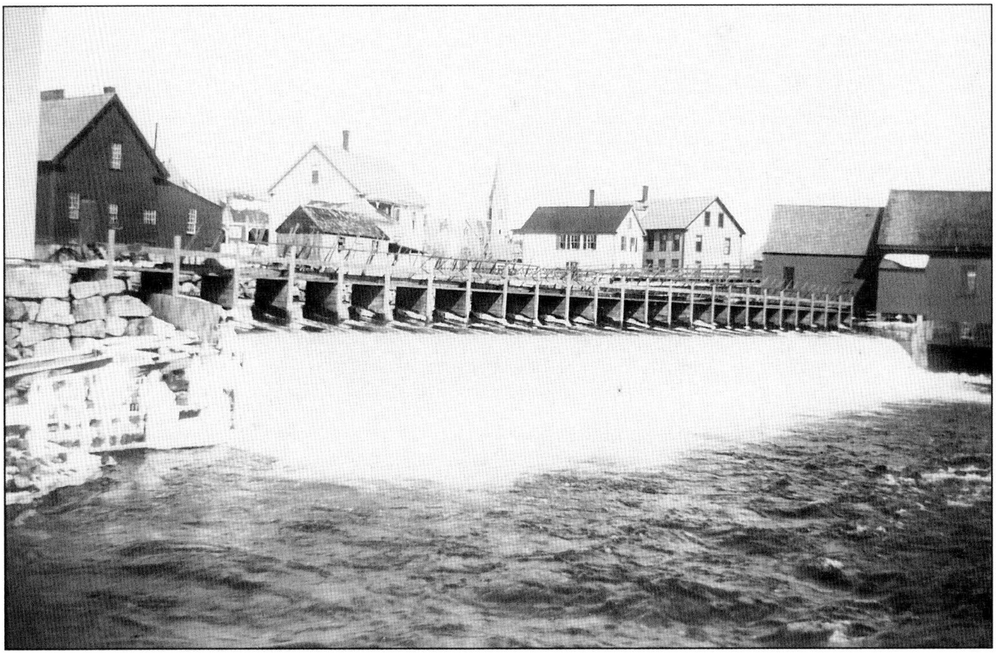

LAKEPORT DAM. Water pours over the 1861 wing dam, with part of the Lake Co. gatehouse visible at right. The steeple of the Trinity Methodist Episcopal Church and two Franklin (McGrath) Square buildings appear in distance at center, with F.R. Adams's West End Grocery and Provision Store, located at 154–156 Elm Street, left of center.

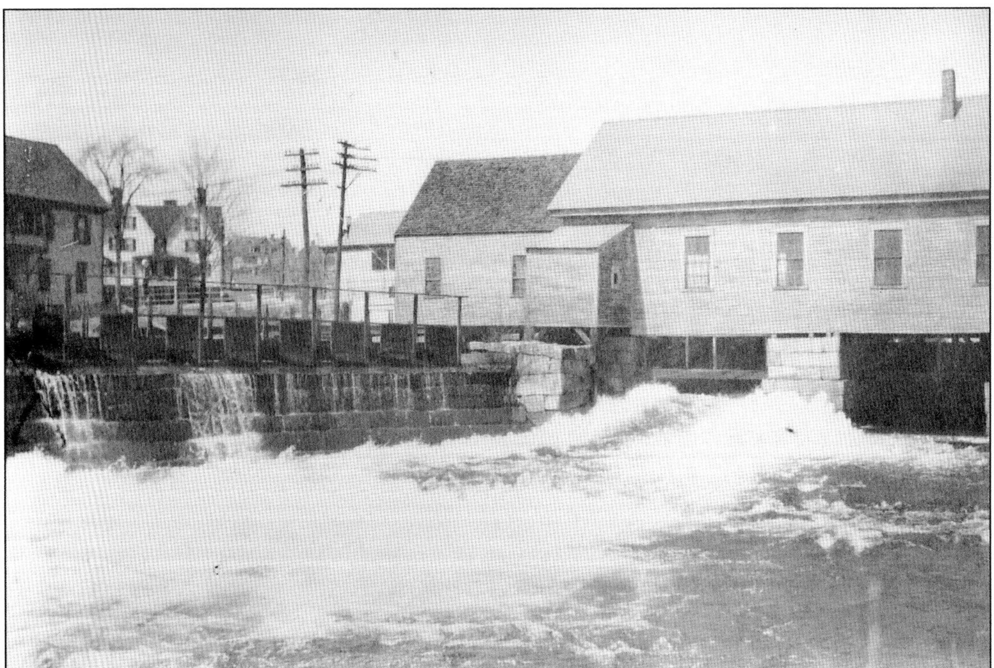

CLOSE-UP OF GATEHOUSE. The main dam (1851) is at right, and a part of the 1861 wing dam is at left. The grocery store at 154–156 Elm Street appears at extreme left.

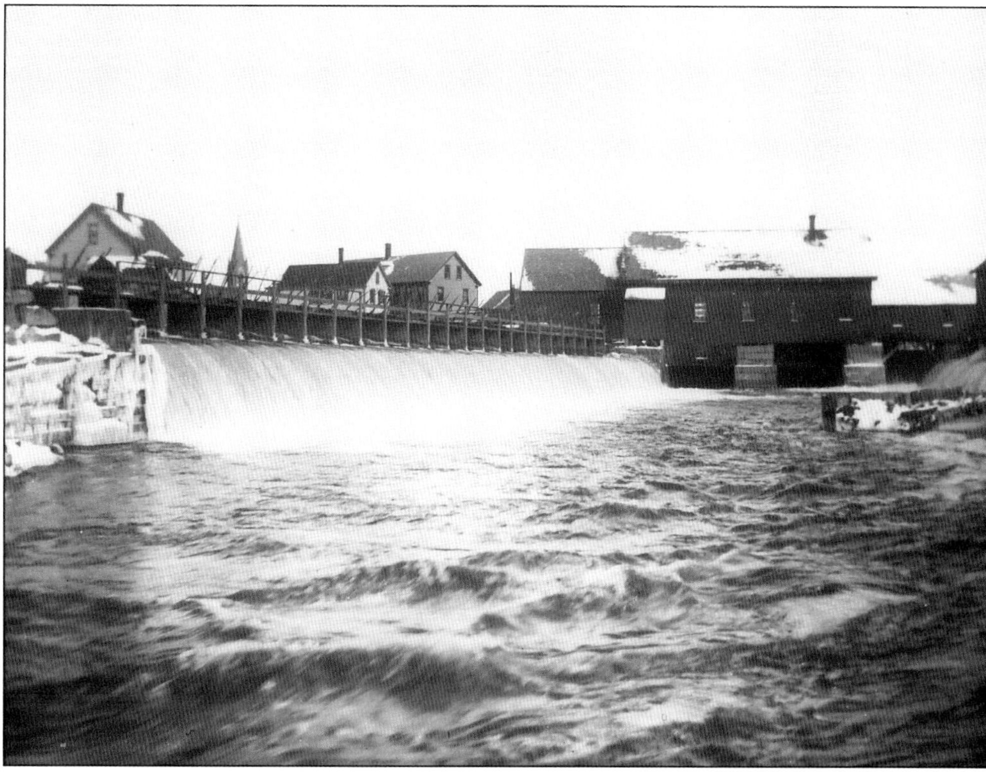

WING DAM AND GATEHOUSE. At first glance, one might mistake the 1861 wing dam (center left), which ran parallel with the river, for the Elm Street Bridge. The bridge, however, is obscured by the gatehouse (right) and runs, of course, at a right angle to the river, from left to right.

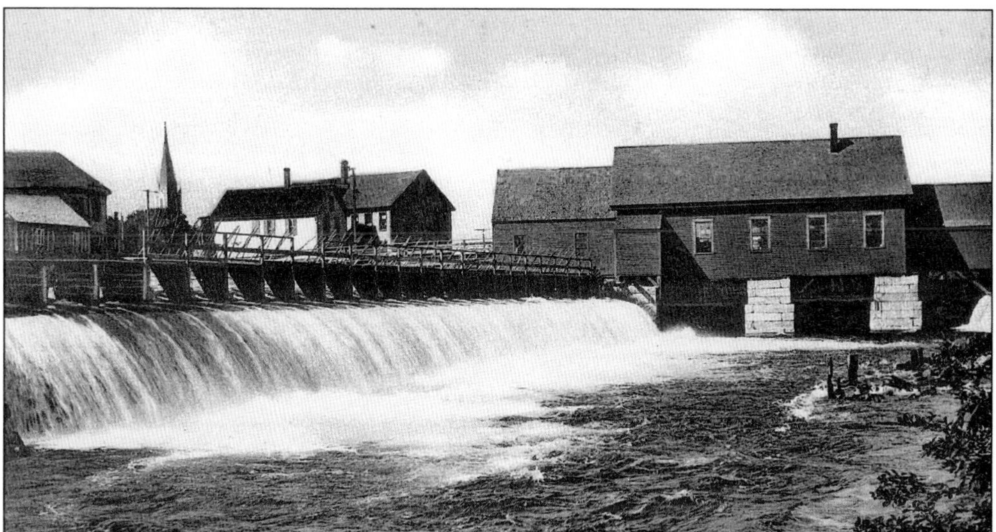

A CLOSER LOOK AT WING DAM AND GATEHOUSE. From left, the 154–156 Elm Street grocery store, the steeple of the Belvidere Street Methodist Church, and two buildings on Franklin (McGrath) Square are visible.

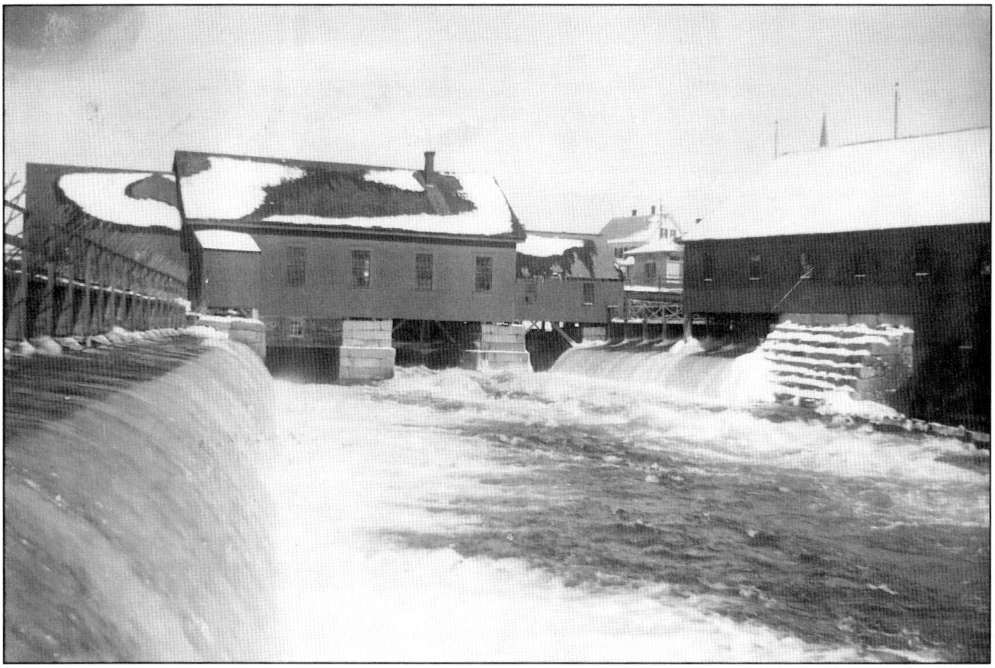

Lakeport Dam in Winter. The gatehouse and main dam appear at center, with the wing dam at left and sawmill at right. The Lake Company office is visible right of center, in front of one of the gabled Fore Street buildings.

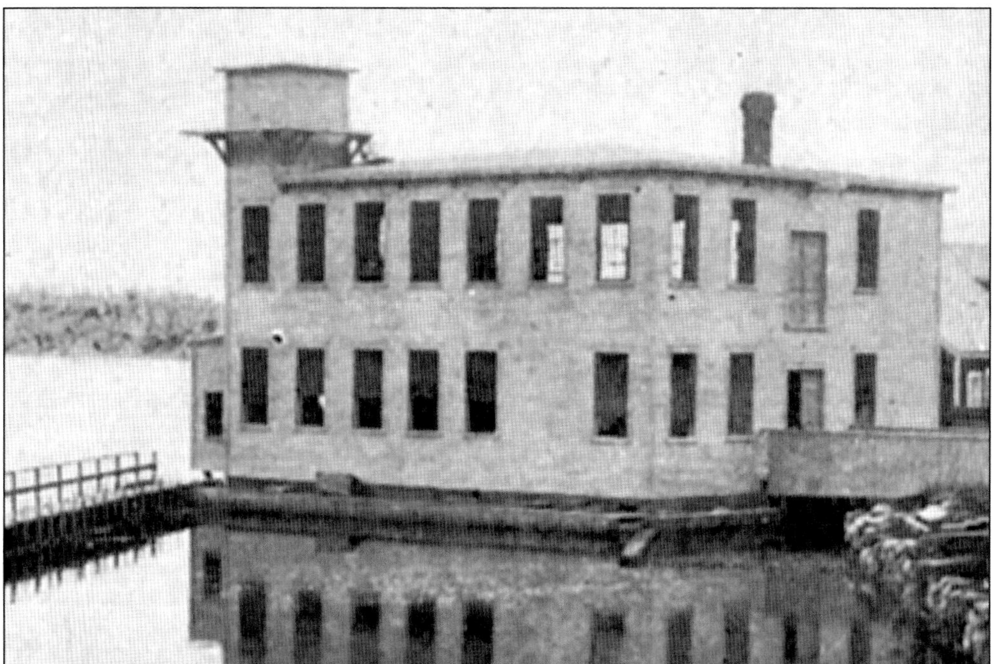

Power Station. Built in 1892–1893, this building at the end of the wing dam housed the generators of the Laconia Electric Lighting Co. until it was destroyed in the Great Fire of 1903. It was rebuilt in brick (see next page).

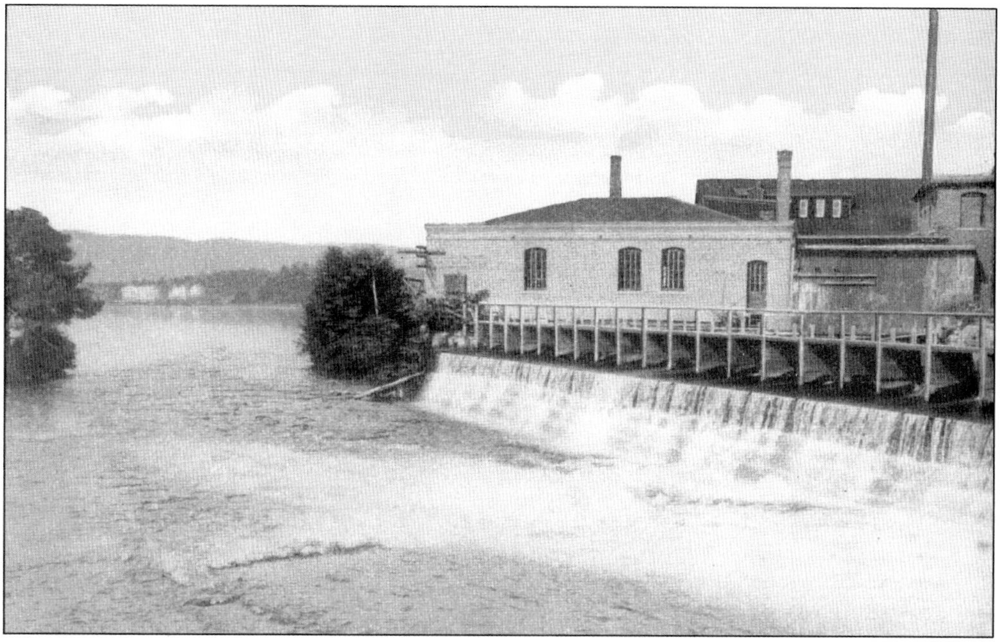

LOOKING DOWNSTREAM FROM GATEHOUSE, SEPTEMBER 4, 1929. The powerhouse of the Public Service Co. of New Hampshire (formerly the Laconia Electric Lighting Co.) appears at the end of the wing dam, with the Boulia-Gorrell Lumber Co. plant at right.

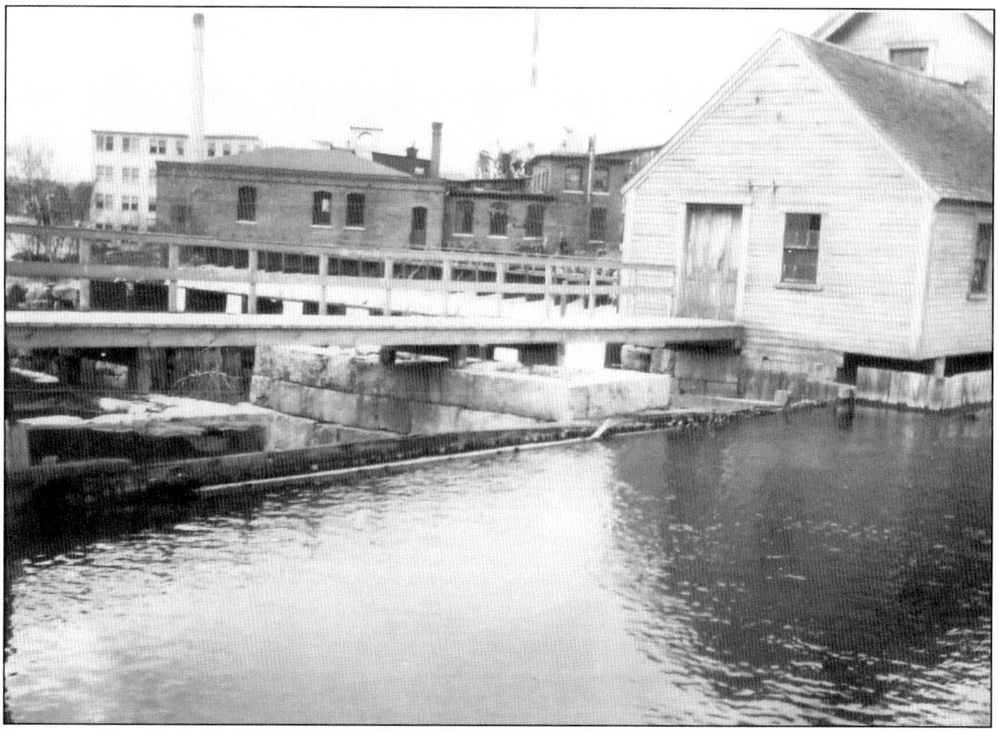

LOOKING DOWNSTREAM FROM DAM. Wood's Mill is the four-story building visible in the distance at left, beyond the powerhouse, with the Boulia-Gorrell plant obscured by buildings at center.

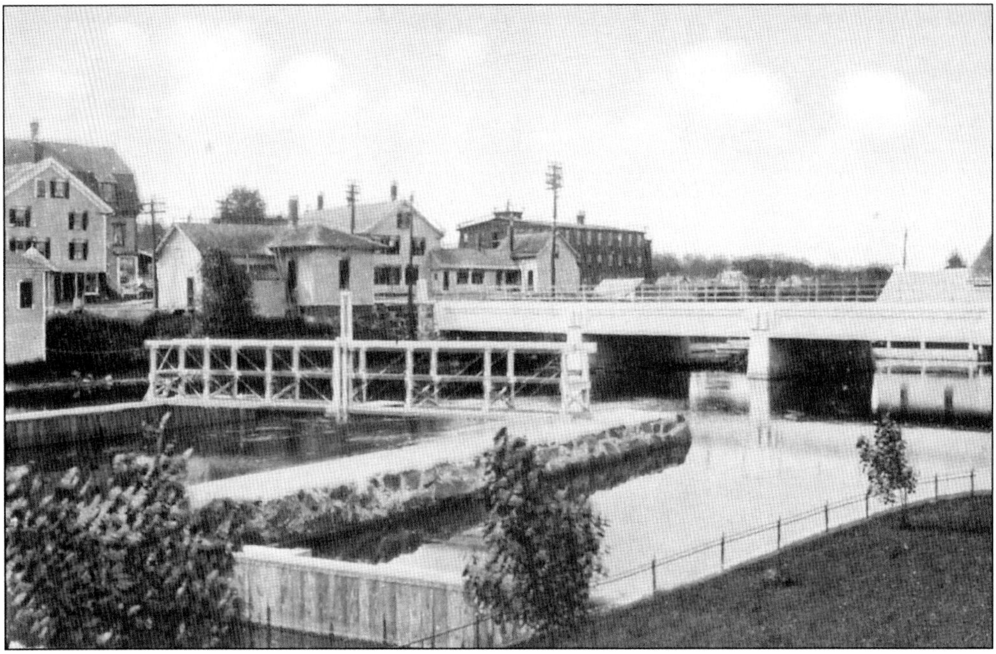

LOOKING DOWNSTREAM TOWARD DAM. A new concrete Elm Street Bridge (opened 1914) is at center and the gambrel roof of the Brawn Block is visible at left. The Halifax Mill looms in the distance at center.

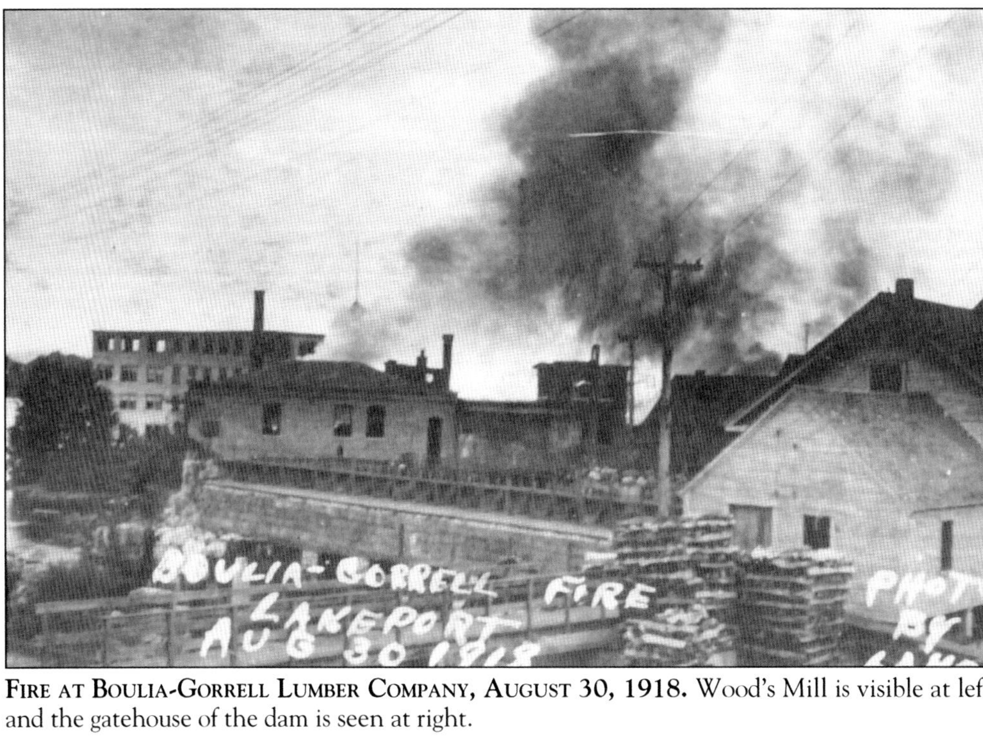

FIRE AT BOULIA-GORRELL LUMBER COMPANY, AUGUST 30, 1918. Wood's Mill is visible at left and the gatehouse of the dam is seen at right.

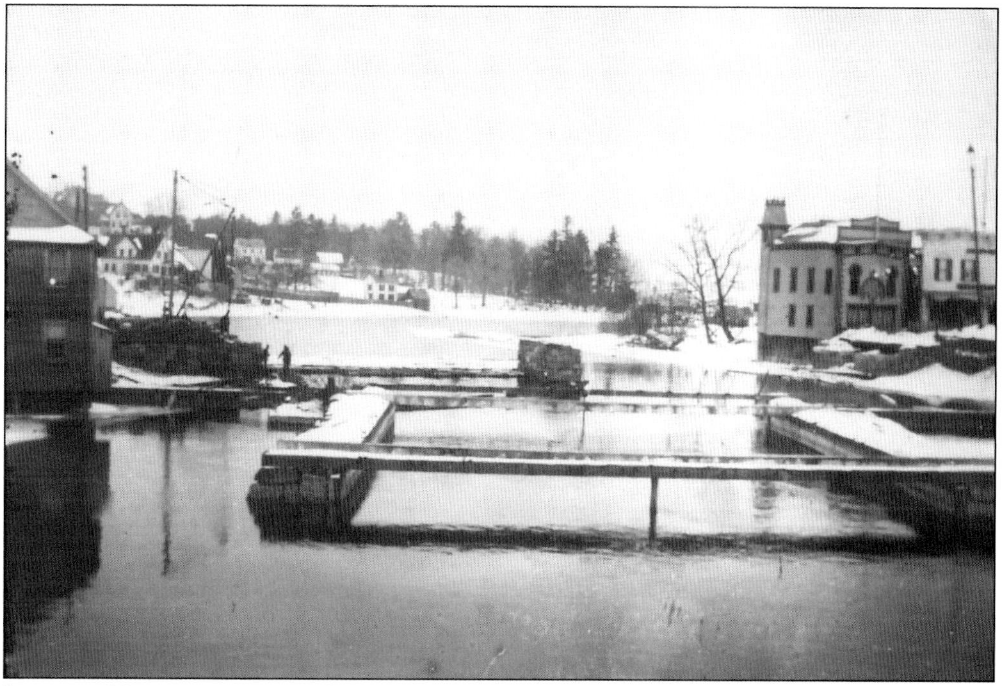

Looking Upriver from Elm Street Bridge, early 1900s. The Niagara Engine House and other Gold Street buildings are seen at right. The center pier of one of a series of earlier Gold Street bridges is visible in the center of the photograph.

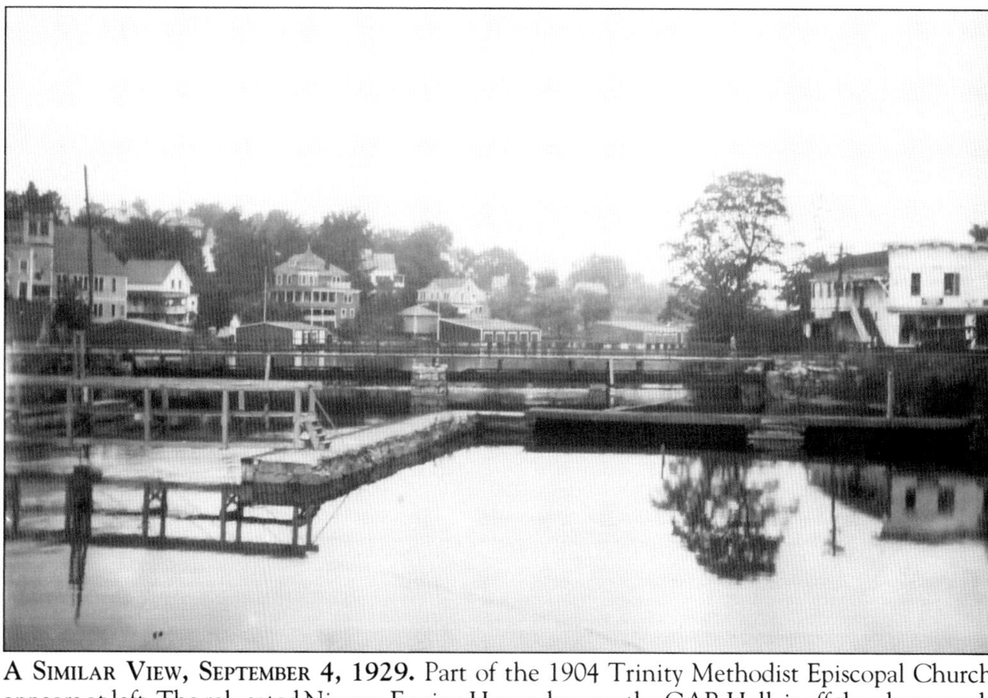

A Similar View, September 4, 1929. Part of the 1904 Trinity Methodist Episcopal Church appears at left. The relocated Niagara Engine House, by now the GAR Hall, is off the photograph at left. The early Folsom Dam (*c.* 1766) was located just beyond the Gold Street footbridge.

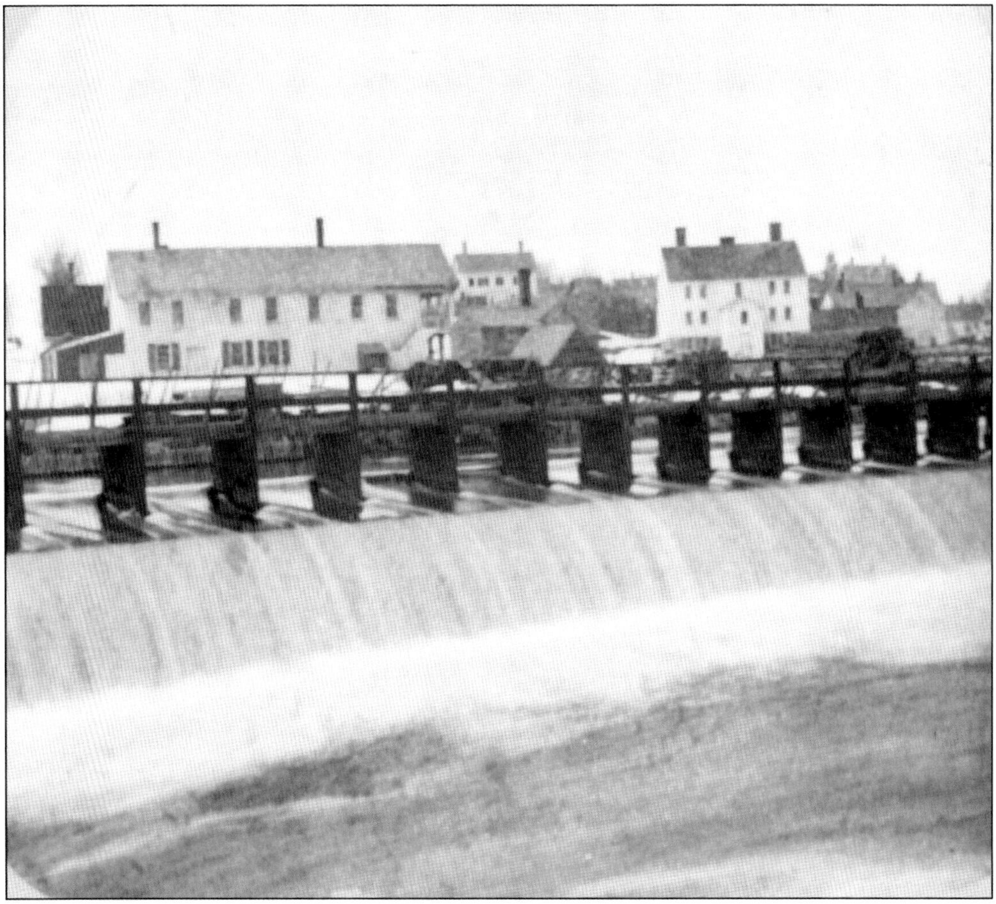

Final Look at the Waterpower of the Lakeport Dam, c. 1870s. Hidden by the superstructure of the wing dam, Elm Street crosses from upper right and rises in the distance at center. Wood's Mill is off the photograph at left. The first settler, Abraham Folsom, built the earliest dam, upriver of the Gold Street Bridge, sometime after 1766. Nathan Batchelder and Stephen C. Lyford built a loose boulder-and-rubble dam c. 1828 on the site of today's substantial stone dam, which was built in 1851. The wing dam (above), built in 1861, was filled in around 1957. Batchelder and Lyford organized the Lake Winnipisiogee Cotton and Woolen Manufacturing Co. in 1831. In 1846, a successor Lake Company was incorporated by Lawrence and Lowell, Mass. manufacturing interests (the so-called Boston Associates), which retained control of the Winnipesaukee watershed until the water rights were acquired by the International Paper Corp. In 1943, the dam was transferred to the Public Service Co. of New Hampshire. Ownership of the dam and its waterpower ultimately passed to the New Hampshire Water Resources Board on March 31, 1958.

Five

WEST SIDE

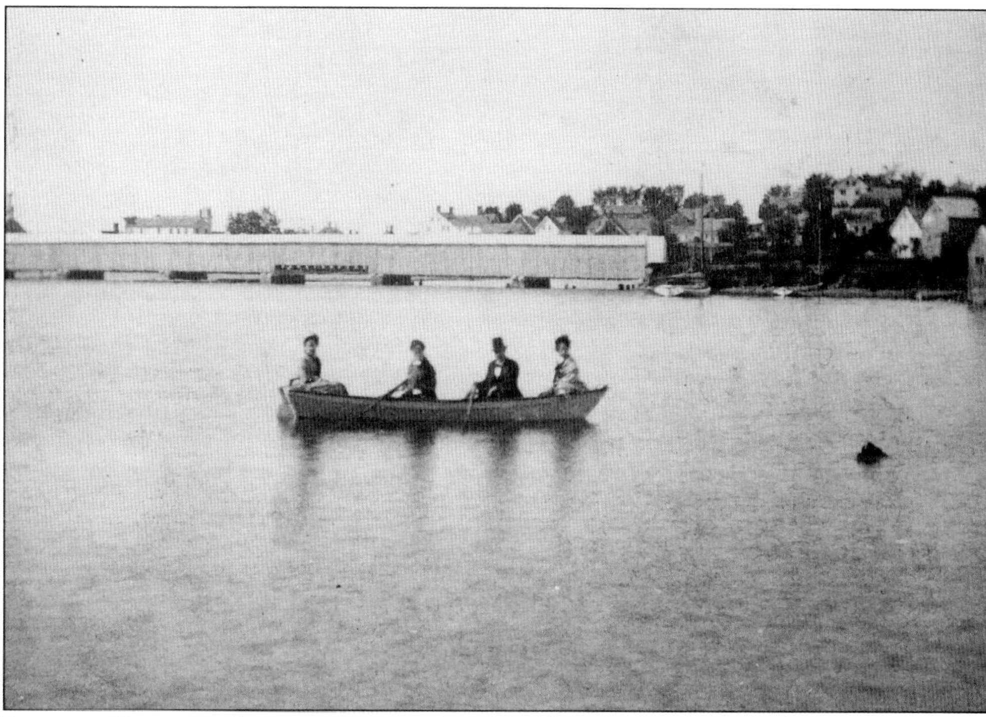

LAKEPORT RAILROAD BRIDGE, C. 1875. A party of boaters enjoys an outing at the lower end of Lake Paugus. The outlet from the lake is obscured by the Boston, Concord & Montreal Railroad bridge, the side trusses of which were protected from the weather by the boarding. By this date, only the sides were covered; there was no roof over the tracks (see also pp. 60–61). Earlier wooden bridges had burned in 1862 and 1872. When the new bridge was built in 1873, one section was placed "at a sufficient elevation from the water to allow of the passage of small boats and rafts of logs, a matter of great convenience to some parties." A steel bridge replaced the wooden spans in 1892.

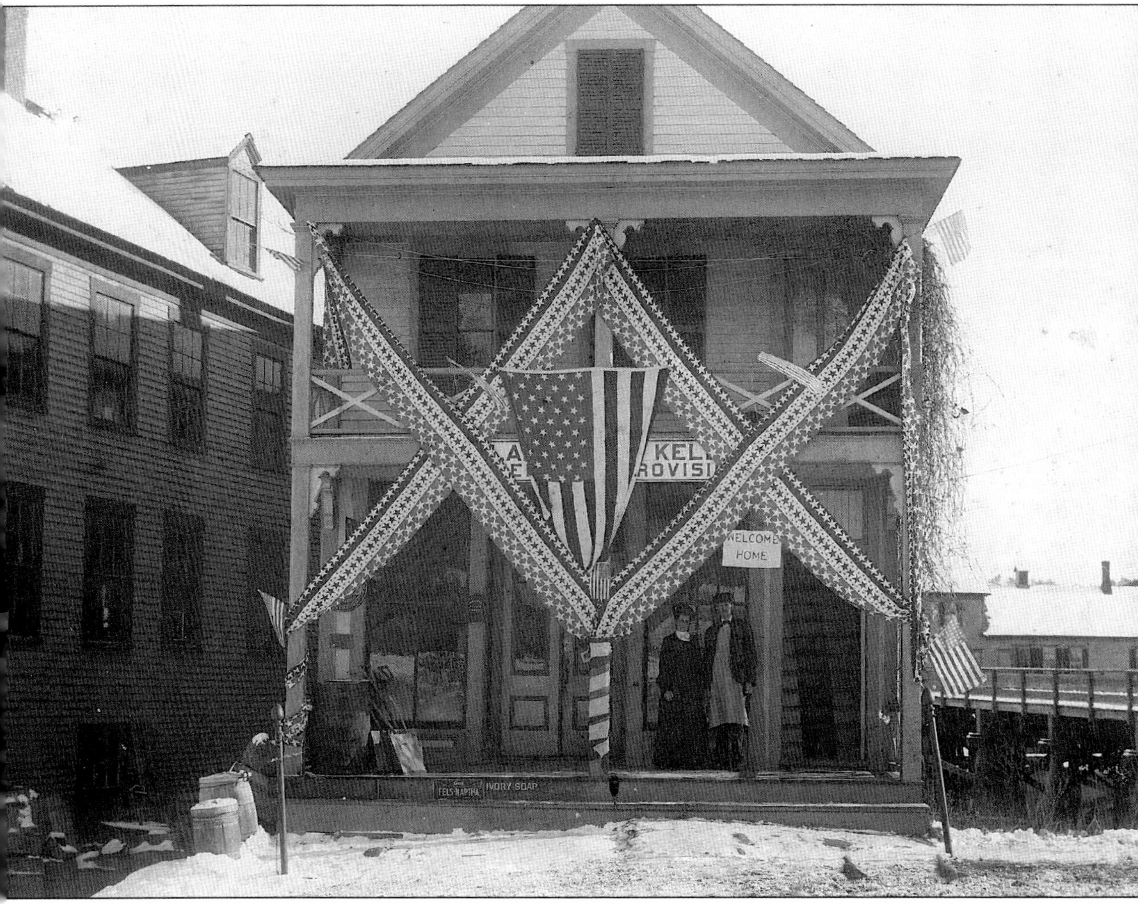

GROCERY STORE, FRANKLIN (LATER MCGRATH) SQUARE, C. 1898. Earlier, John R. Leavitt had conducted a grocery store in this building. The proprietors at 166 Gold Street, in this view, were Oscar A. Flanders and George E. Kelly. The reason for the bunting and "welcome home" sign is unknown, though it is tempting to speculate that they may have been in recognition of the return of Laconia's Company K, New Hampshire National Guard, from Spanish-American War service in 1898. Part of the 1890 Tetley Box Shop, remodeled by Isaac B. Sakansky in 1935 and later occupied for some years by the Baker antiques and second-hand business, is visible at left. The Elm Street Bridge is seen at right. In 1922, the city council redesignated Franklin Square as McGrath Square, to honor the memory of Earl O. McGrath, 26th Division, the first Laconia soldier killed in action in World War I.

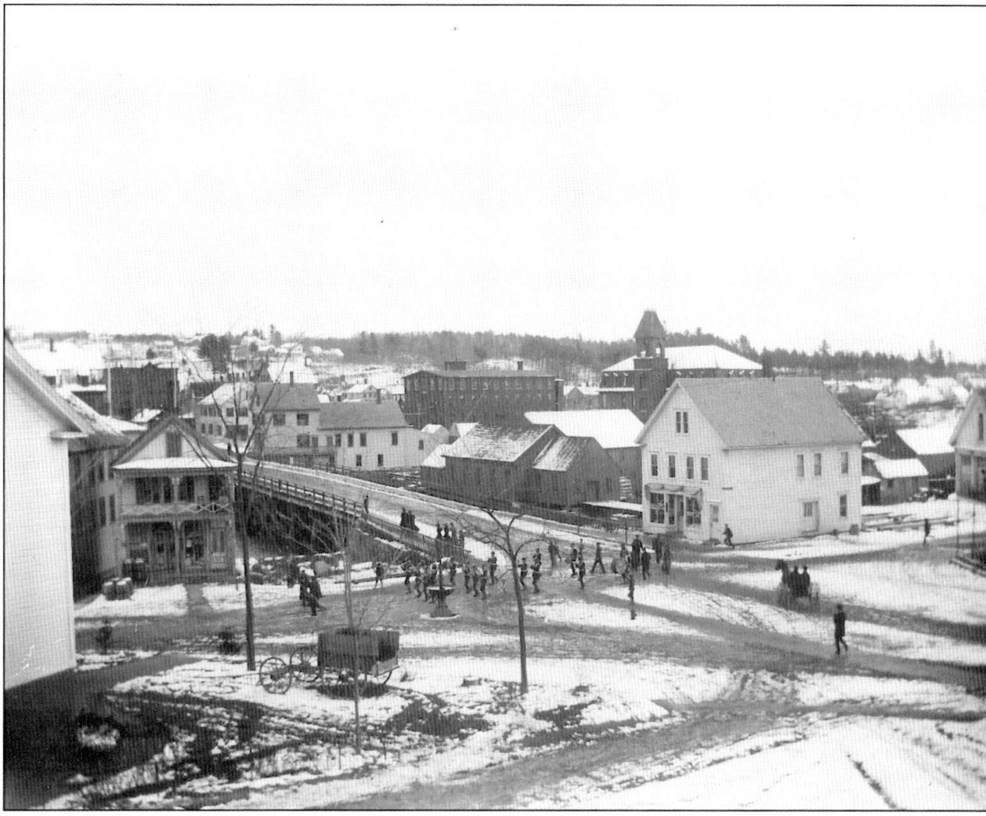

Franklin (McGrath) Square, Looking toward Union Avenue. Flanders & Kelly store (see previous page) is at left; F.R. Adams's West End Grocery and Provisions Store (see p. 76–77) is at right.

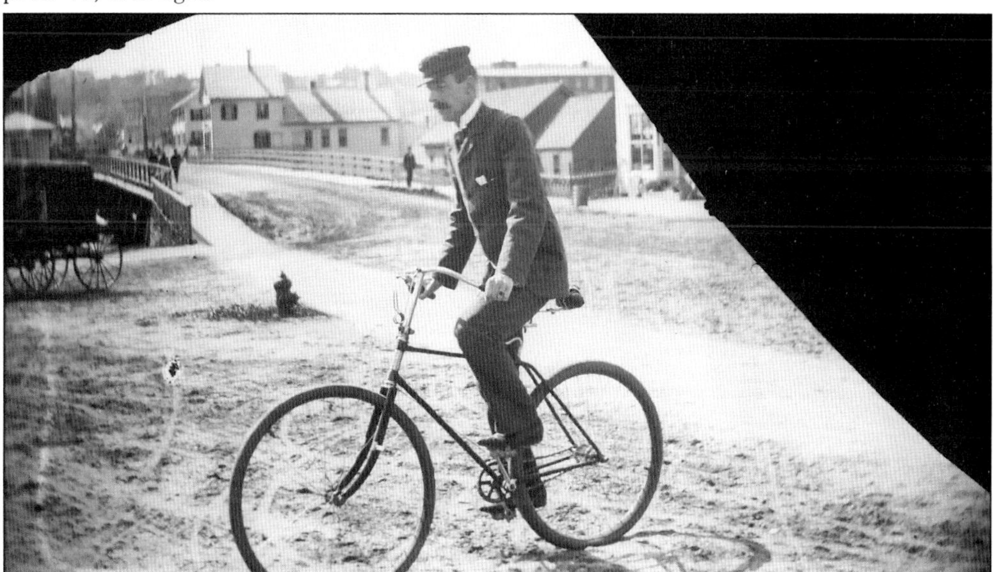

Bicyclist Named Bundy, in Franklin (McGrath) Square, c. 1895. The Elm Street Bridge is in the background, with the Lake Co. office (built 1885) visible in the distance at left.

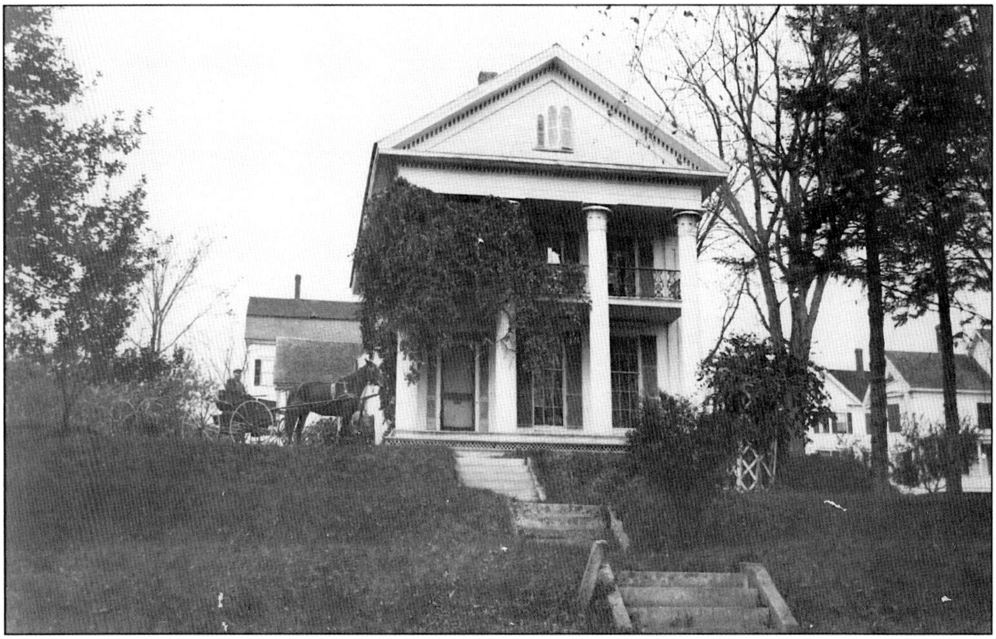

Moses Sargent House. Gracing the high ground above the terraces and stone steps, this landmark at 43 Franklin Street was built in the Greek Revival style by Moses Sargent, a textile industrialist here and in Belmont. By 1903, the house had passed into the possession of Horace H. Wood, though he resided in the gambrel-roofed dwelling to the rear, facing Fairmount Street. Both houses were destroyed in the Great Fire of 1903. Although the mansion was lost, the steps are still there, today leading to a small Cape Cod-style home.

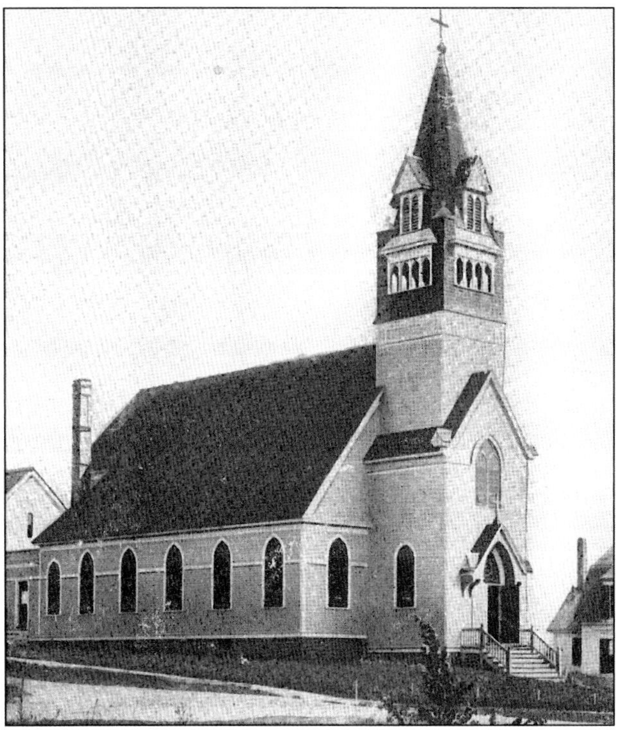

Our Lady of the Lakes Church, c. 1906. Located at the corner of Fairmount and Washington Streets, the church was built in 1905 and razed in 1966. A new church had been constructed directly across the street in 1965.

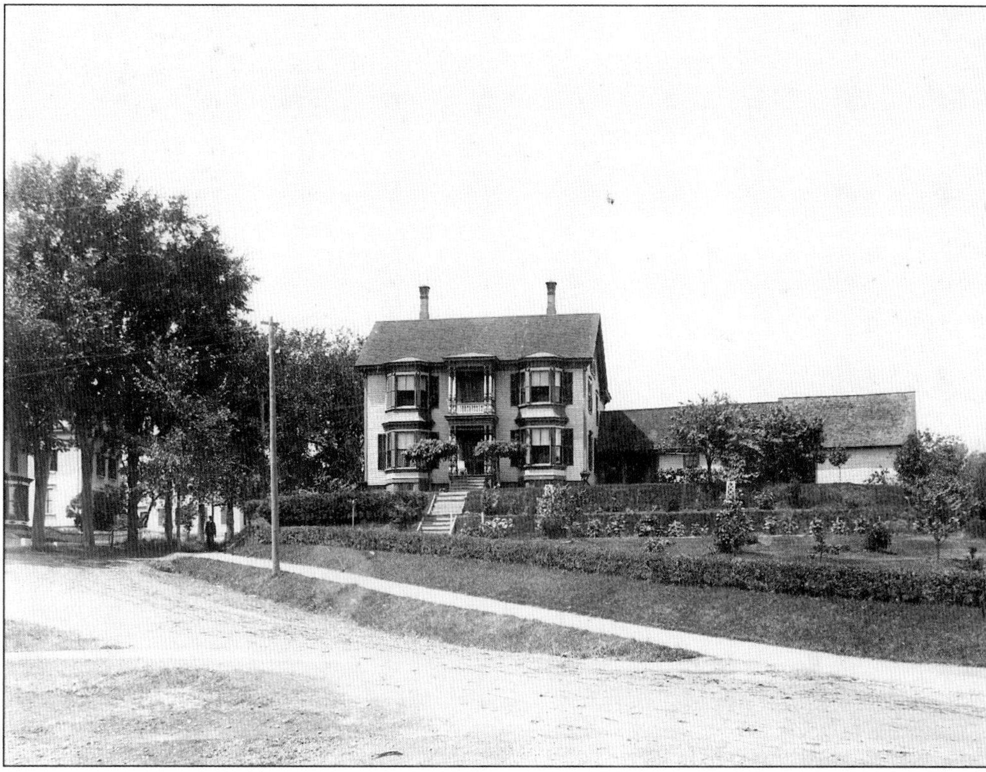

Rowe House at 193 Elm Street, c. 1895. This structure burned in the Great Fire of 1903.

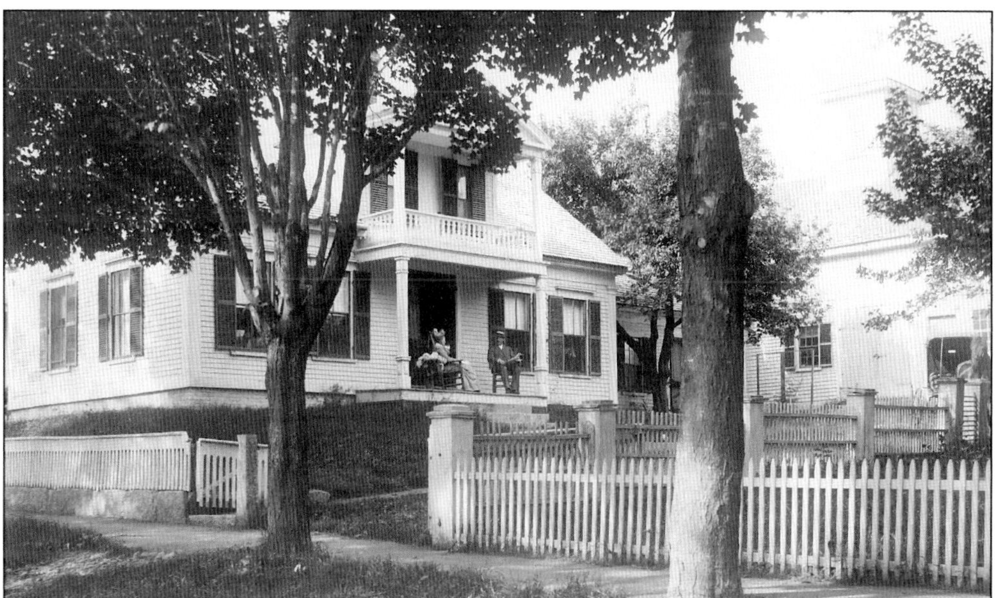

First Parsonage of Free Will Baptist Church. The residence of Dr. Freeman A. Durkee at 243 Elm Street was destroyed in the Great Fire of 1903. The house had served as the parsonage of the Lake Village Free Will Baptist Society from 1887 to 1893.

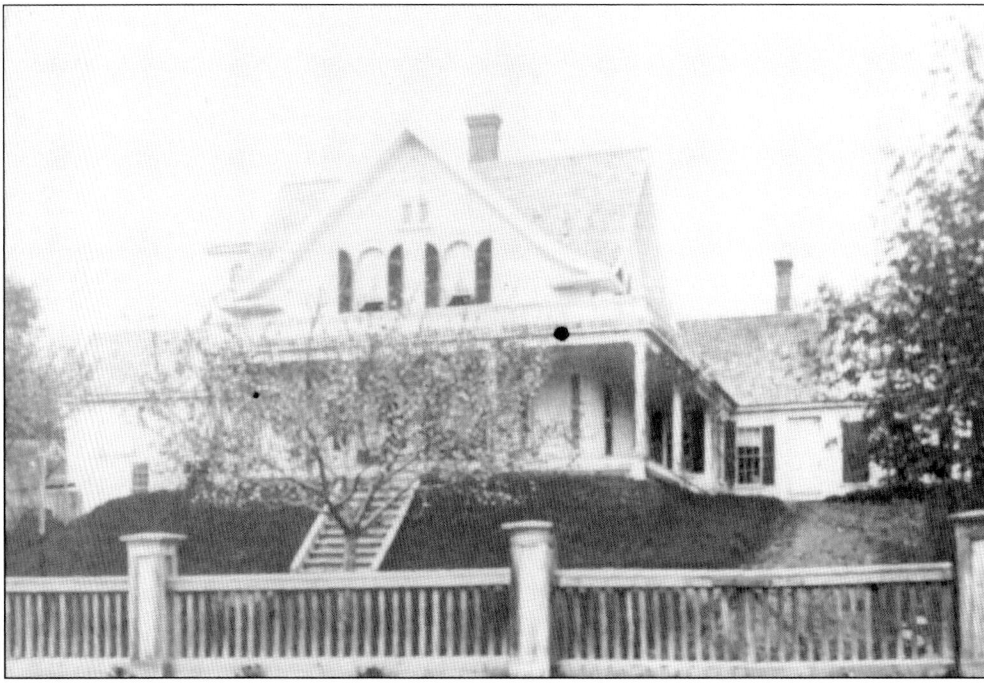

Albert T.L. Davis House, 75 Franklin Street. This house was the only building in this area to escape the Great Fire of 1903.

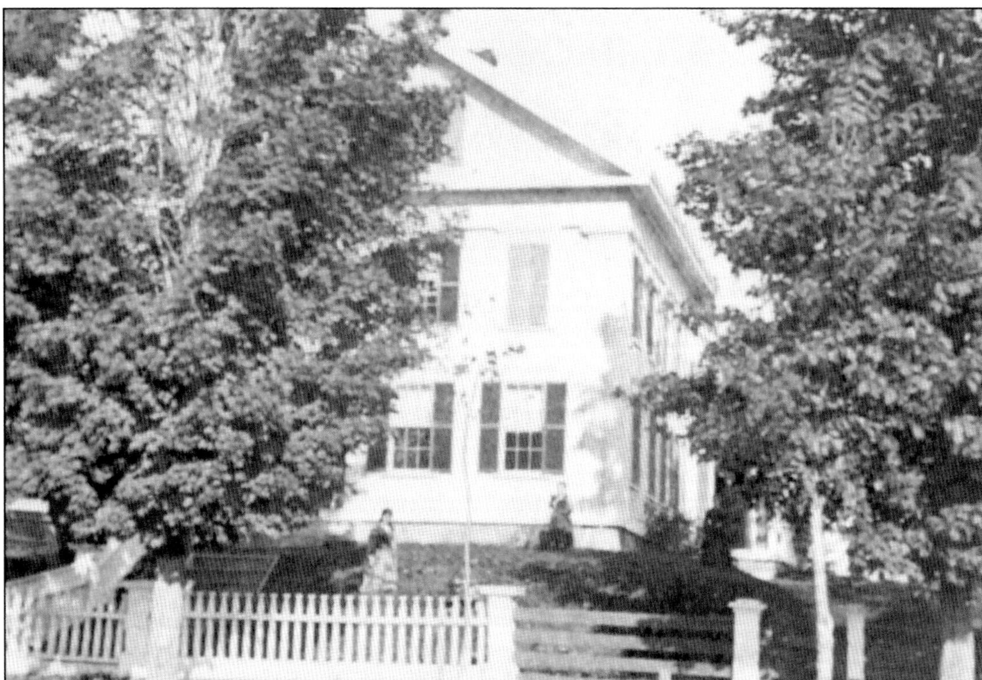

Harrison O. Heywood House. Built *c.* 1850, this was later the home of Mr. and Mrs. Leon J. Merchand. Located at 255 Elm Street, on the southeast corner of Elm and School Streets, it was destroyed in the Great Fire of 1903. Heywood was Mrs. Merchand's father.

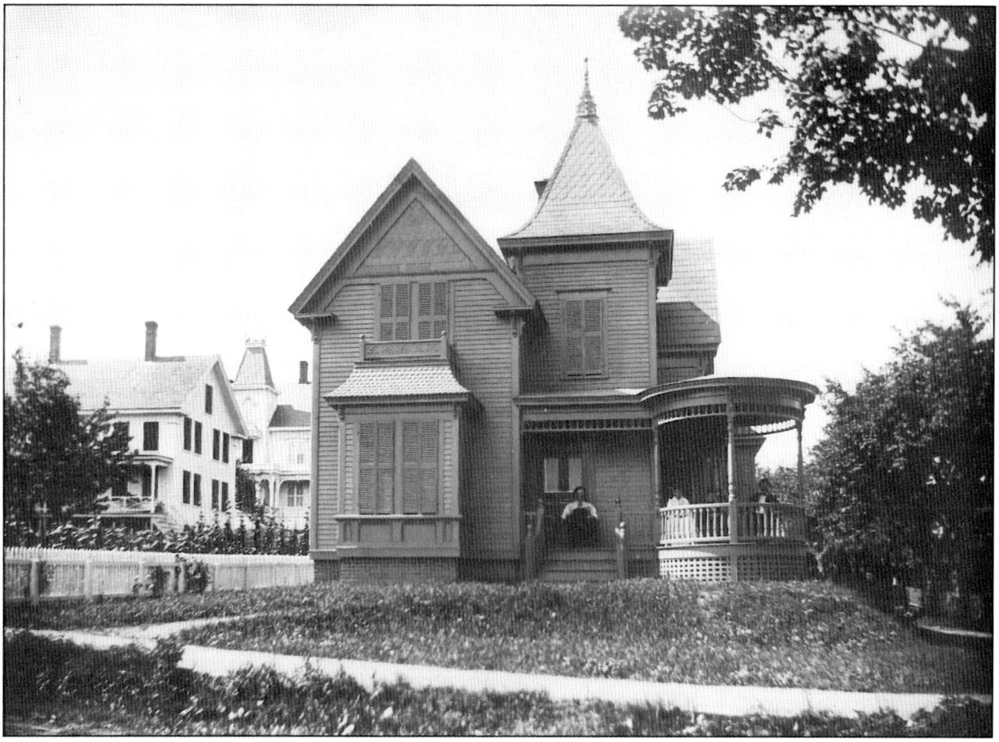

Bert M. Hutchins House, 76 Fairmount Street. This house was also destroyed in the Great Fire of 1903. In the distance at left, the tower of the Clarence Plummer House (built and initially occupied by B. Frank Drake in the summer of 1882) is visible. It was one of the few on Washington Street to survive the fire.

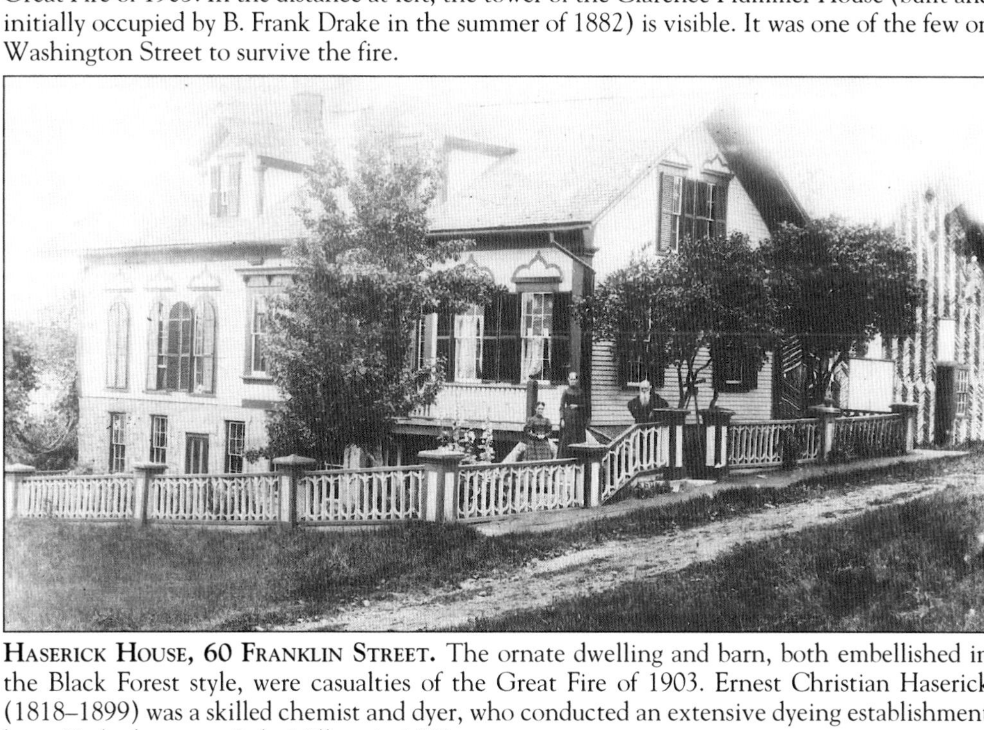

Haserick House, 60 Franklin Street. The ornate dwelling and barn, both embellished in the Black Forest style, were casualties of the Great Fire of 1903. Ernest Christian Haserick (1818–1899) was a skilled chemist and dyer, who conducted an extensive dyeing establishment here. He had come to Lake Village in 1853.

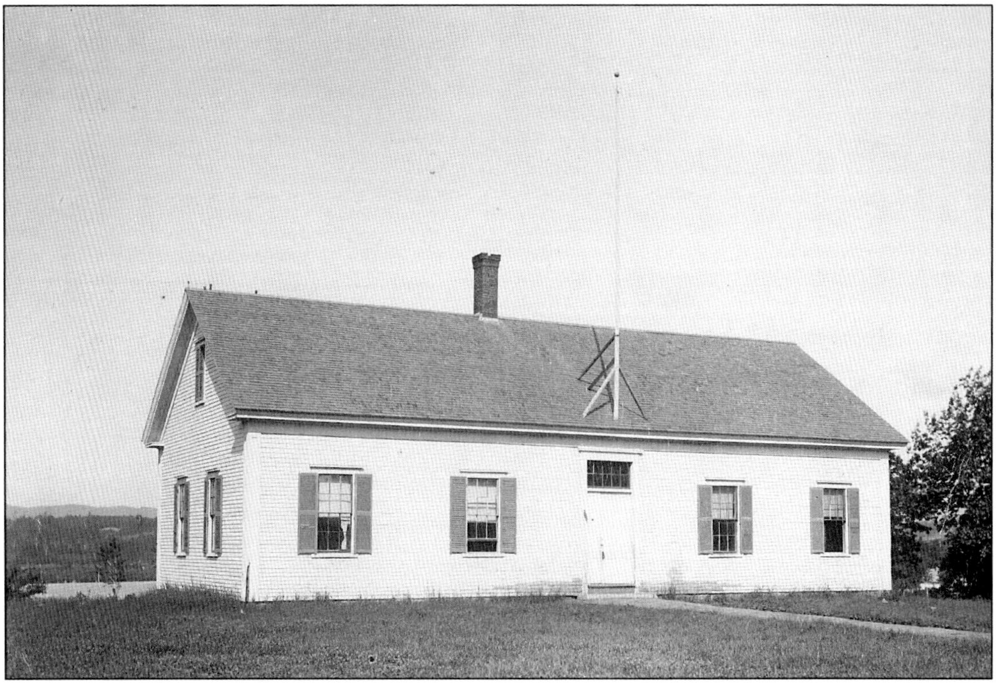

Washington Street School. Built in 1864, this structure was located near the southeast corner of School Street. The wooden building was replaced in 1902–1903 by one of brick, which survived the Great Fire of 1903.

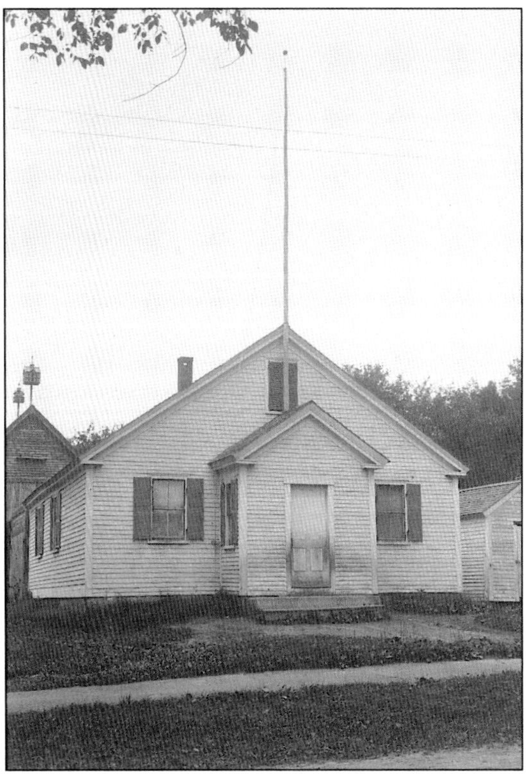

School Street School. Built in 1844, this building was used as a school until February 2, 1903, when the new Washington Street School opened. The old schoolhouse was then used by Hose Co. 6 for only three months until it was destroyed in the Great Fire of 1903.

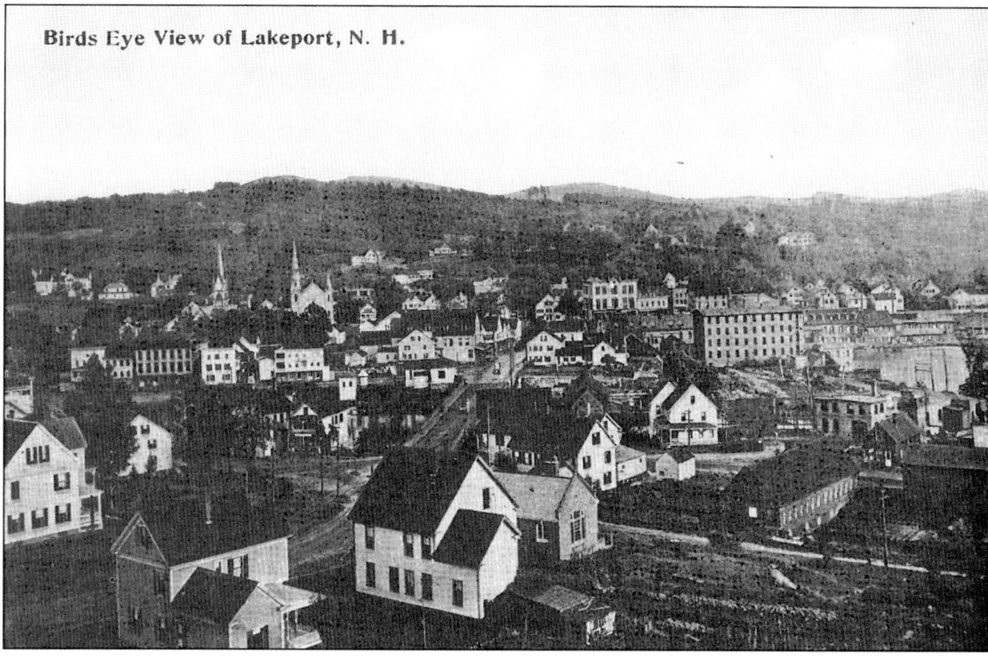

BIRD'S EYE VIEW OF LAKEPORT, C. 1910. In this commercial postcard, the photographer was located on the high ground southwest of Elm Street, looking toward Union Avenue. The Goss Reading Room (opened 1907) appears at lower center, beyond the two-and-one-half-story frame dwelling.

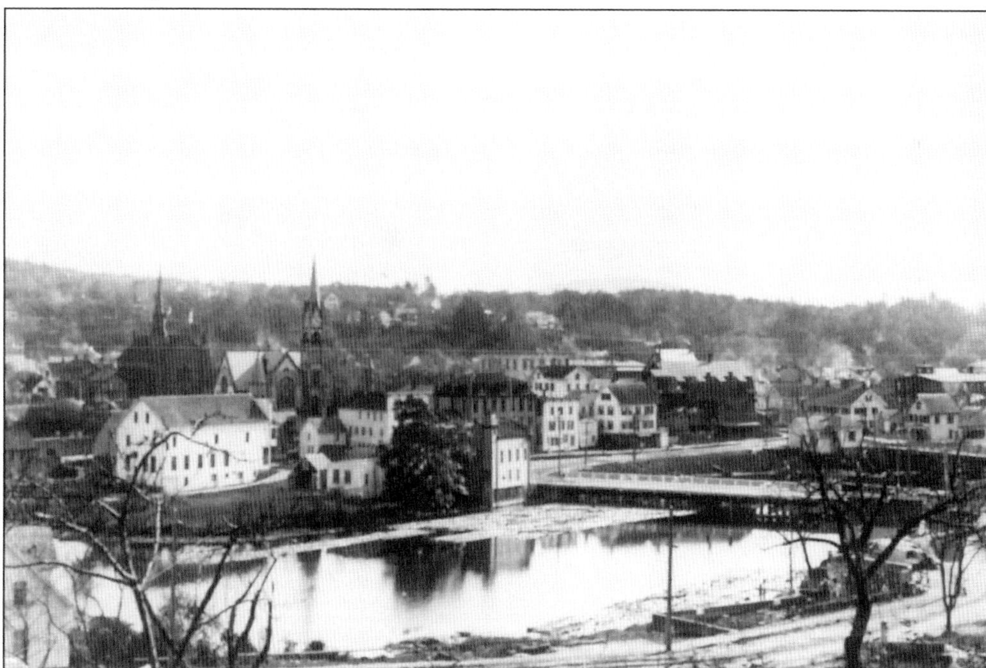

AREA BETWEEN RIVER AND RAILROAD, FROM ABOVE BELVIDERE STREET. In this *c.* 1890 view, both the Gold and Elm Street Bridges are visible at right, along with the Niagara Engine House (center) in its original location at the northeast end of the Gold Street Bridge.

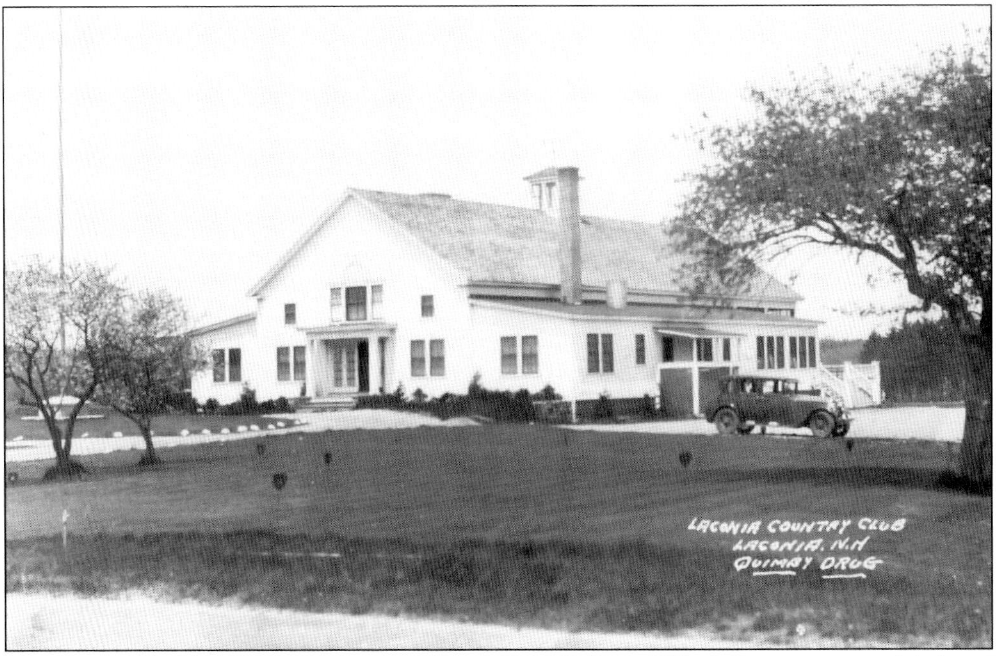

Original Clubhouse of Laconia Country Club. This rambling structure, remodeled and expanded in 1922 from a large barn on the Sanborn property, burned November 9, 1965.

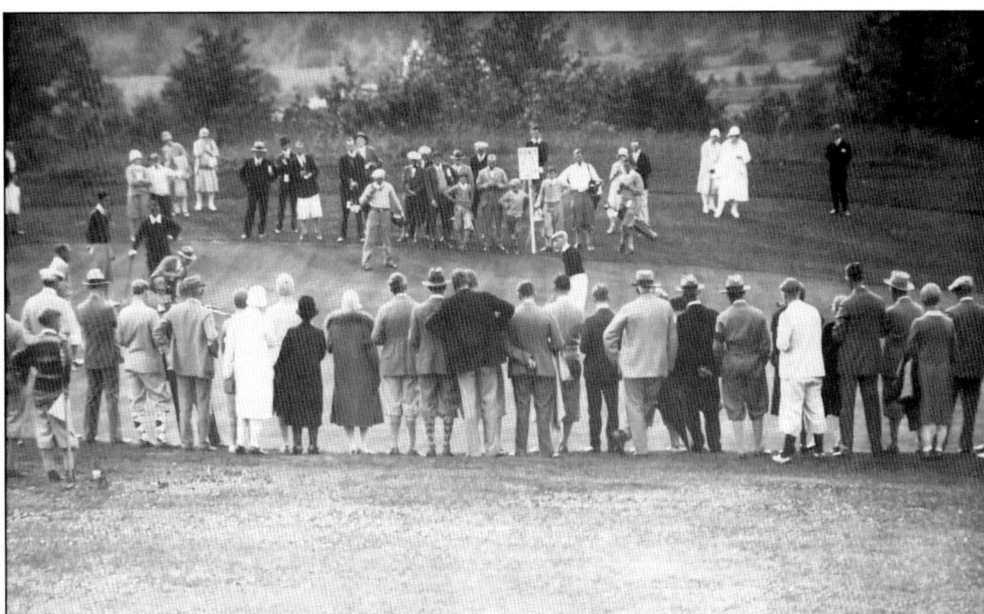

Early Activities at Laconia Country Club. Spectators watch intently in this late 1920s or early 1930s view.

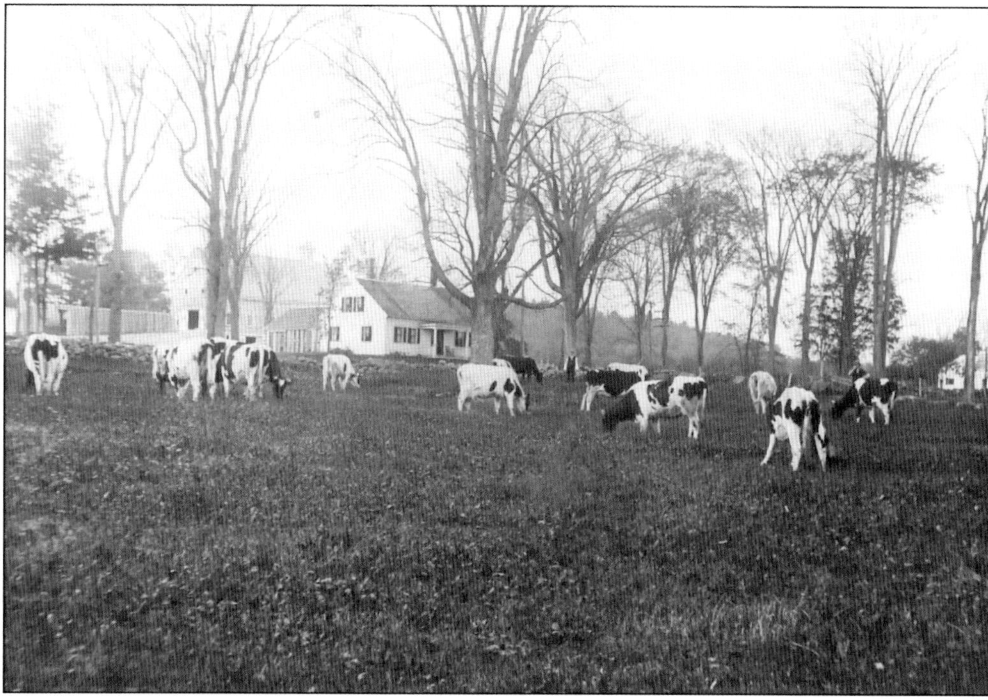

Joshua Woodman House on Laconia State School Property, c. 1920. Cows graze in the pasture opposite one of the earliest surviving dwellings (in distance, left of center) of what is now Laconia. Dating from c. 1785, the Woodman House was dismantled and re-erected near Gilmanton Corner in 1985.

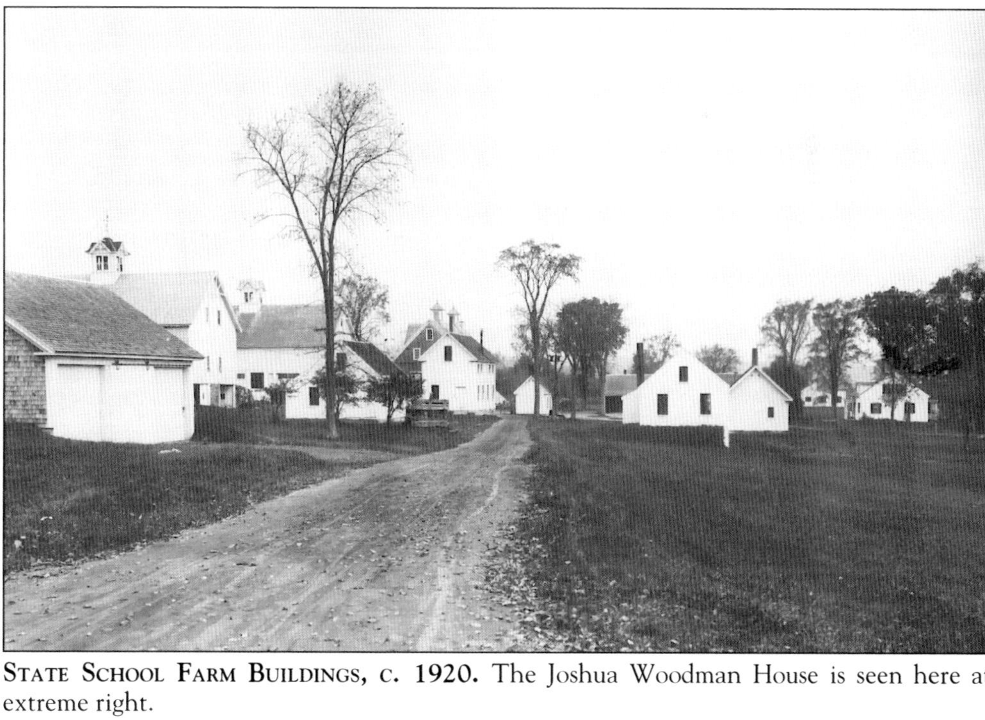

State School Farm Buildings, c. 1920. The Joshua Woodman House is seen here at extreme right.

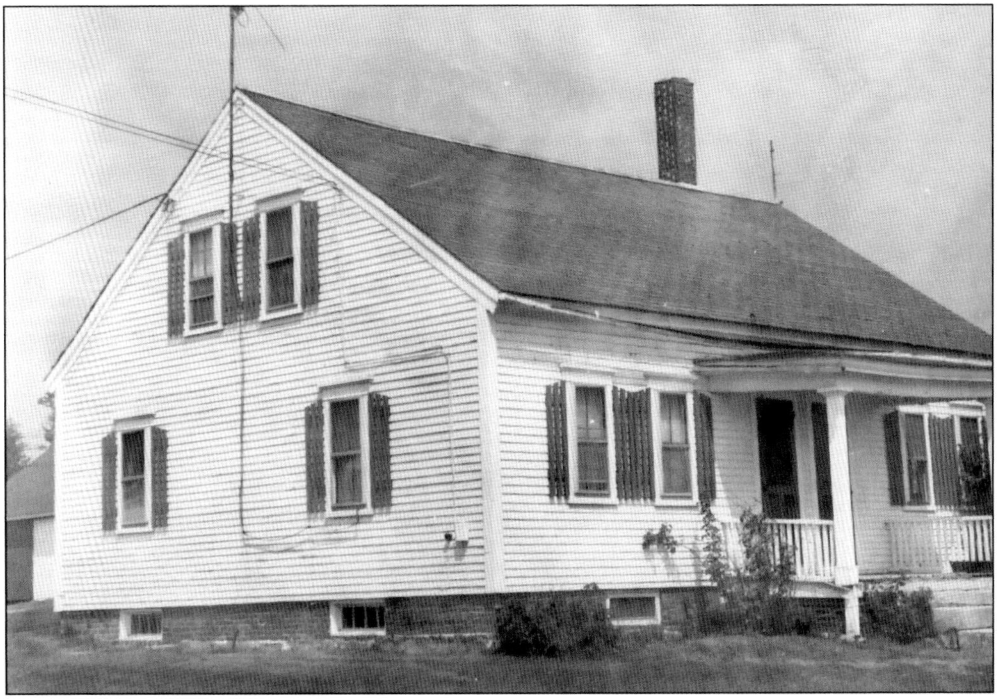

Close-up of Woodman House. Capt. Joshua Woodman was moderator of the Meredith town meeting in 1785. His heirs sold the property in 1879 to John Frank Crockett, who carried on the farm until his death in 1901, after which it was sold to the State of New Hampshire for use by the State School.

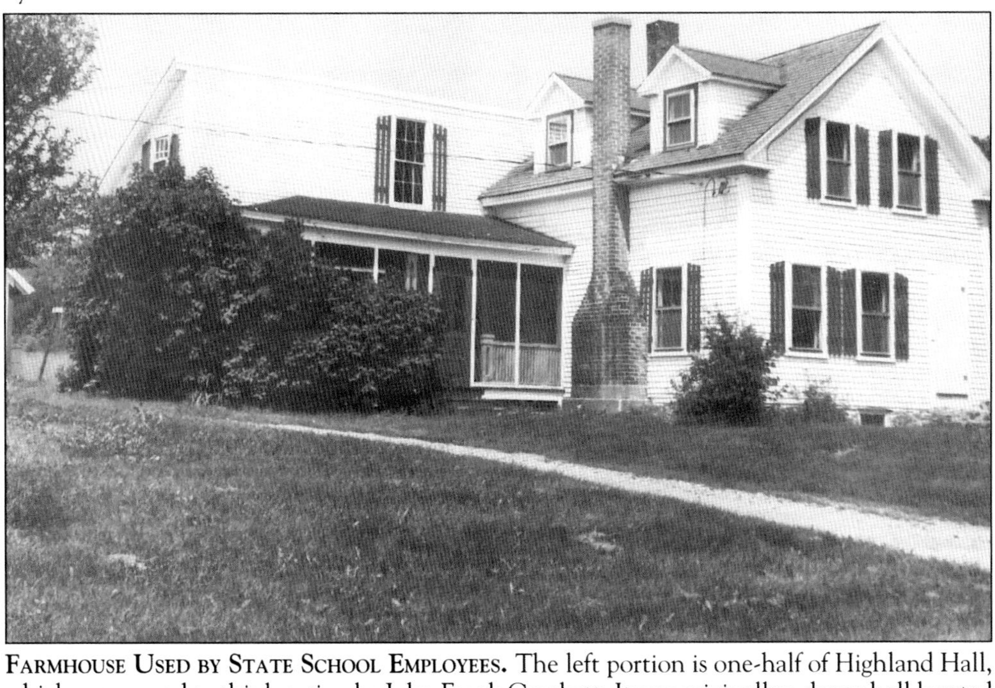

Farmhouse Used by State School Employees. The left portion is one-half of Highland Hall, which was moved to this location by John Frank Crockett. It was originally a dance hall located on the northeast side of the Parade Road, just beyond the old pound.

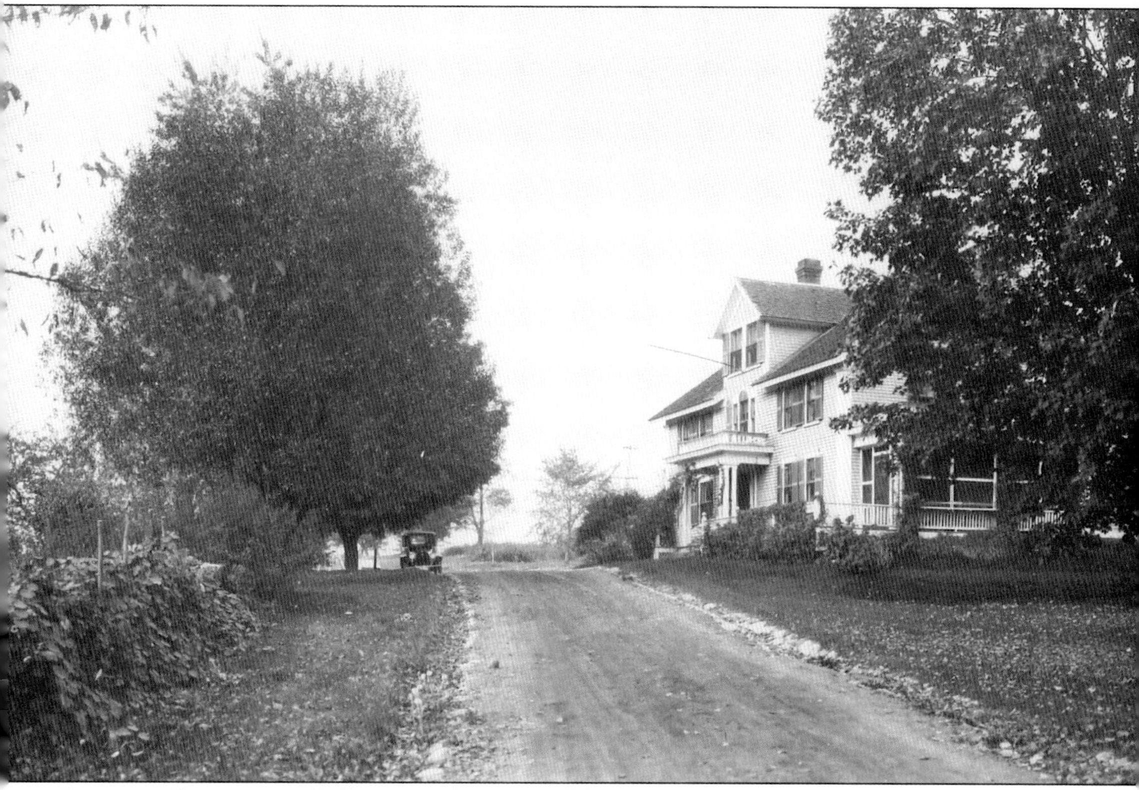

CROCKETT FARMHOUSE. William Crockett, one of the first settlers of the town of Meredith, built a log house on this site, and Joshua Crockett built a frame house here in 1771. The building was used as the first superintendent's home and, for many years, was the LSS Administration Building after the State of New Hampshire acquired the property on January 10, 1902. The rambling, 12-room landmark was razed as a training exercise for firemen in 1961.

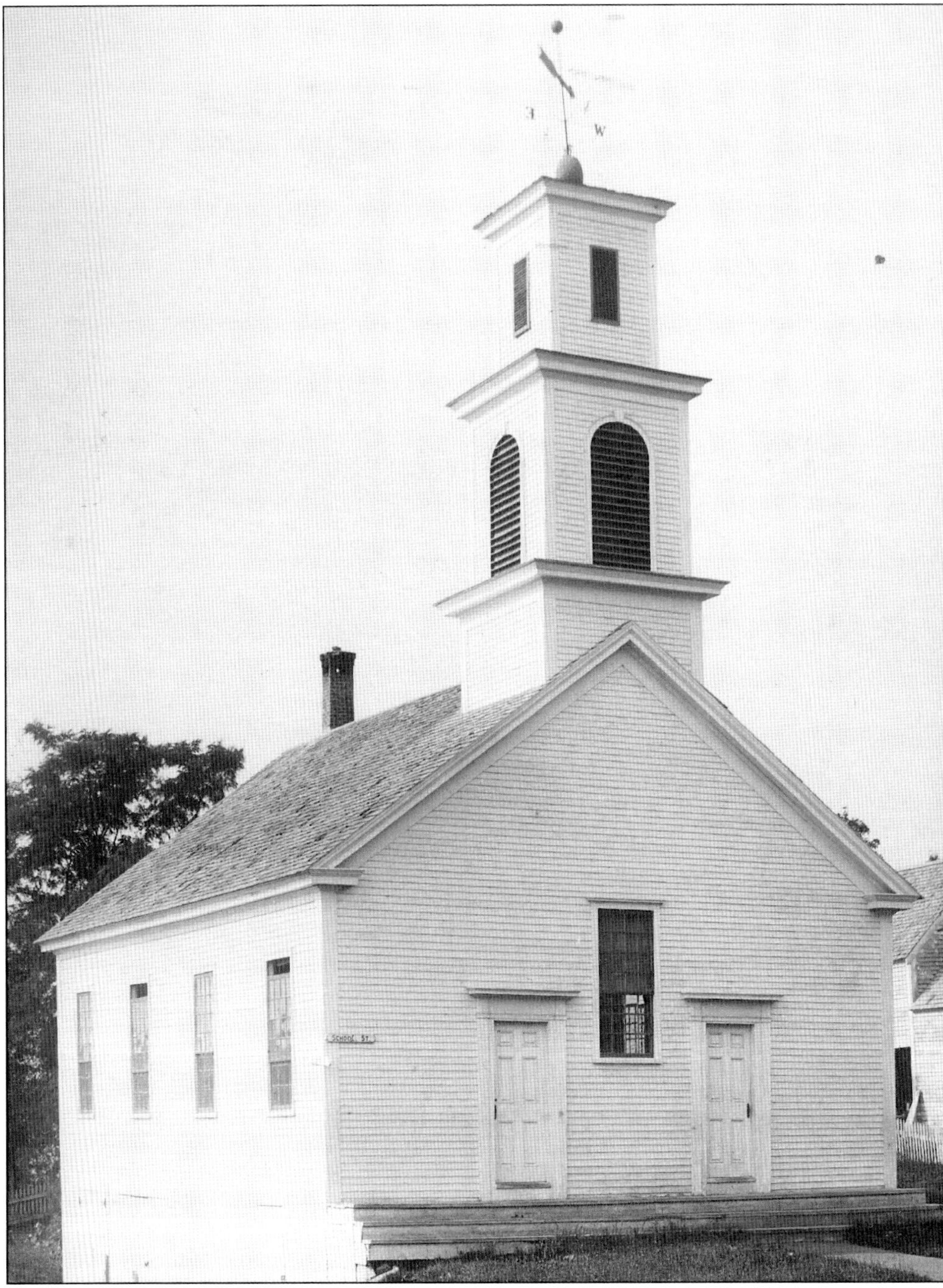

ADVENT CHURCH, NORTH STREET. Known as the North Church, this building was originally located on the Parade Road, between Laconia and Meredith, before it was taken down and moved to the southwest corner of North and School Streets in 1865. The structure was destroyed in the Great Fire of 1903. Later, the Adventists acquired the 1904 building (see bottom p. 99) of the Trinity Methodist Episcopal Church. In 1832, the Adventists had erected a chapel on Gold Street on the site (see pp. 48–49) later occupied by William G. Cram as a grain store.

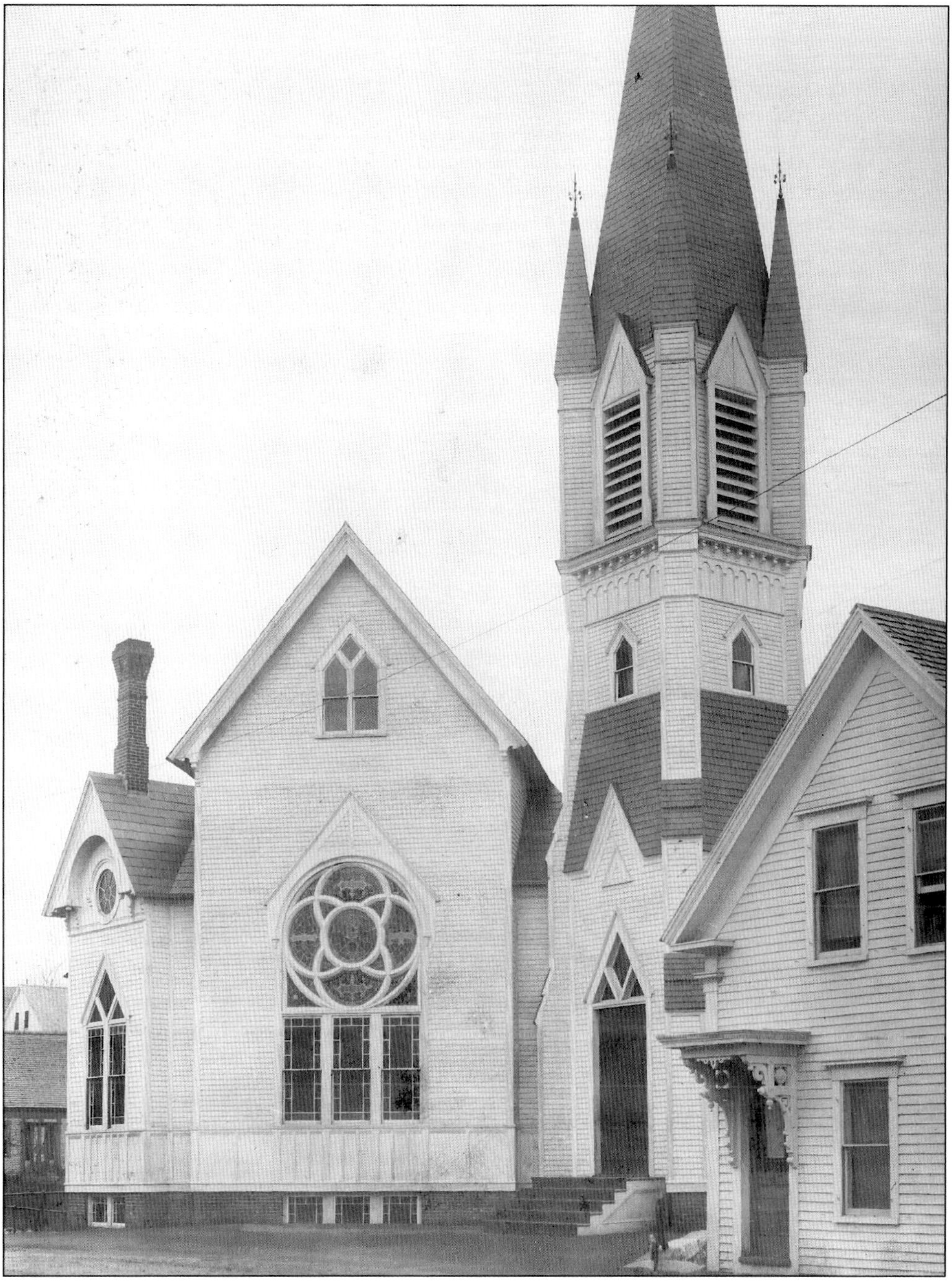

ORIGINAL TRINITY METHODIST EPISCOPAL CHURCH, FROM BELVIDERE STREET. Dedicated February 16, 1892, this building was destroyed in the Great Fire of 1903 (see bottom of p. 110). Earlier, the Methodists had worshipped in a chapel on Fairmount Street, and in the former Advent Chapel on Gold Street, among other locations.

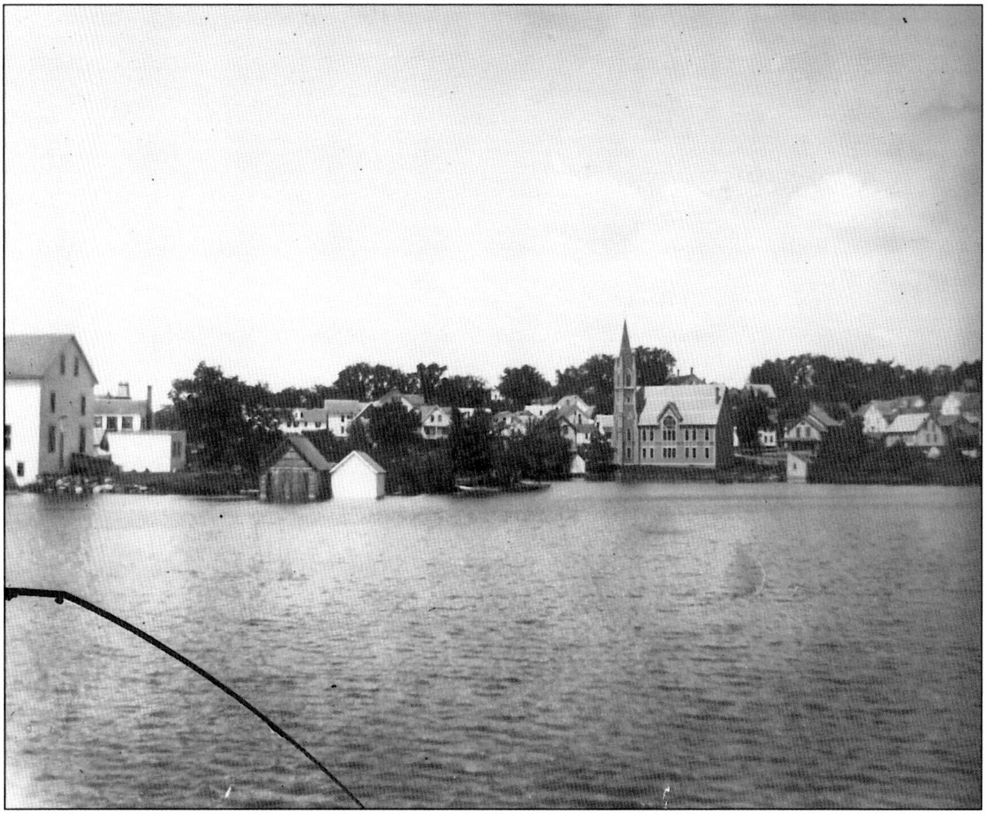

Original Trinity Methodist Episcopal Church and Surrounding Structures, Belvidere Street.

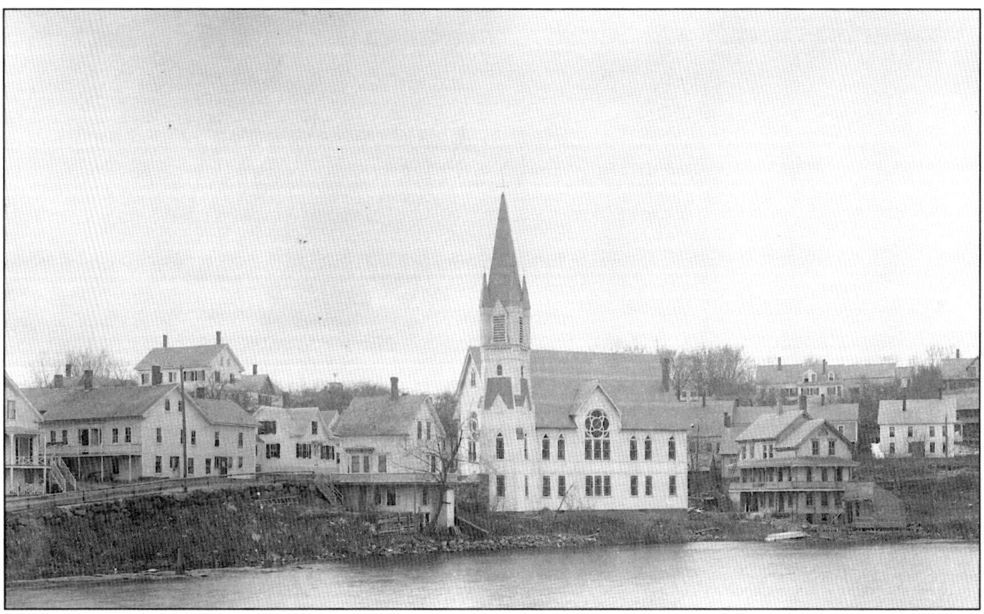

Another View of Original Trinity Methodist Episcopal Church.

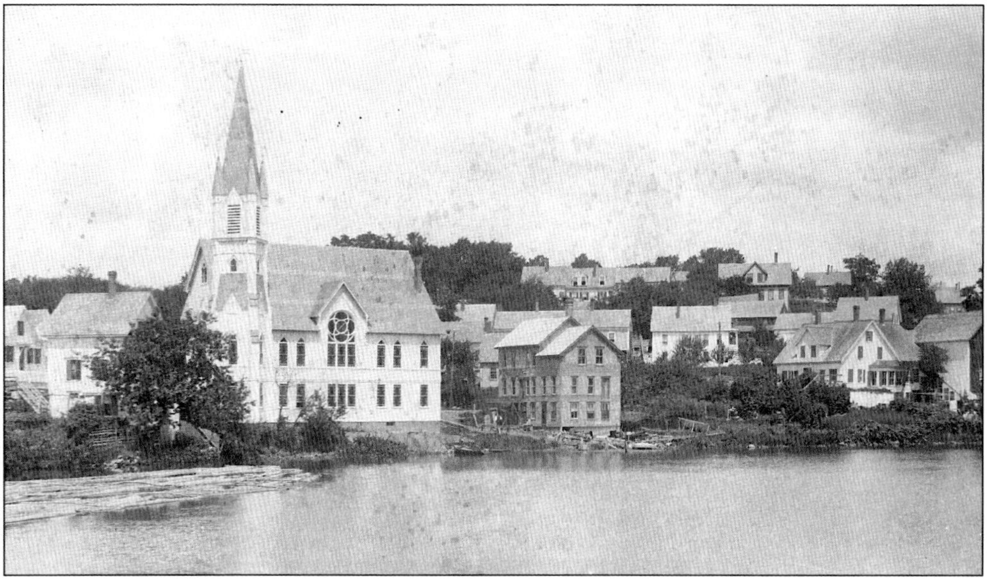

ORIGINAL TRINITY METHODIST EPISCOPAL CHURCH, 25 BELVIDERE STREET, c. 1900.

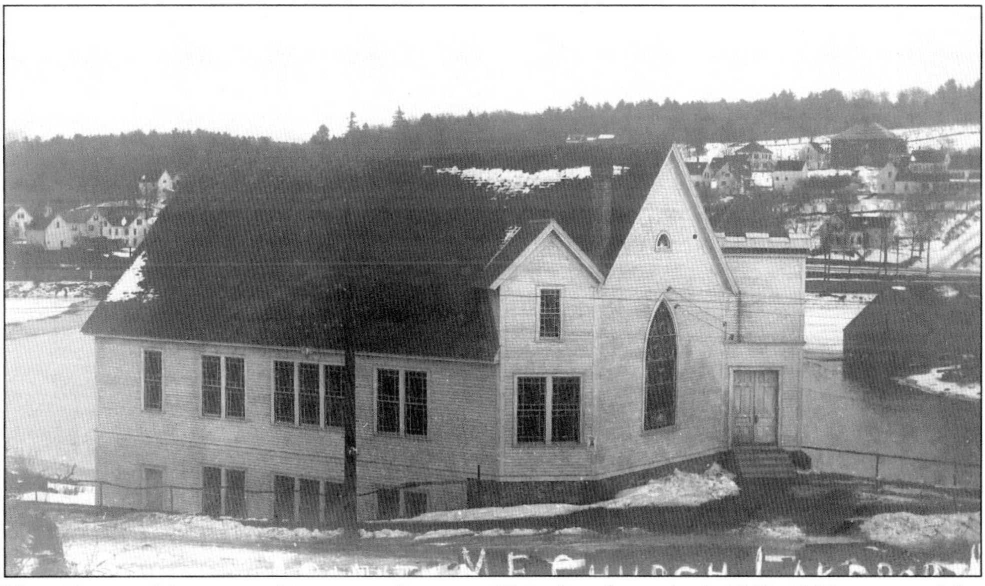

NEW TRINITY METHODIST EPISCOPAL CHURCH. This church was built 1903–1904 on site of the structure destroyed in the Great Fire of 1903. After Trinity Methodist merged with the Weirs Methodist Church in 1963, the Belvidere Street edifice was transferred, February 18, 1964, to the Second Advent Christian Church.

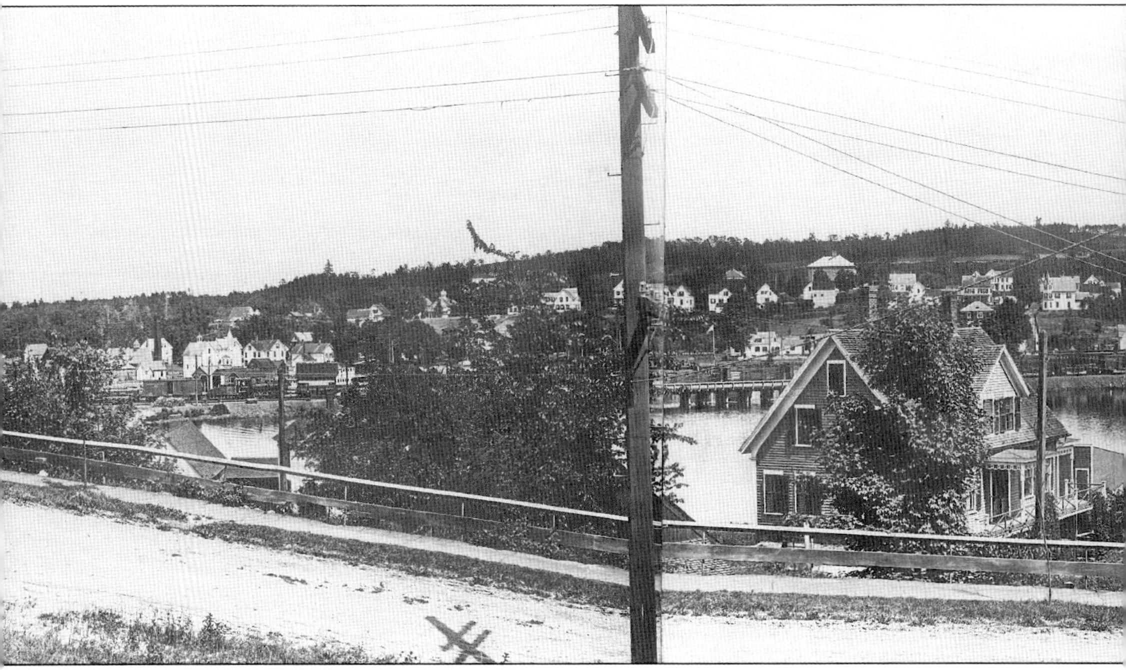

Panoramic View from North Street across Lake Paugus, c. 1910. North Street (foreground) begins off the photograph at right. Today, Sheridan Street branches off at the

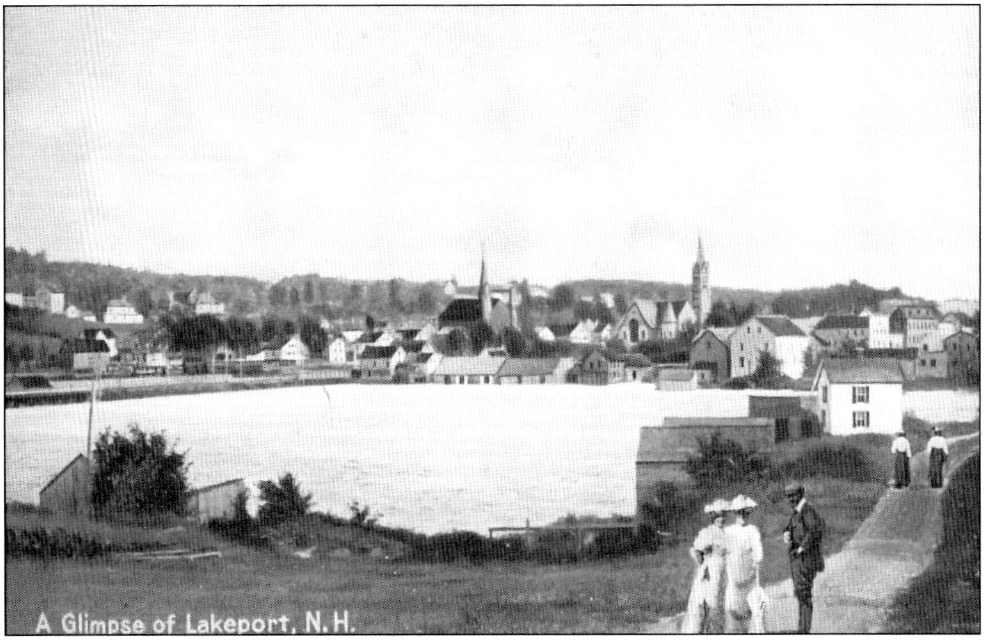

An Earlier View, with Railroad Bridge Visible at Left.

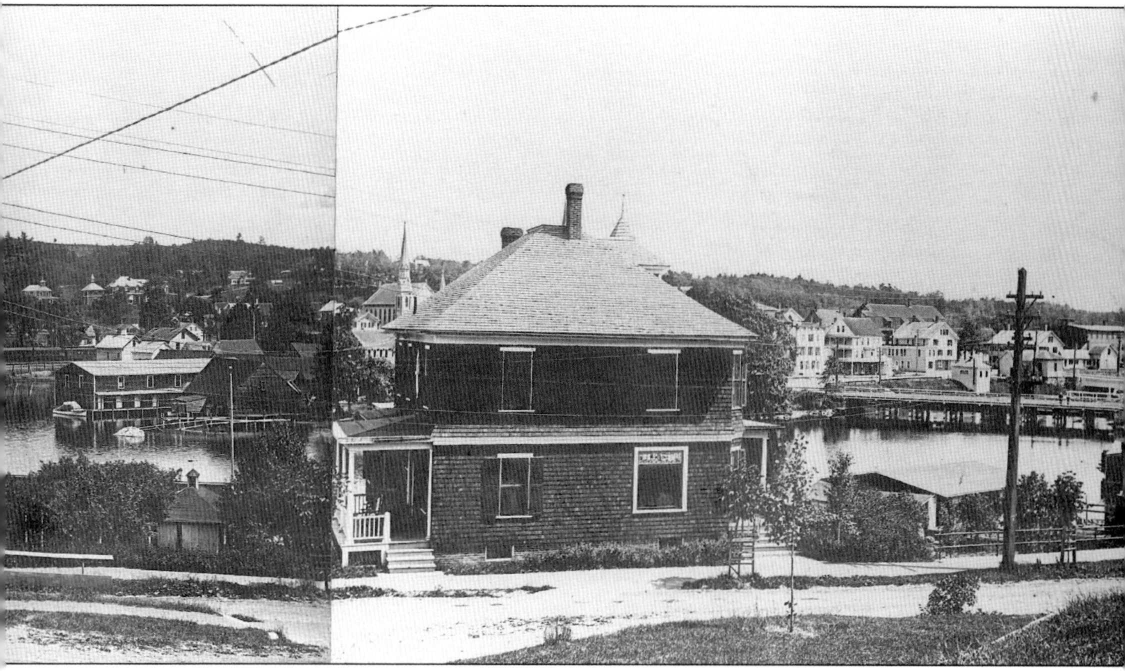

house with the hip roof (17 North Street), at right. The railroad bridge is visible at left and the Gold Street Bridge is seen at right.

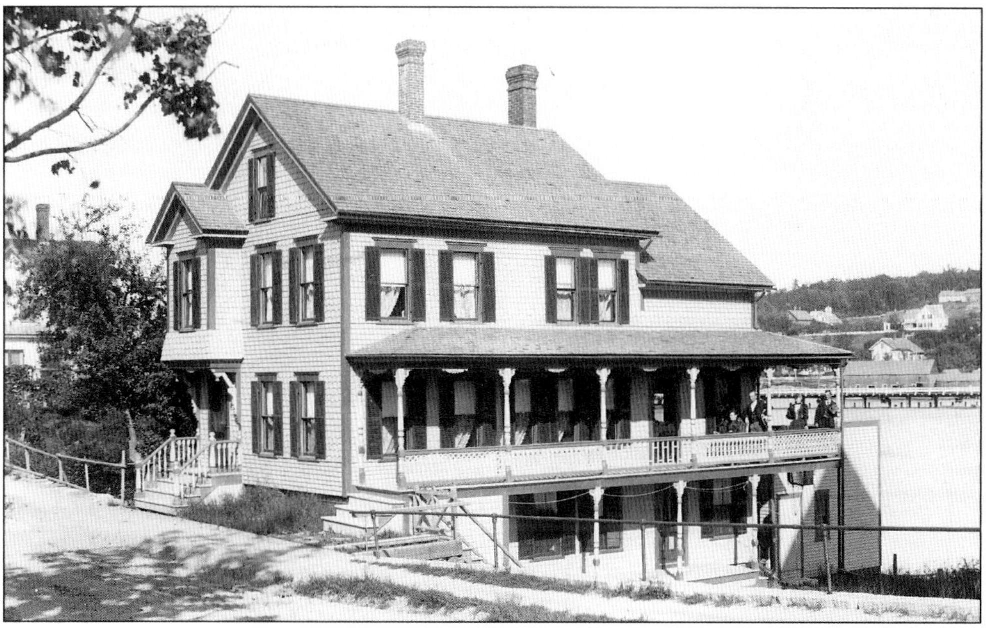

Dr. Phillip Z. Hart House, 5 North Street, with Railroad Bridge Visible at Right. Dr. Hart's house burned in the Great Fire of 1903.

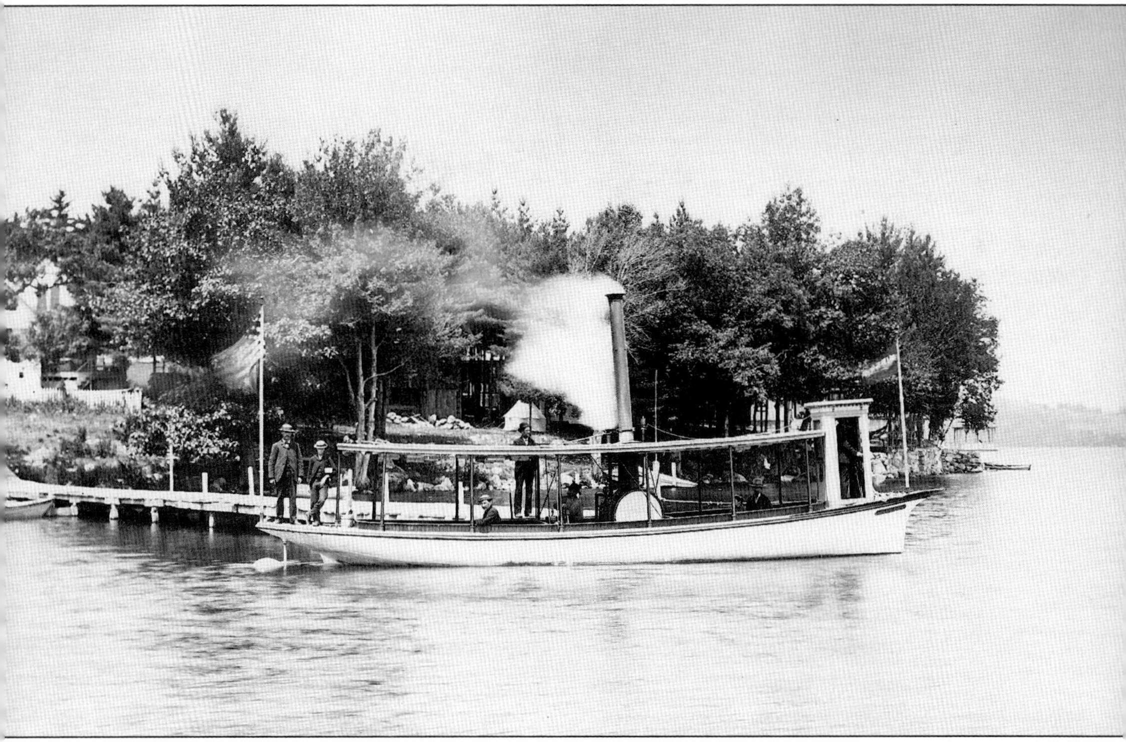

STEAMER *MINEOLA*, C. 1885. Built at Newburg, New York, in 1877, she was shipped here by rail in July of that year. "Probably no boat on the lake ever brought in as large dividends to its owners . . . She was the first steamer on the lake, large enough for freight and passenger business, to be fitted with a screw propeller."

Six

The Great Fire of 1903

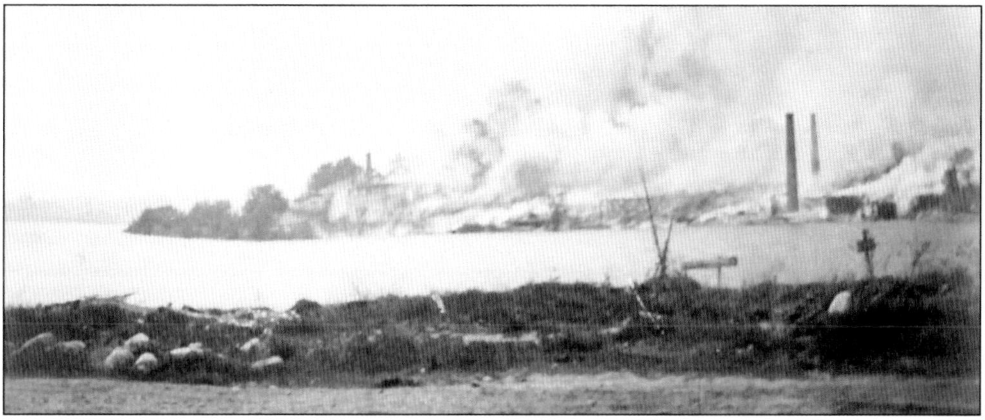

H.H. Wood Mill during the Great Fire of May 26, 1903. According to *The Laconia Democrat*, at about 2 p.m., "the fire started in the boiler house of the H.H. Wood mill, and spread so rapidly that before the fire alarm signal was completed almost the entire mill was in flames. There were about two hundred operatives at work in the mill and some of them barely had time to escape from the doomed building." When firemen reached the scene, the flames had already spread to the woodworking establishment of Boulia, Gorrell, & Co. and the power station of the Laconia Electric Lighting Co., both at right.

A strong southwest wind from Lake Opechee drove sparks from the burning buildings up among the residences on Belvidere Hill, "and it was quickly seen that Lakeport was booked for a most disastrous conflagration. A general fire alarm was at once sounded, bringing all of the fire-fighting apparatus in the city to the fire." Concord, Franklin, and Dover promptly sent steam fire engines by special train, and Meredith and Tilton sent hose carriages and men. But the wooden buildings, "with shingles dry as tinder for lack of rain for many weeks, offered the most inflammable material for the sheets of flame and showers of sparks which were driven by the fierce wind directly up the hill, and in less than an hour, the flames had jumped from house to house until almost every residence on Washington street, Elm street, Belvidere street, and North street was a roaring conflagration," in addition to almost total destruction in the Franklin Street area.

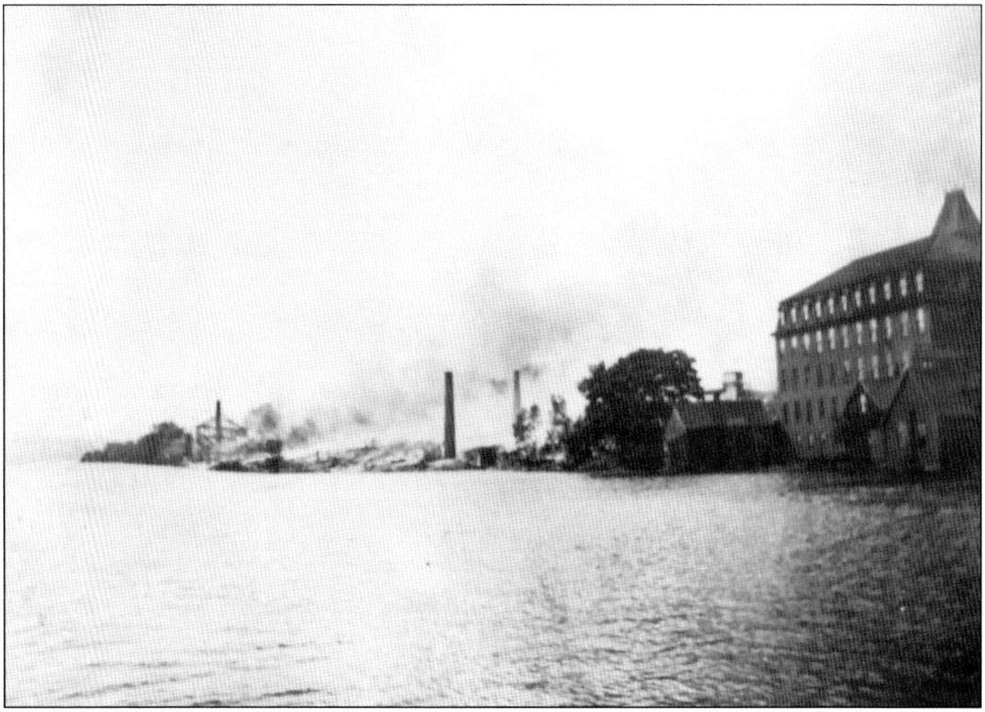

Another View of the H.H. Wood Mill and Boulia-Gorrell Lumber Co. during the Fire. At right is the Bayside Mill, on the other (east) side of the river.

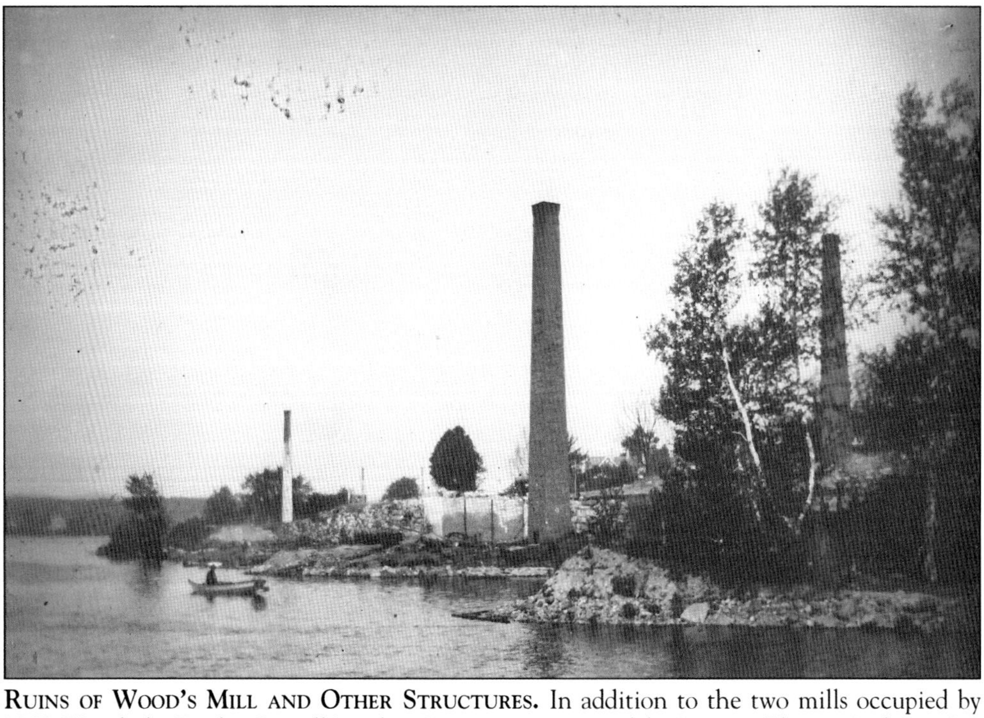

Ruins of Wood's Mill and Other Structures. In addition to the two mills occupied by H.H. Wood, the Boulia-Gorrell Lumber Co., power station of the Laconia Electric Lighting Co. and the Lake Co. (Riverside) Gristmill were destroyed, along with two blacksmith shops.

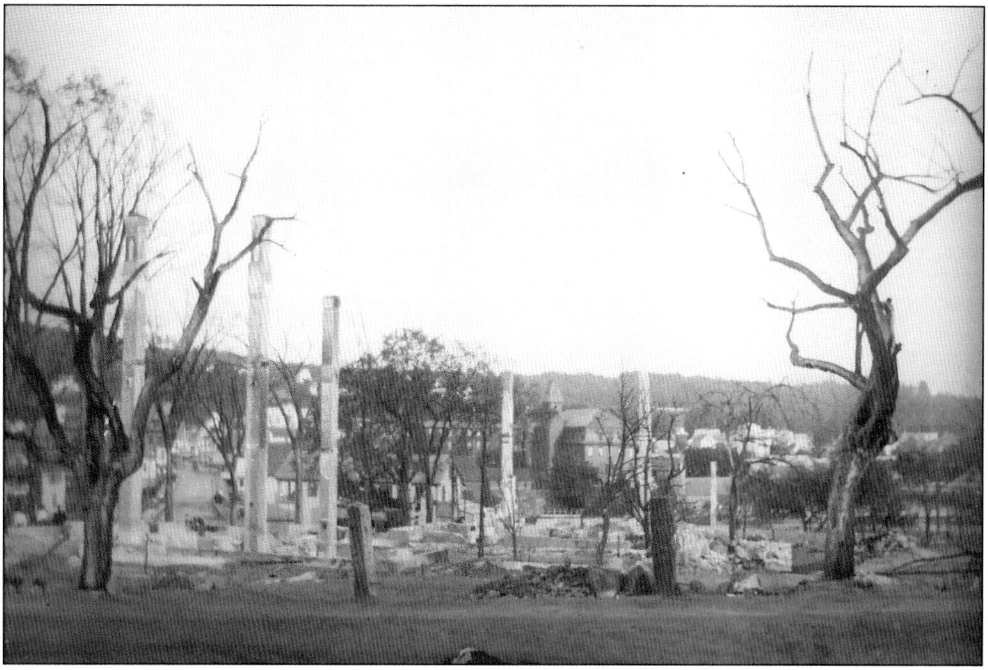

MORE RUINS. The Halifax and Bayside Mills, across the river, are visible at center.

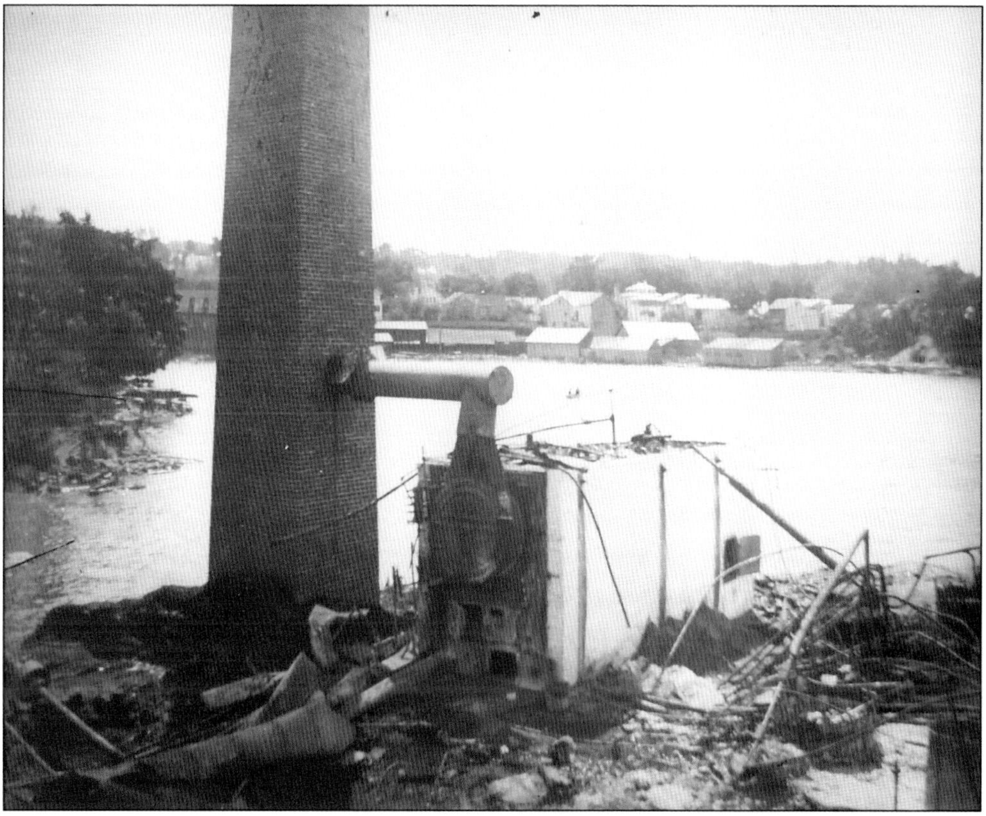

RUINS OF BOILER HOUSE, WOOD'S MILL.

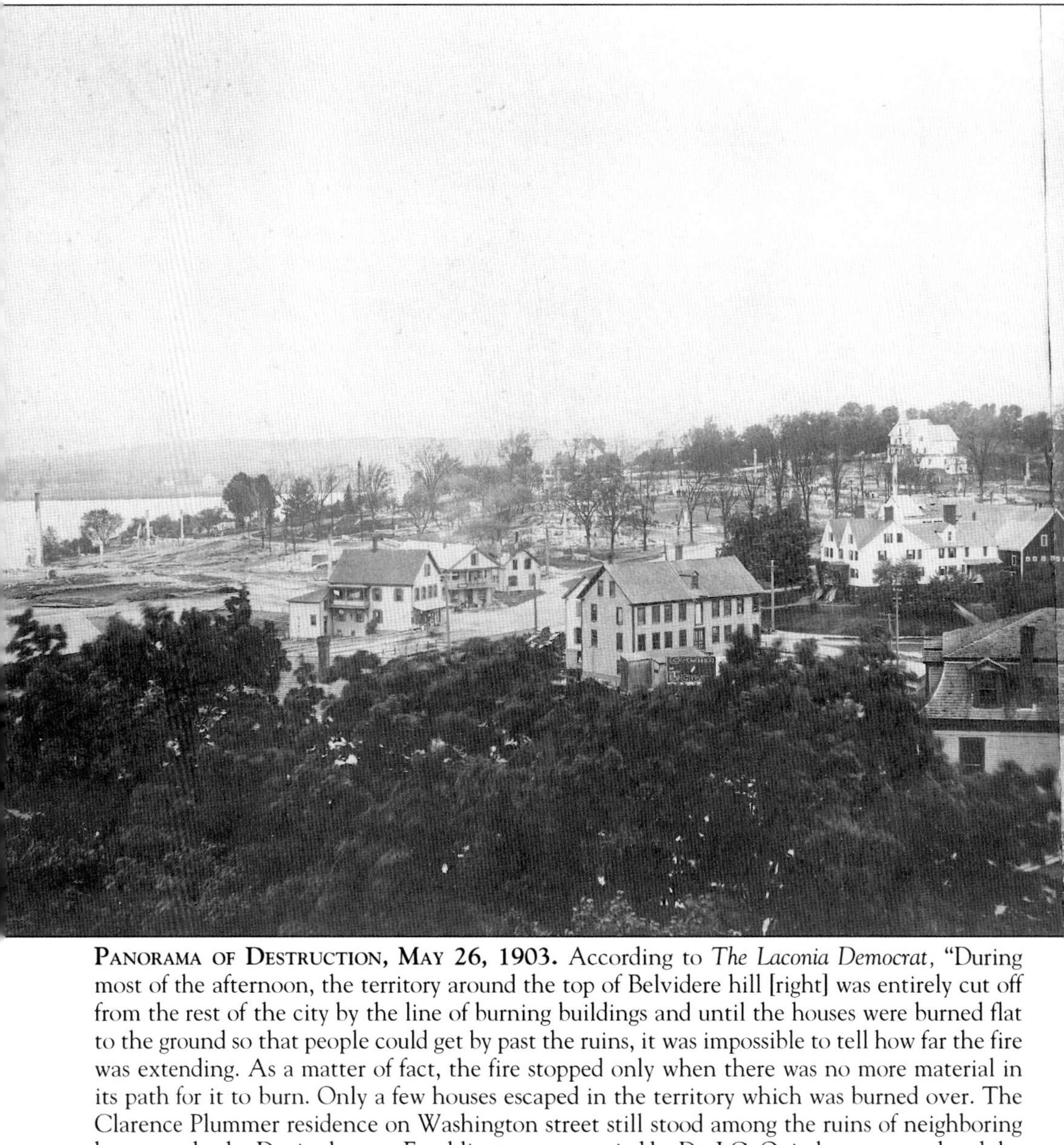

Panorama of Destruction, May 26, 1903. According to *The Laconia Democrat*, "During most of the afternoon, the territory around the top of Belvidere hill [right] was entirely cut off from the rest of the city by the line of burning buildings and until the houses were burned flat to the ground so that people could get by past the ruins, it was impossible to tell how far the fire was extending. As a matter of fact, the fire stopped only when there was no more material in its path for it to burn. Only a few houses escaped in the territory which was burned over. The Clarence Plummer residence on Washington street still stood among the ruins of neighboring homesteads; the Davis place on Franklin street, occupied by Dr. J.G. Quimby, was saved and the

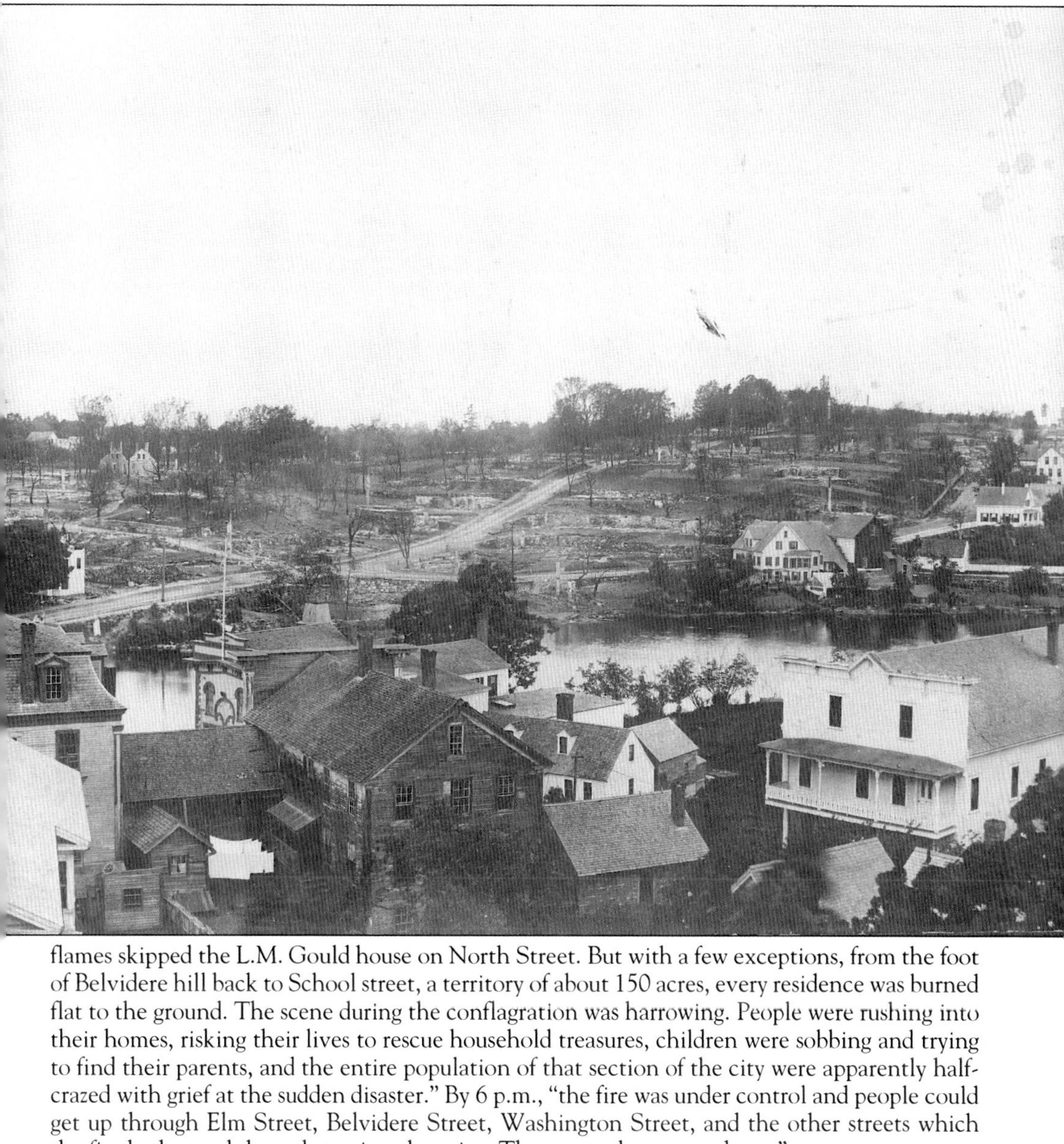

flames skipped the L.M. Gould house on North Street. But with a few exceptions, from the foot of Belvidere hill back to School street, a territory of about 150 acres, every residence was burned flat to the ground. The scene during the conflagration was harrowing. People were rushing into their homes, risking their lives to rescue household treasures, children were sobbing and trying to find their parents, and the entire population of that section of the city were apparently half-crazed with grief at the sudden disaster." By 6 p.m., "the fire was under control and people could get up through Elm Street, Belvidere Street, Washington Street, and the other streets which the fire had passed through to view the ruins. The spectacle was a sad one."

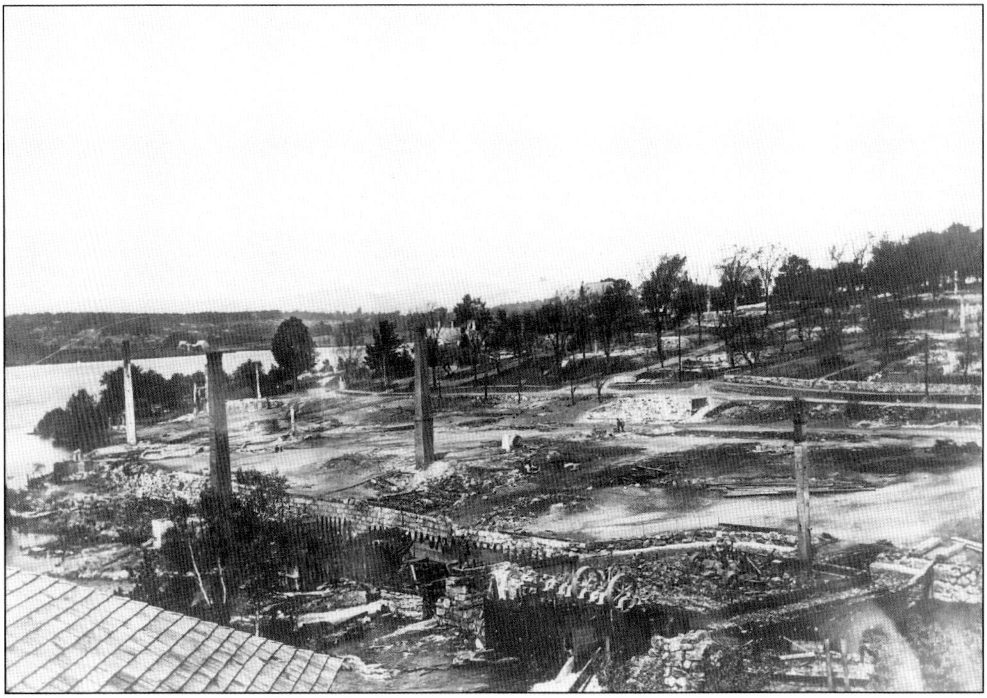

BAYSIDE COURT AND FRANKLIN STREET AFTER THE FIRE. Washington Street appears at top center.

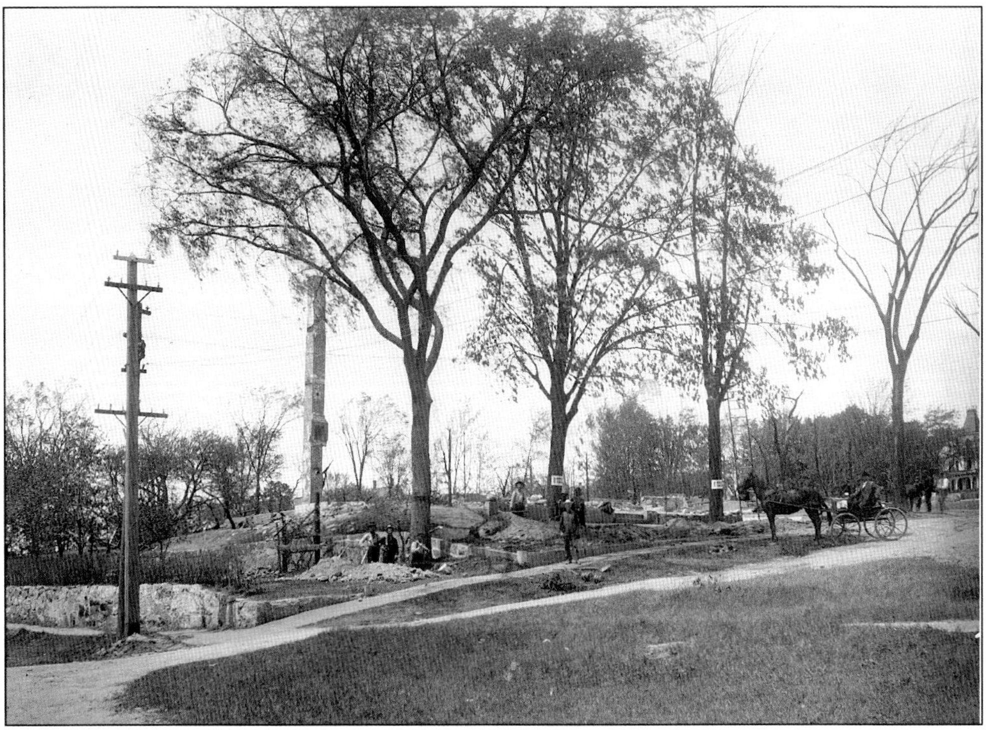

MORE RUINS FROM FRANKLIN STREET. Part of the Drake-Plummer House is visible at extreme right.

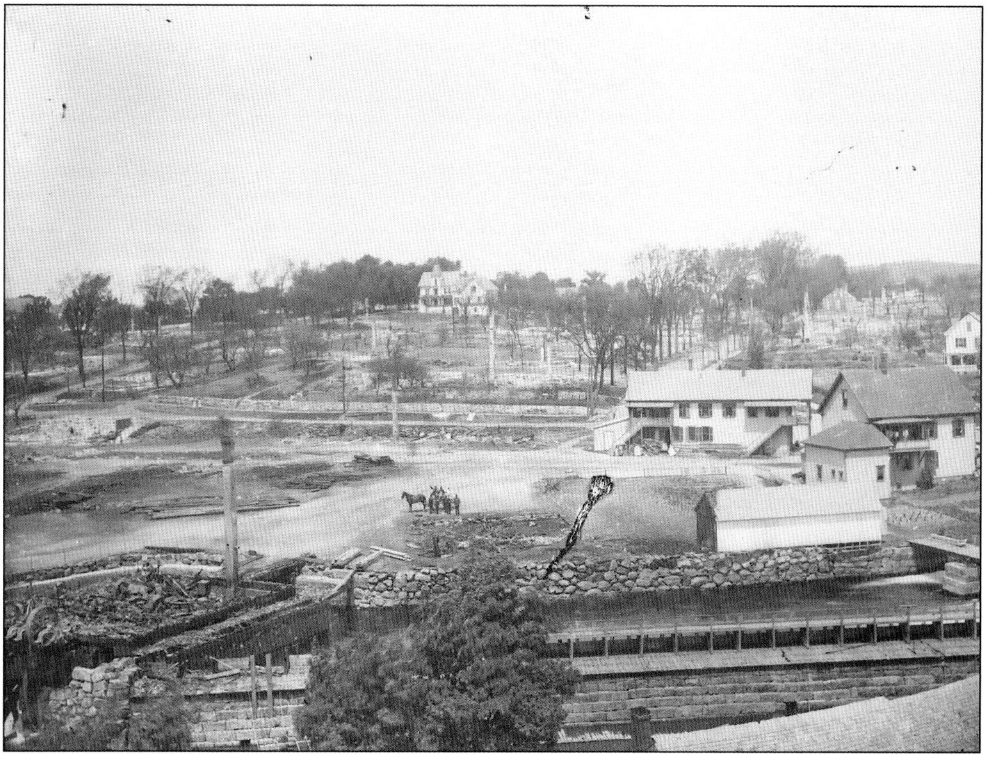

BAYSIDE COURT AND FRANKLIN STREET AFTER THE FIRE. The wing dam appears at bottom, and the ruins of the Laconia Electric Lighting Co. plant are at left. The B.F. Drake-Clarence Plummer House at 43 Washington Street, which escaped the flames, is at top center.

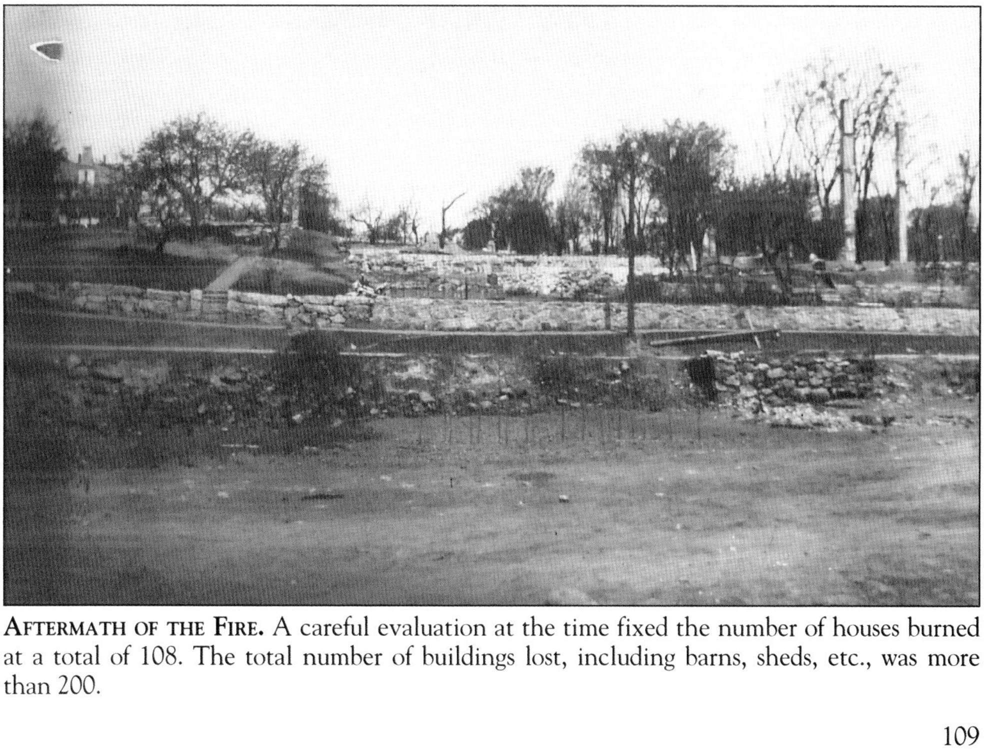

AFTERMATH OF THE FIRE. A careful evaluation at the time fixed the number of houses burned at a total of 108. The total number of buildings lost, including barns, sheds, etc., was more than 200.

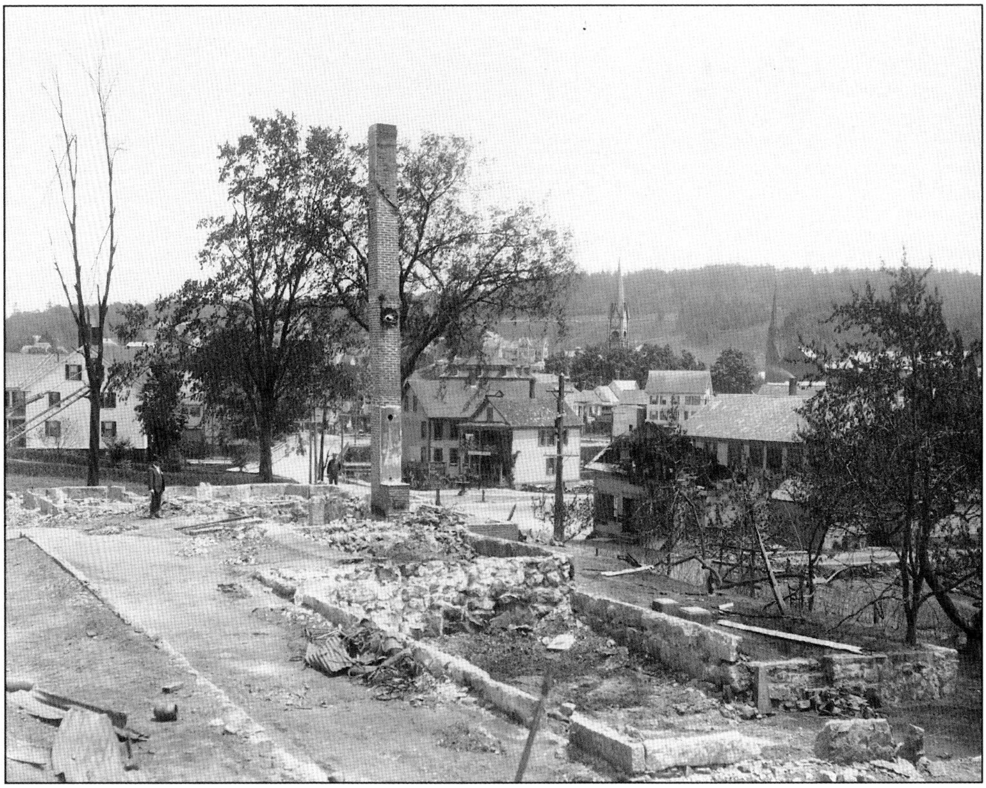

RUINS OF RESIDENCE OF DR. OSSIAN W. GOSS, ELM STREET. The Goss Reading Room was later constructed on this site. The Folsom-Batchelder House, spared by the flames, is at left and Franklin (later McGrath) Square buildings appear to the right of the chimney.

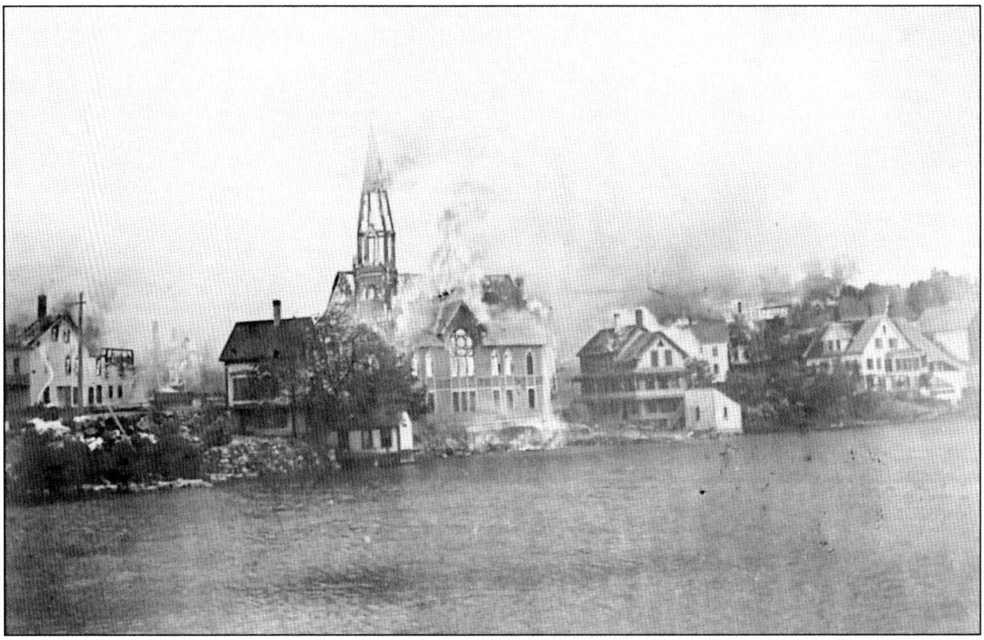

TRINITY METHODIST EPISCOPAL CHURCH ON FIRE.

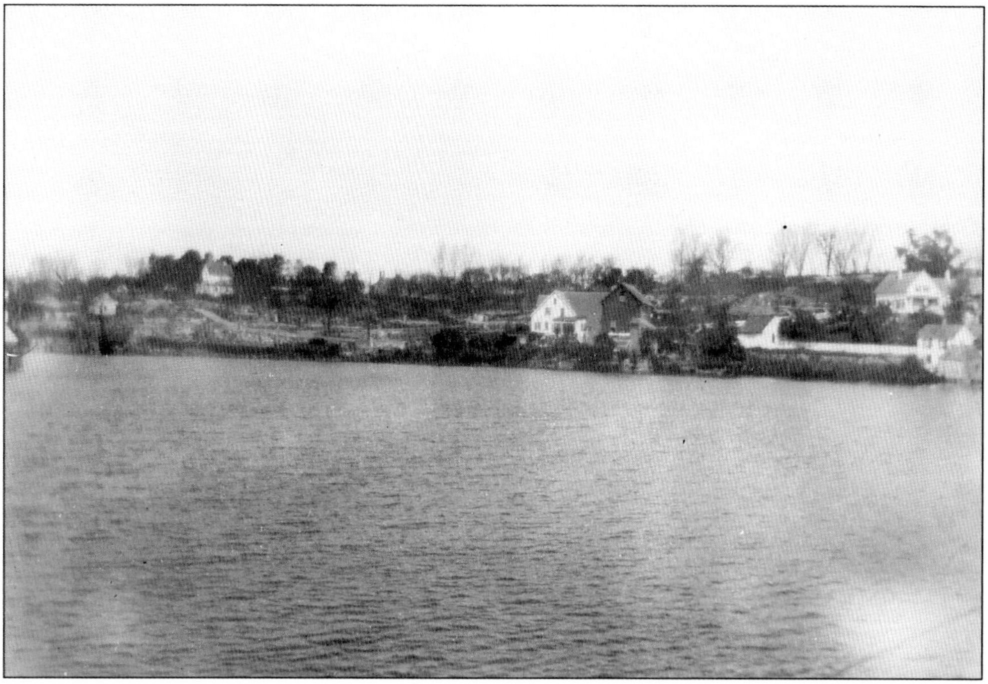

Aftermath, North Street Area. The Trinity Methodist Episcopal and North (Advent) Churches, on this side of Belvidere Hill, were also casualties of the fire.

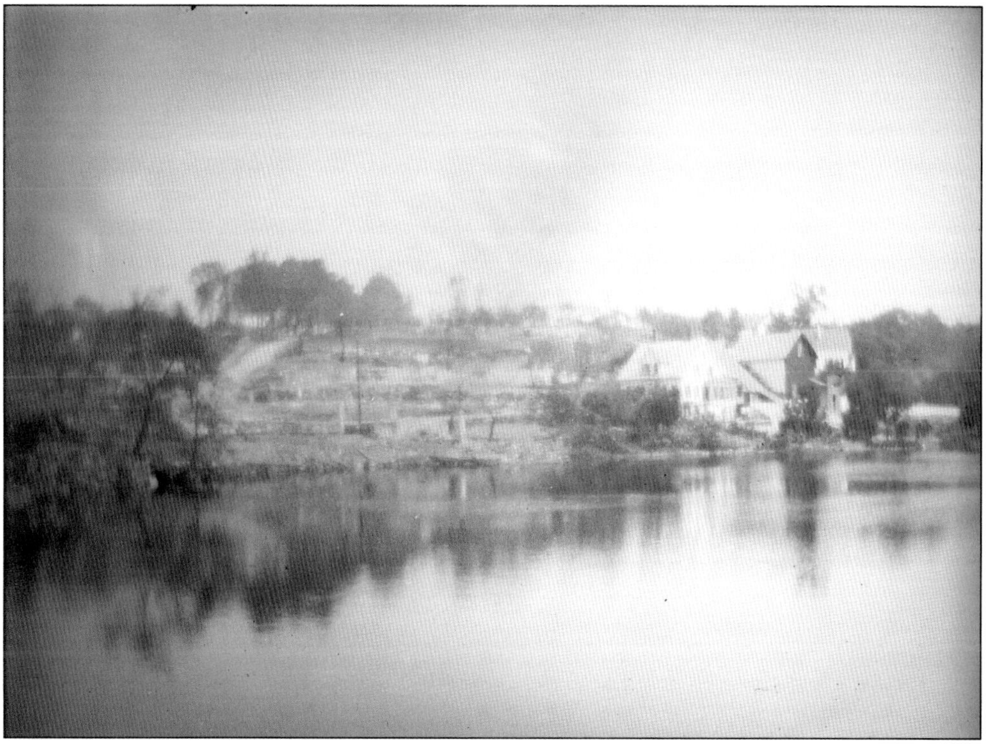

Belvidere and North Streets after the Fire. The total value of property destroyed, from Bayside Court and Franklin Street to Belvidere Hill, was established at more than $400,000.

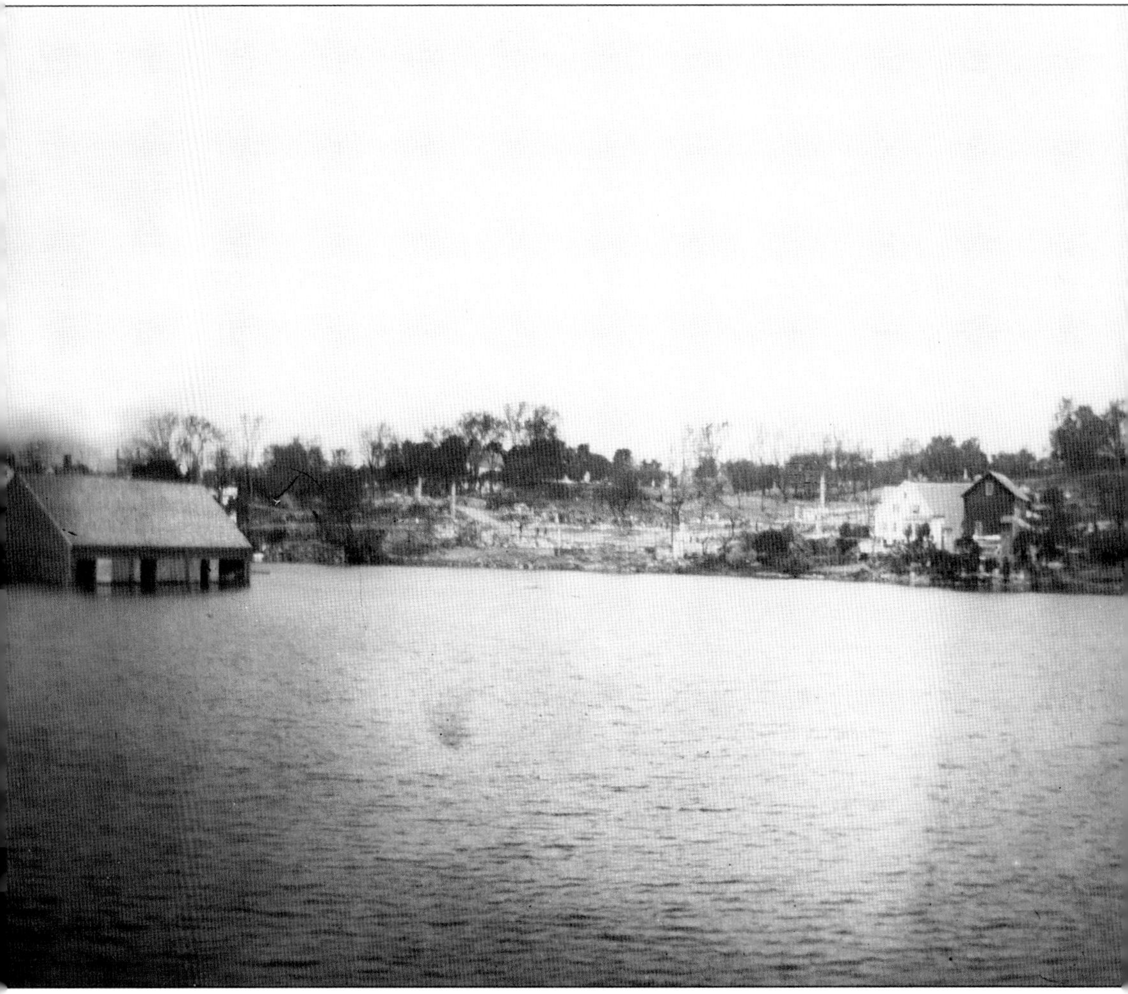

North and Belvidere Streets after the Fire. *The Laconia Democrat* reported that, "The beautiful shade trees, which made this portion of the city one of the pleasantest for residential purposes, were all blackened and killed and in many cases were stripped naked of their bark. The streets were full of telephone and electric wires, and full-burned household furniture. The pretty residences of a few hours previous were a mass of coals, and only the chimneys standing gaunt against the sky-line marked the locations of former homes. Poultry, cats, dogs and even pigs wandered around the streets trying to find their former homes, while the recent owners were also wandering aimlessly around the ruins, sadly contemplating the havoc which had been wrought in such a short time."

Seven

East Side to Black Brook

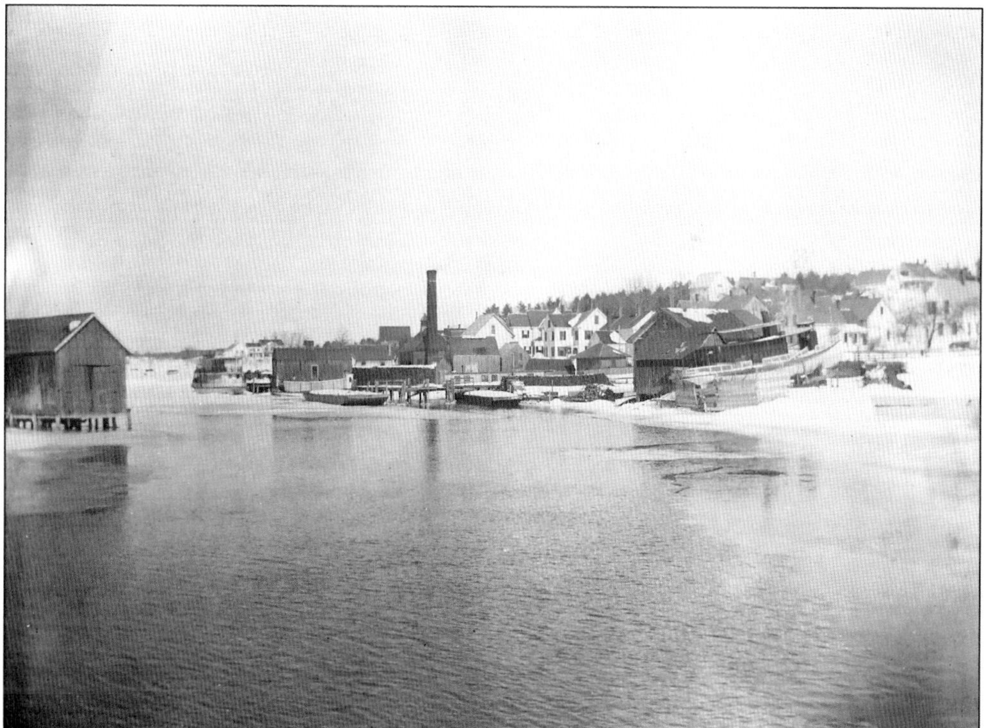

Lake Paugus and Union Avenue from Gold Street Area, c. 1888. The chimney of the Laconia Water Works is at center; the boat yard is at right. The railroad bridge is off the photograph at left.

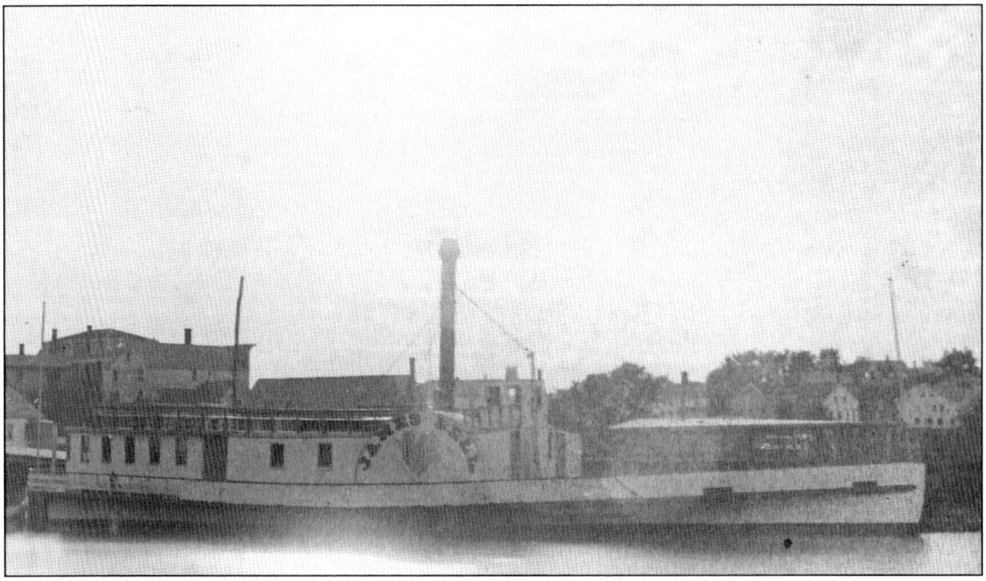

STEAMER *JAMES BELL,* NEAR RAILROAD BRIDGE. Built in 1866–1867 at Center Harbor, she was retired in 1886 after 18 years of service carrying excursionists and towing logs.

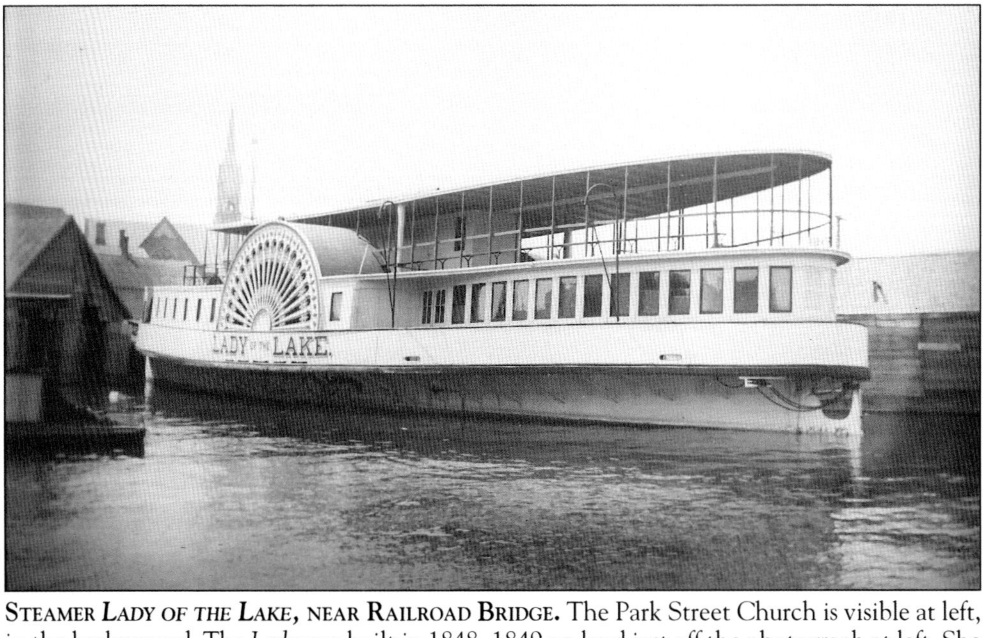

STEAMER *LADY OF THE LAKE,* NEAR RAILROAD BRIDGE. The Park Street Church is visible at left, in the background. The *Lady* was built in 1848–1849 on land just off the photograph at left. She made her last trip on September 14, 1893.

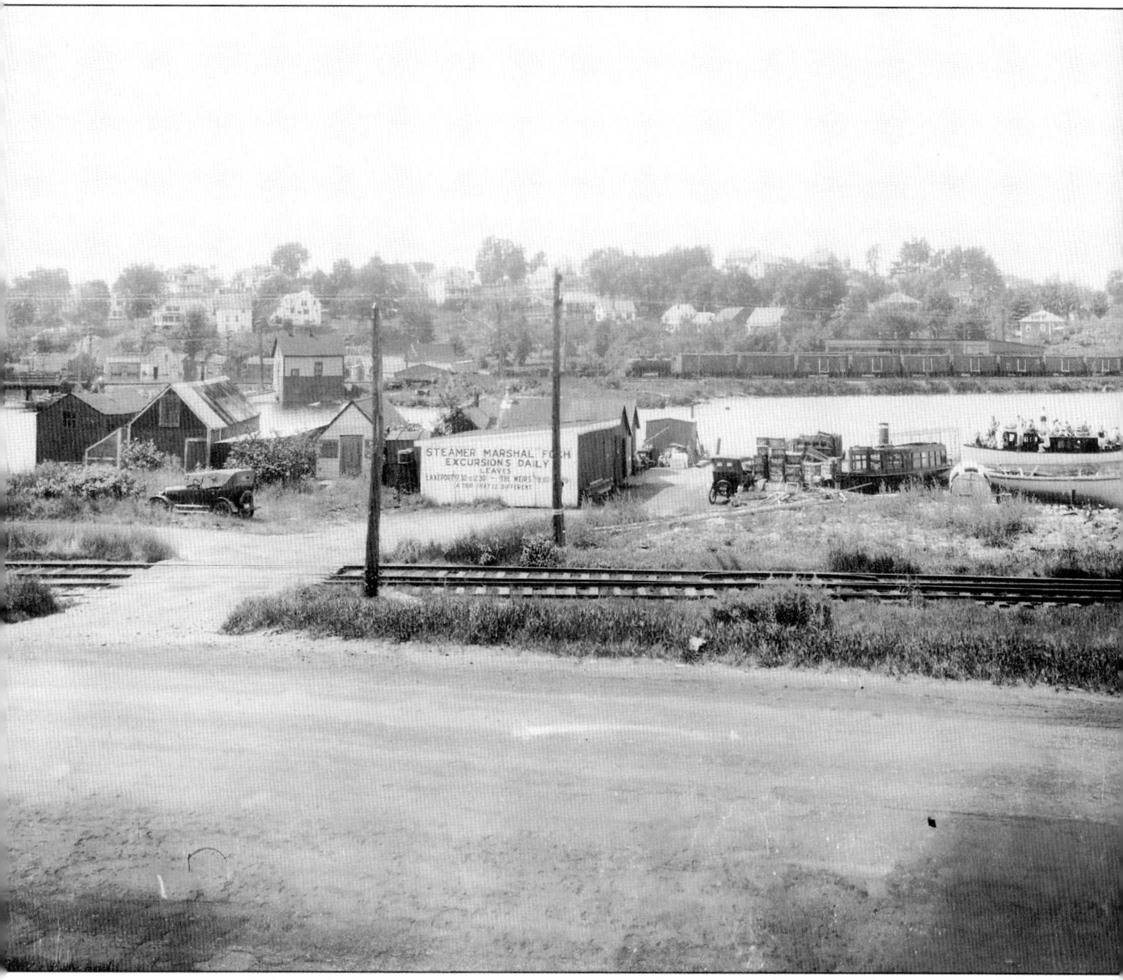

DOCKS ON SITE OF TODAY'S IRWIN MARINE. Across Lake Paugus, a train of ice cars is visible, with the railroad bridge at left. The steamer *Marshal Foch* departed on daily excursions from this location. Many small steamboats had wharves in this locale. Tracks of the Lake Shore Railroad (1890–1935) appear in the foreground. The photographer is standing on Union Avenue.

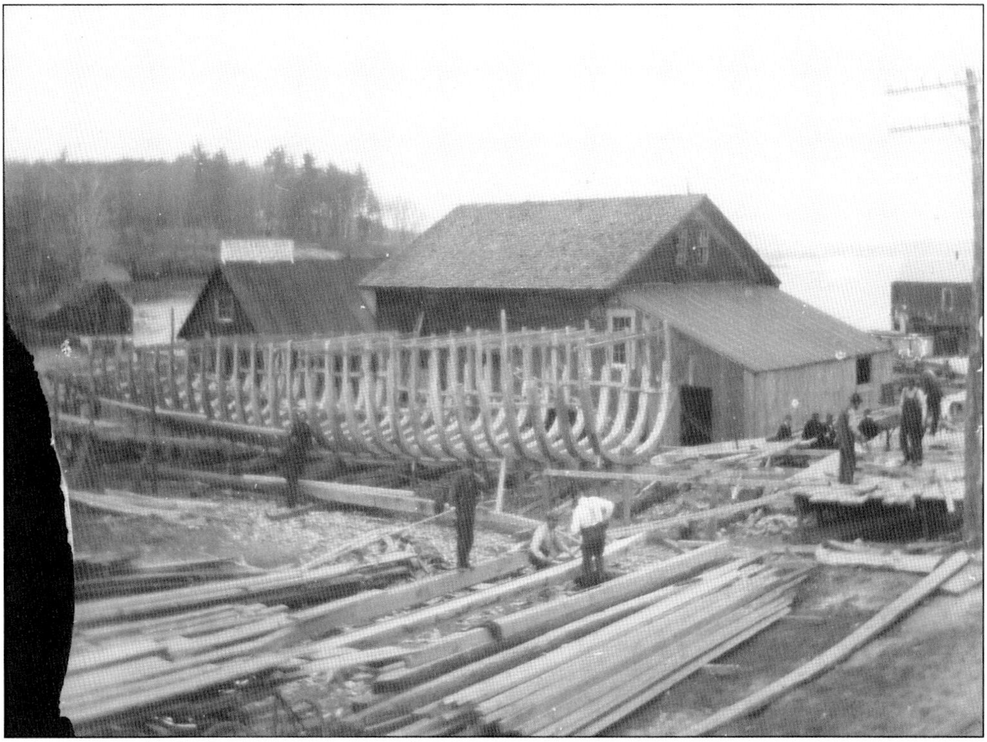

Boatyard. The hull of a steamer is under construction.

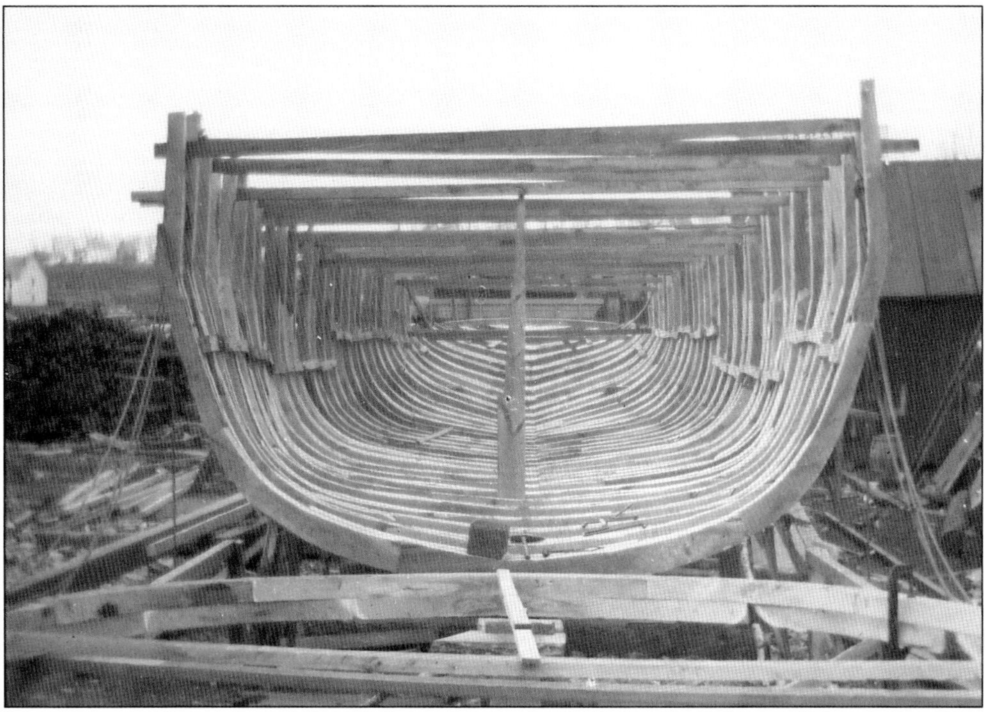

Another View of Construction. Although not identified on the glass-plate negative, the hull resembles that of the *Governor Endicott*.

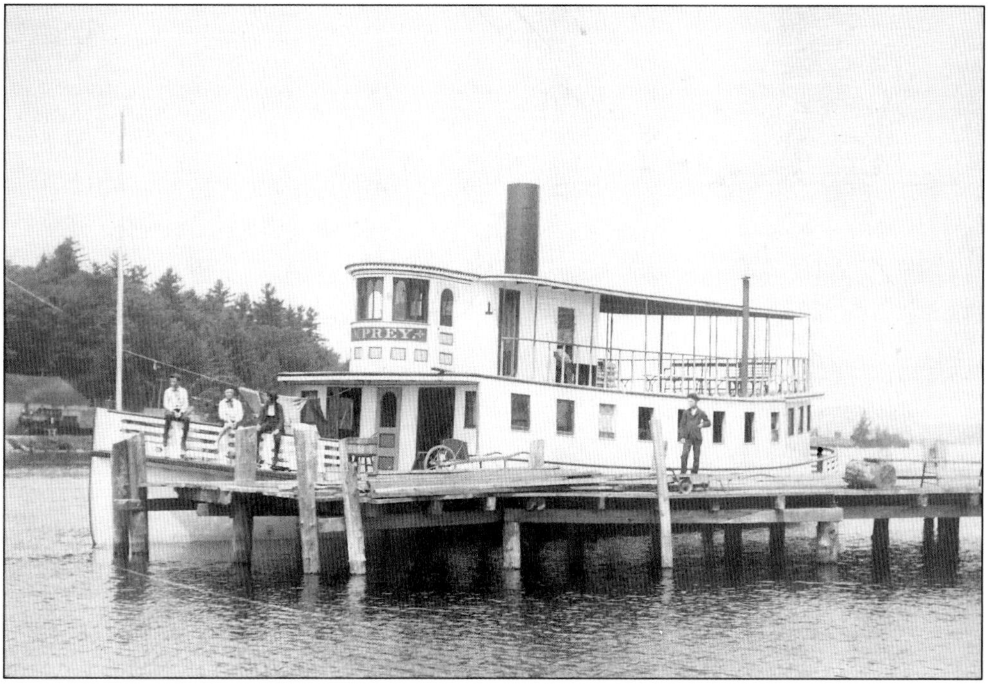

STEAMER *LAMPREY*, C. 1890, SAME LOCATION. In the background, a locomotive heads south toward the railroad bridge on the west side of Lake Paugus.

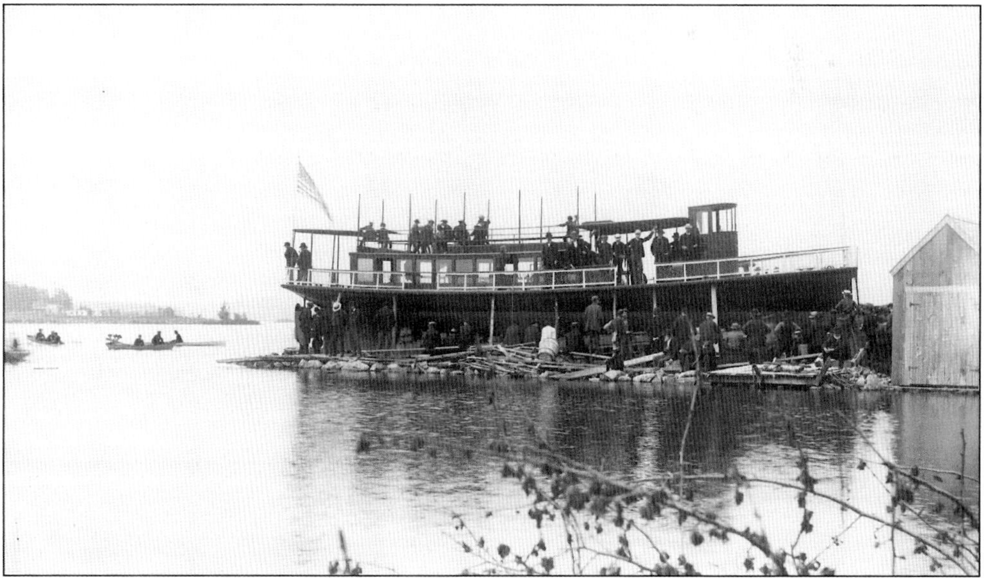

CAPTAIN BROWN'S *EAGLE*, 1886. Built that year by Capt. Herbert A. Blackstone, she burned at Long Island in 1903.

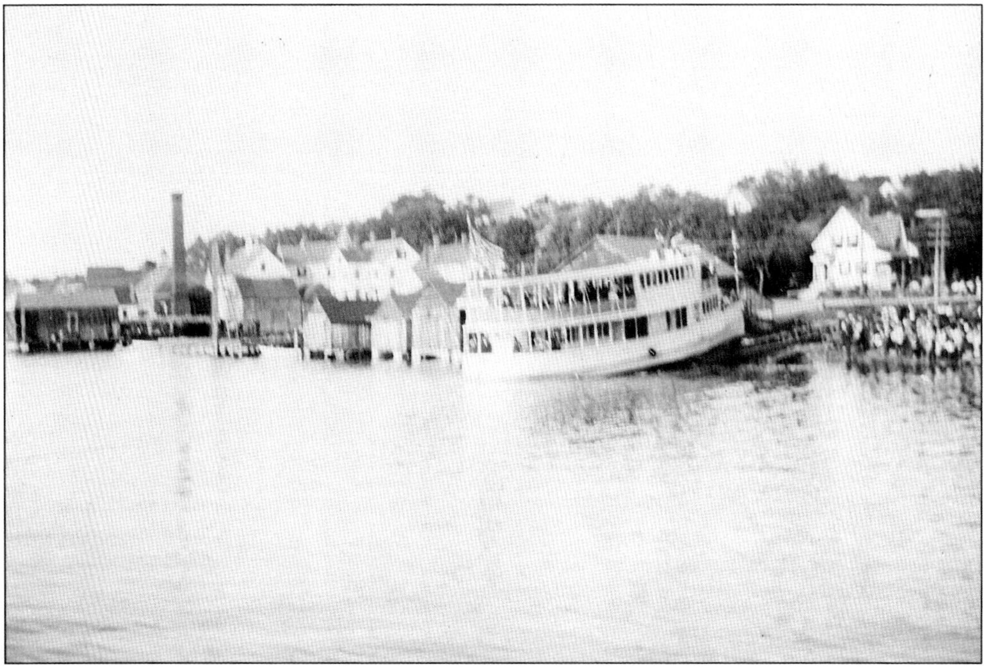

ANOTHER VIEW OF BOATYARD, WITH *GOVERNOR ENDICOTT* IN MID-LAUNCH. The tall chimney of the Laconia Water Co. is visible at left.

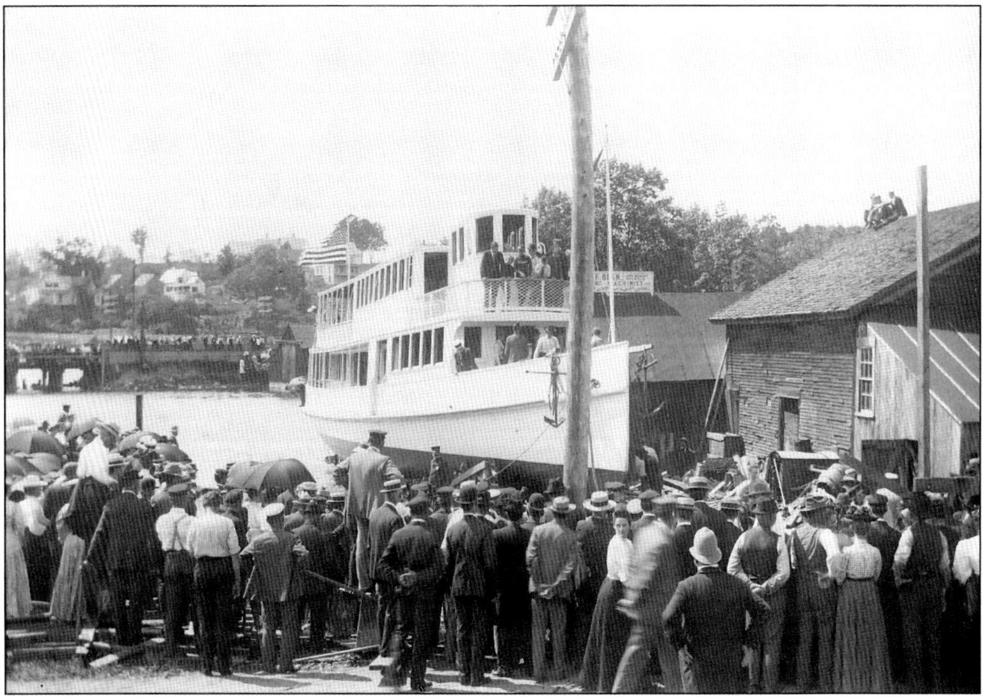

LAUNCHING OF *GOVERNOR ENDICOTT*, JULY 20, 1905. When the keel snagged on the ways, stopping the launch, a rope was carried across the water and attached to a locomotive. "Two or three yanks were successful" and she "slid gracefully into the water." The steamer, which carried as many as 500 passengers, was dismantled at Lakeport in April 1928.

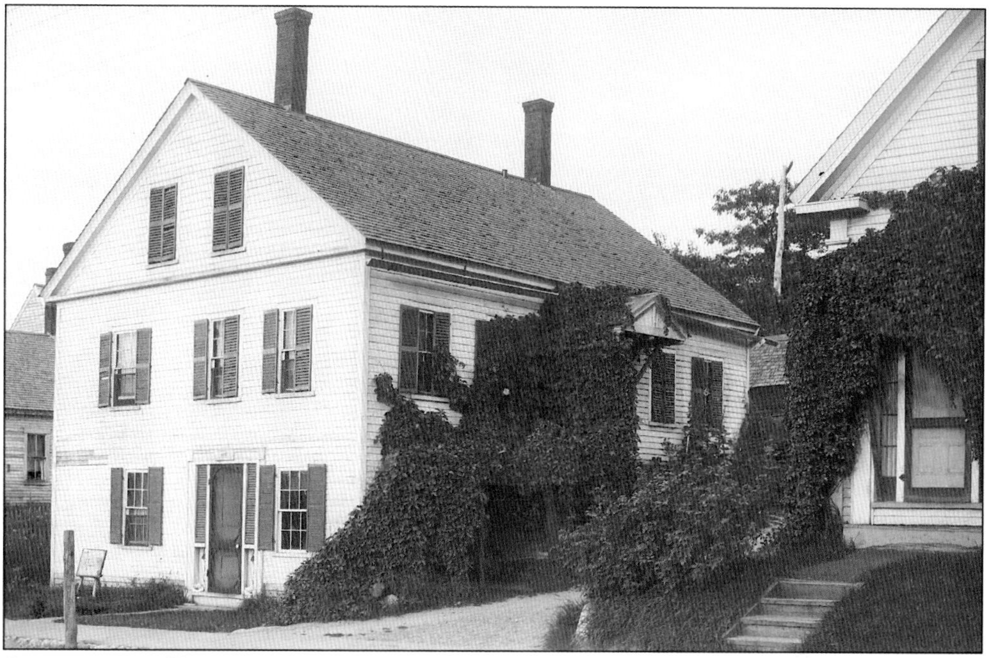

Chapel, later Tenement House, 879 Union Avenue. When the Free Will Baptists outgrew their earlier quarters, Benjamin J. Cole and John Davis 2nd built this chapel at the northeast corner of Harrison Street (visible at center), where the congregation worshipped from 1843–1844 to 1852. The site is now a parking lot.

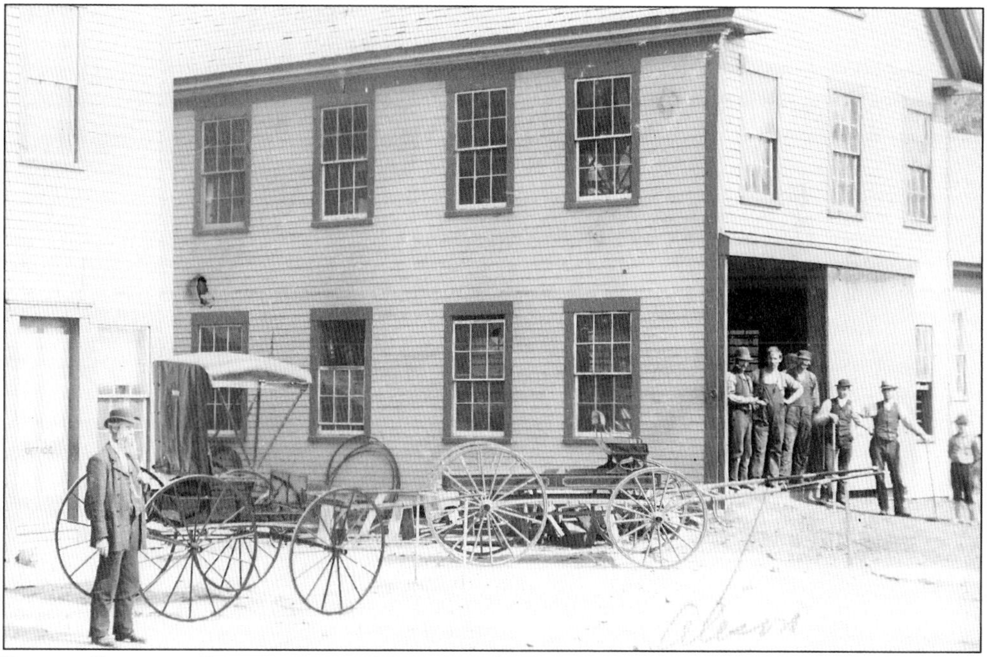

Rublee Carriage Shop, 168–172 Mechanic Street. Henry L. Rublee stands at left. His son Alson is second from the left in the group at the doorway. Today the site, opposite the former Crane Manufacturing Co. plant, is occupied by the drive-up Lakeport Post Office. Father and son were successive leaders of Rublee's Band, a local institution.

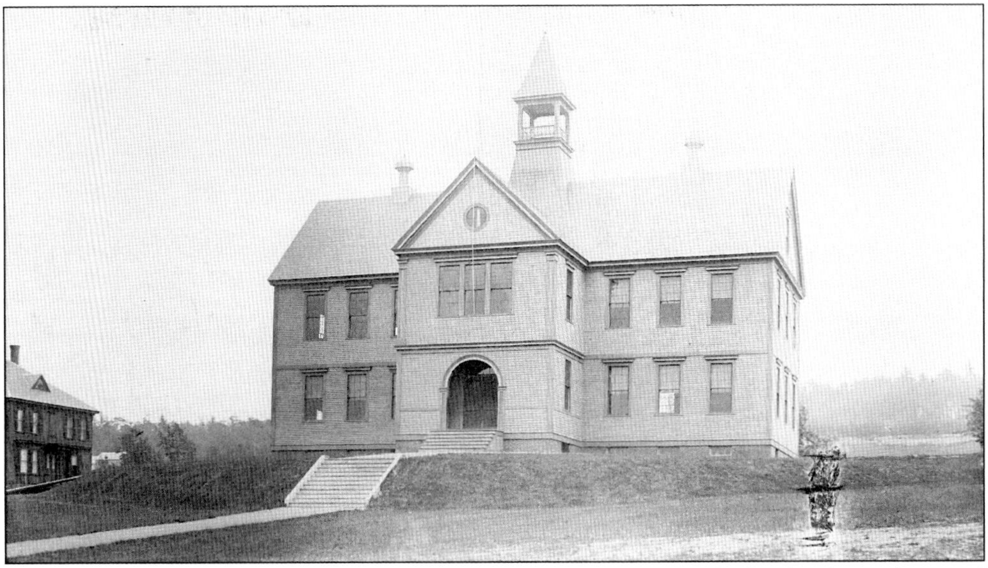

Lakeport High School, Mechanic Street. Built 1886–1887, the high school was destroyed by fire in 1905 and replaced by the brick Mechanic Street School in 1905–1906.

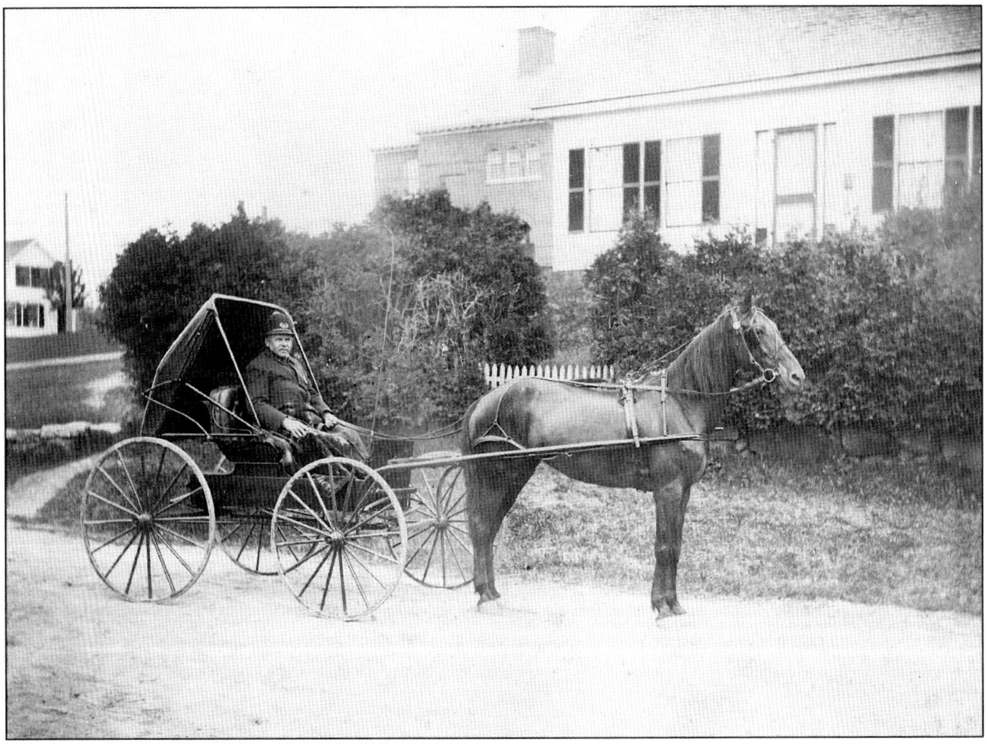

Horace E. Rowen (1854–1934), Police and Truant Officer, on Mechanic Street. He was also the agent of the New Hampshire Woman's Humane Society, in which capacity he investigated complaints of cruelty to animals.

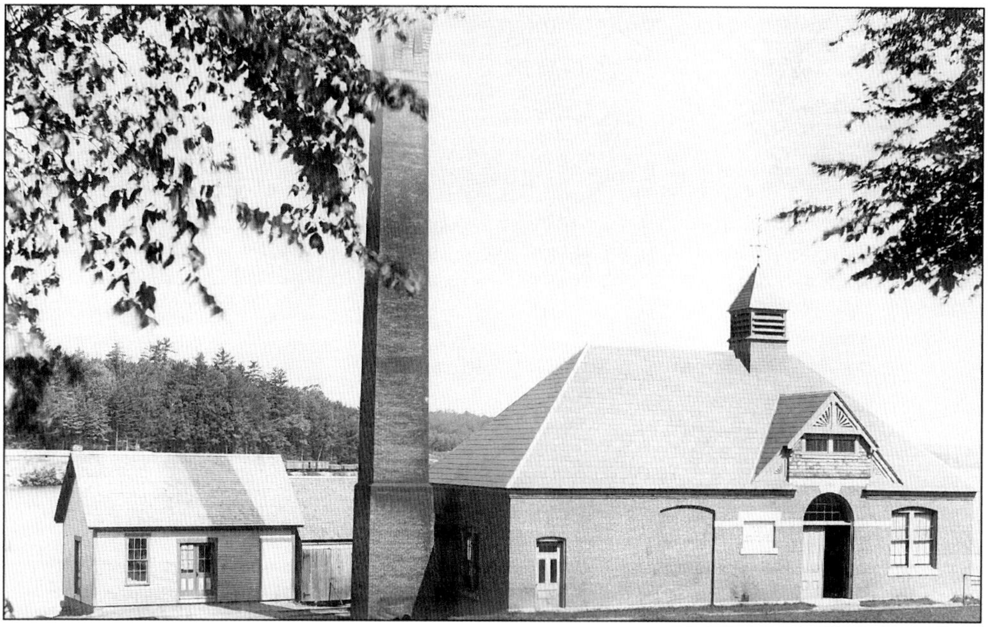

Pumping Station of Laconia Water Company. Built in 1885, the system was in operation by December of that year.

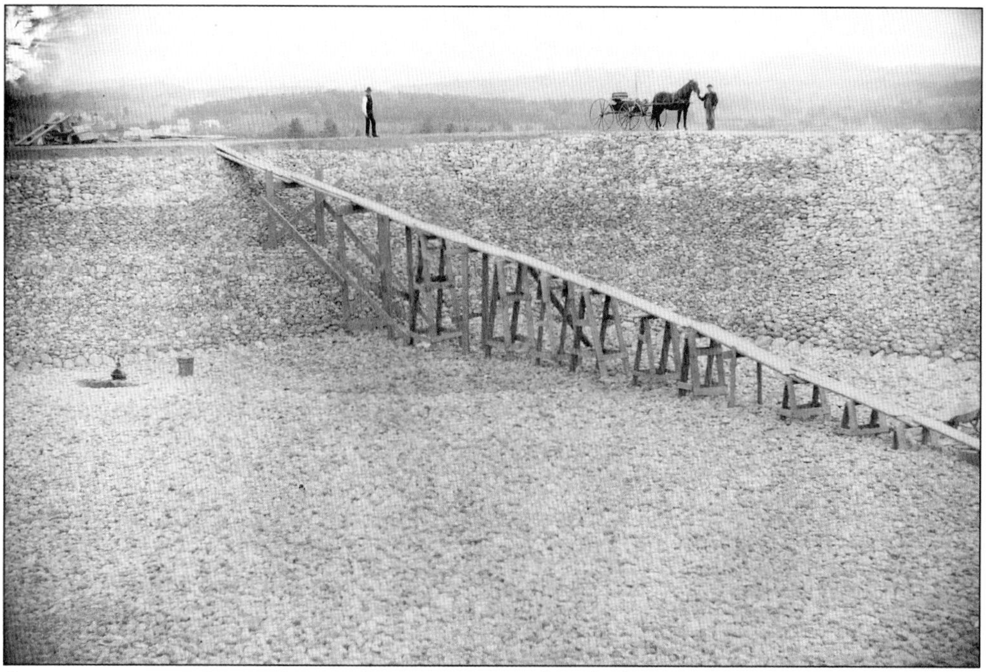

Construction of Stark Street Reservoir. Two hundred feet above the lake, the reservoir was 90 by 135 feet at the bottom, 153 by 198 feet at the top, and 21 feet deep, with a capacity of 2,750,000 gallons. It was paved on the bottom and sides with cobblestones.

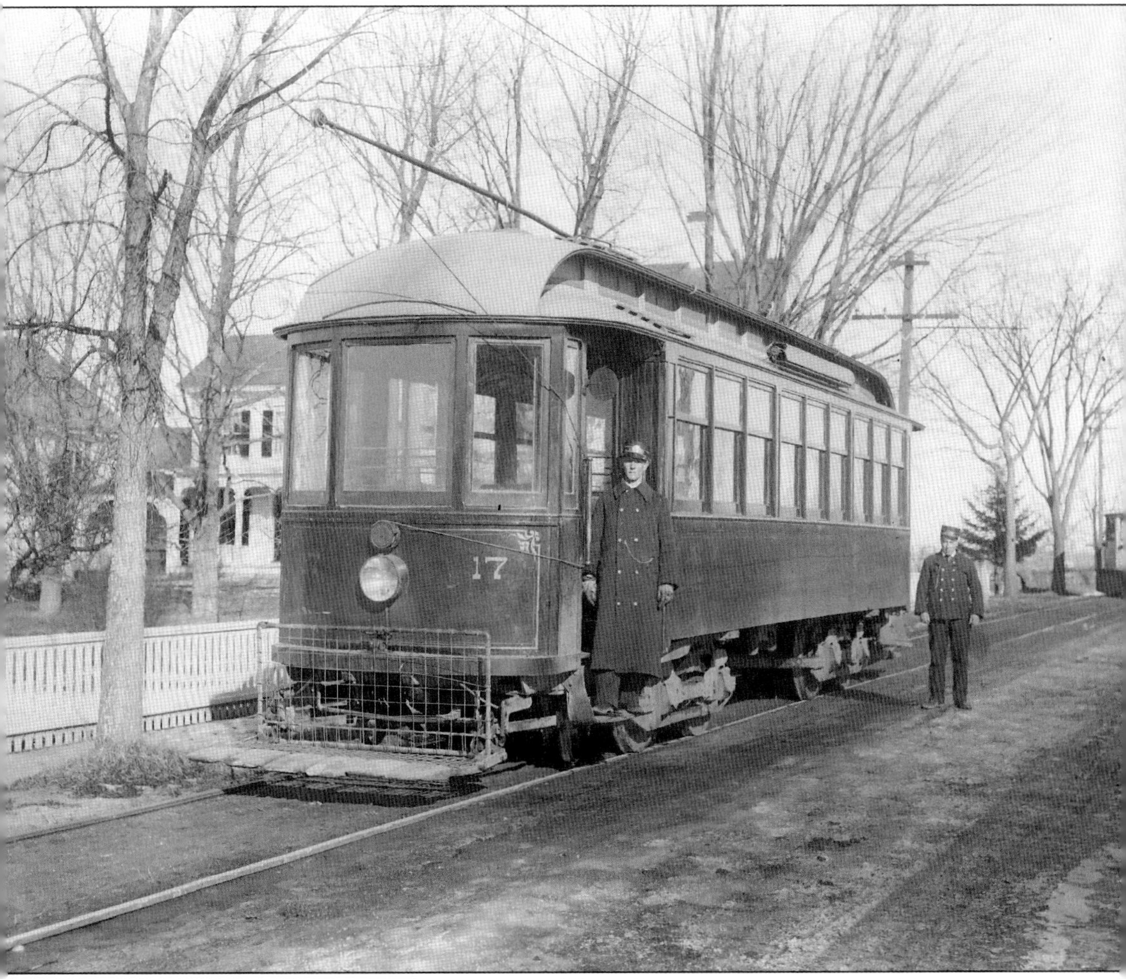

Trolley Car on Union Avenue, 1906. Nelson Doucette, motorman, and George Conant, conductor, pose for the camera. Part of the Squire Clark House (long occupied by his daughter Claribel) is visible at left. The Laconia Street Railway's snowplow "Terror" appears at right. Samuel Clement Clark (1832–1897) was an attorney at Lakeport for 40 years, a clerk of court, a member of the legislature, a director of the Laconia National Bank from the time of its organization, and one of the original promoters and directors of the Laconia and Lakeport Horse Railroad. In later years, Hathaway House was located in the handsome structure and Summerfield's, a restaurant, had quarters in the barn. Today, the principal occupant of the property is the Plant Petaler.

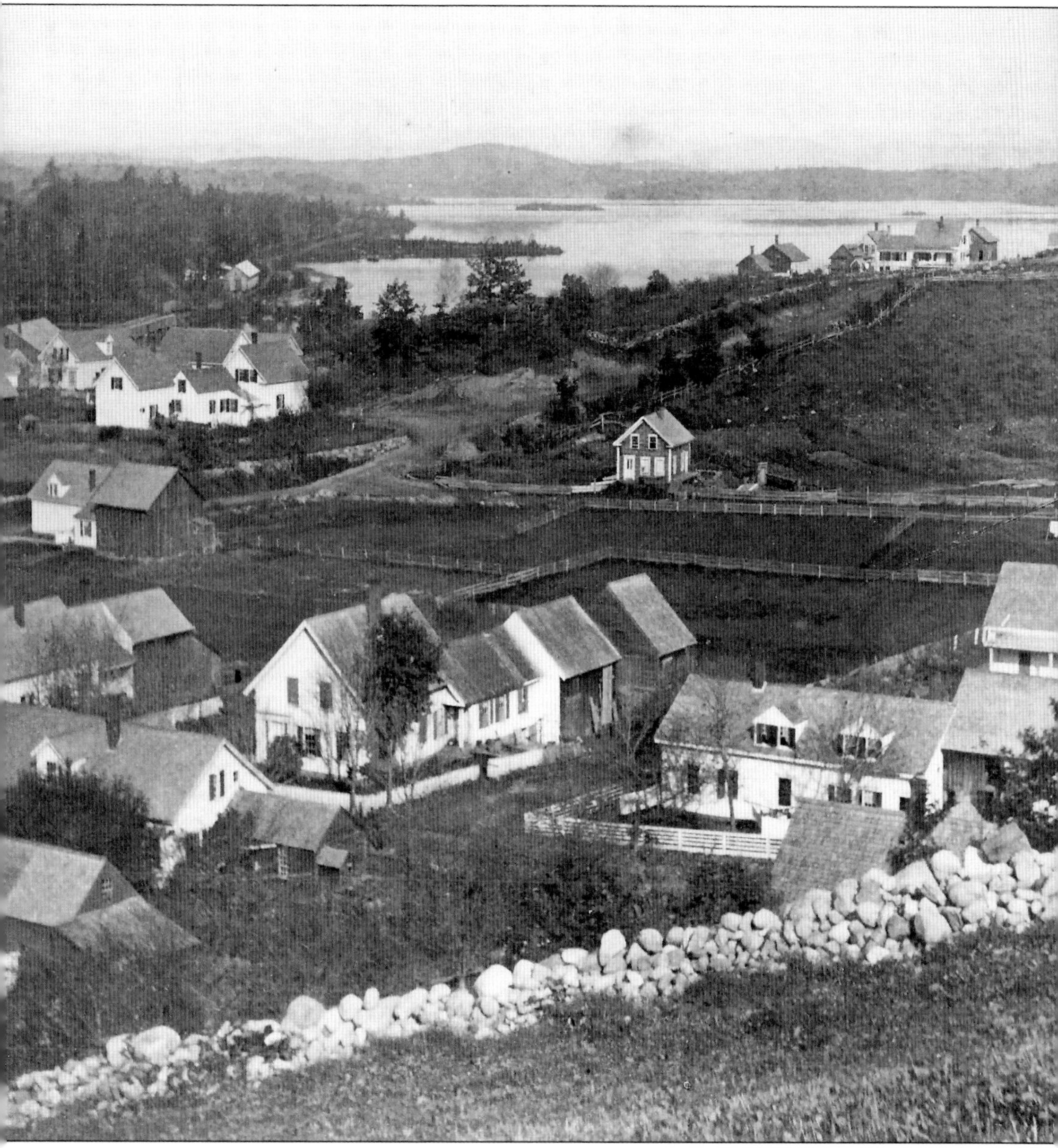

LAKE PAUGUS FROM COLE'S HILL, C. 1875. Mechanic Street is at top and Locke's Hill at top right. Lakeport High School (see top of p. 120) would later be built just off the photograph in the upper right-hand corner. Valley Street would be off the photograph at right.

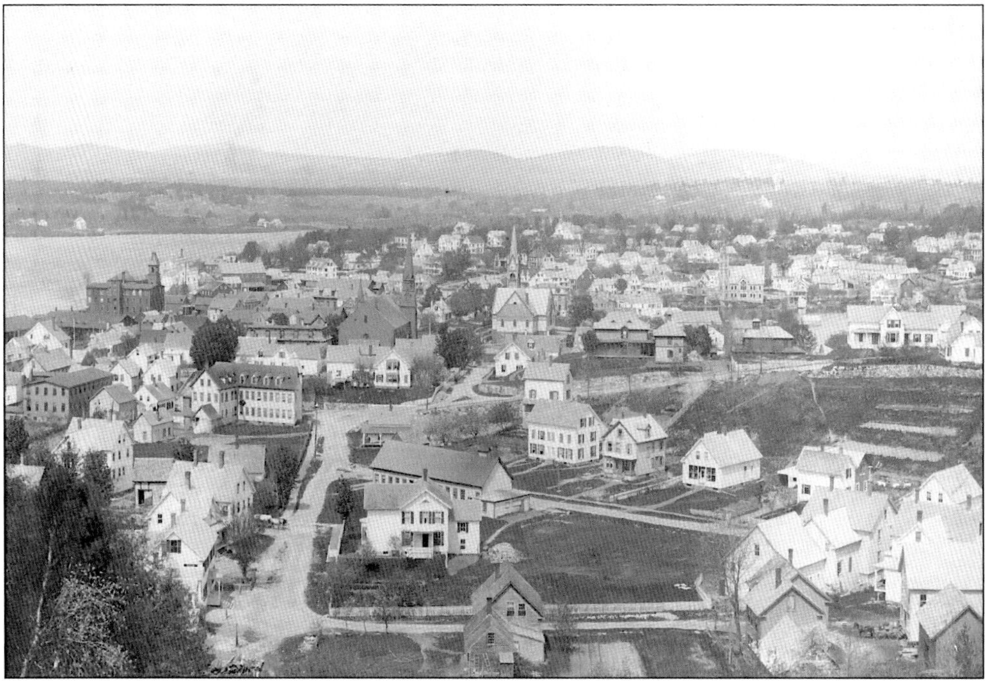

ANOTHER VIEW FROM COLE'S HILL, WITH LAKE OPECHEE AT LEFT. Mechanic Street runs from left to right at center; Valley Street runs diagonally at lower center.

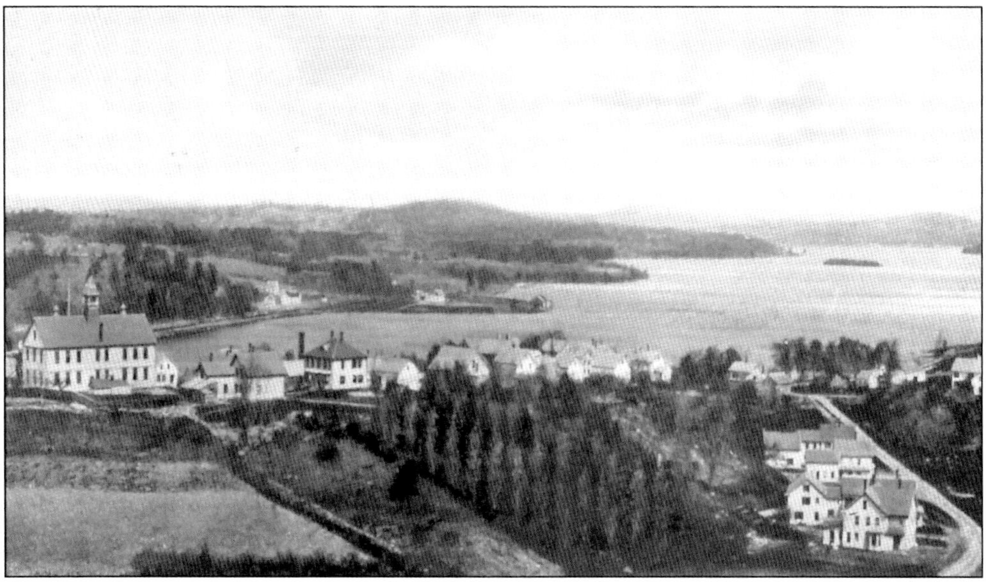

LAKE PAUGUS FROM COLE'S HILL. Lakeport High School (see top of p. 120) is seen at left on Locke's Hill, and Valley Street is at right.

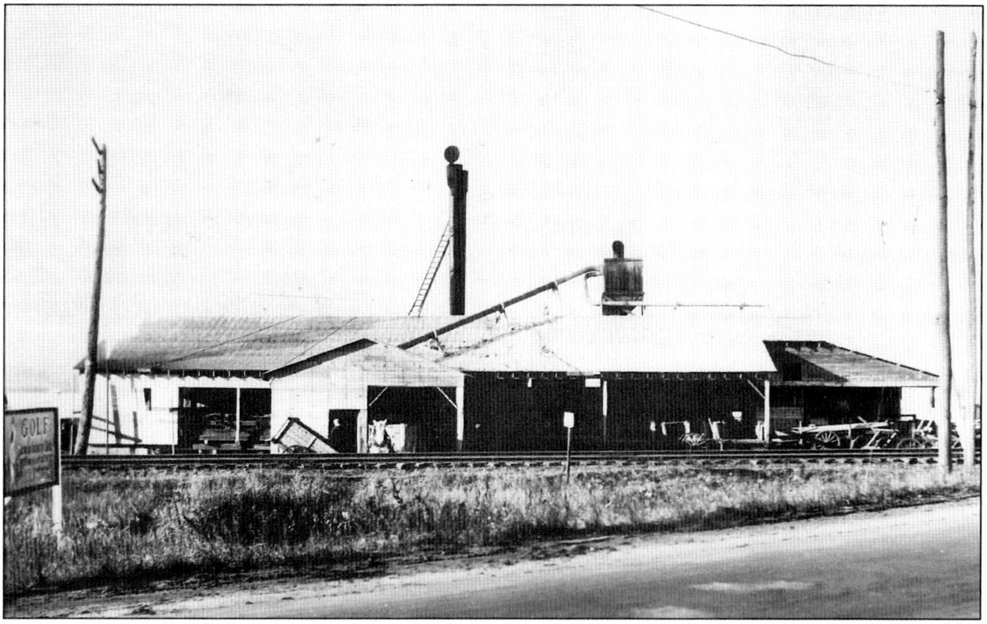

Chase & Veazey Plant at Black Brook Crossing. The site off the photograph at right is occupied today by a Burger King restaurant.

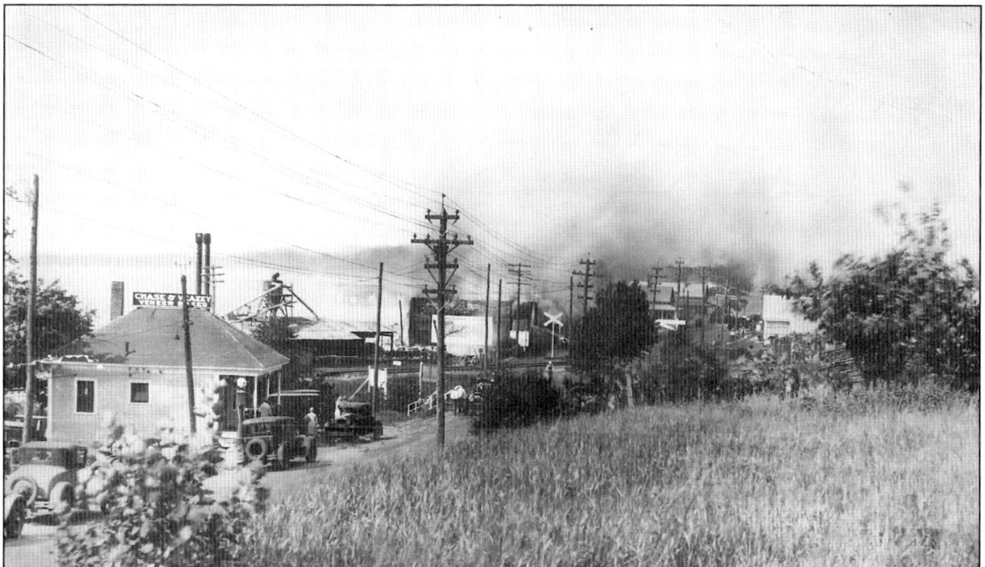

Lakeport Ice Co. Fire, June 12, 1929. A blaze in the Rudzinski stables adjoining the Chase & Veazey lumber mill (left) spread to the large icehouse of the Lakeport Ice Co. (at right), which soon became a mass of flames. The stables and icehouse were completely destroyed. Meanwhile, the huge icehouse (see next page) of the Independent Ice Co. (further right, obscured by smoke) had become covered with burning embers that started small fires, but these were extinguished. *The Laconia Evening Citizen* for June 12, 1929, noted that, "The firemen made a remarkable fight in the face of heavy winds and are being commended this afternoon for allowing no heavy damage to buildings other than the two above mentioned." The Black Brook railroad crossing appears at center of the photo.

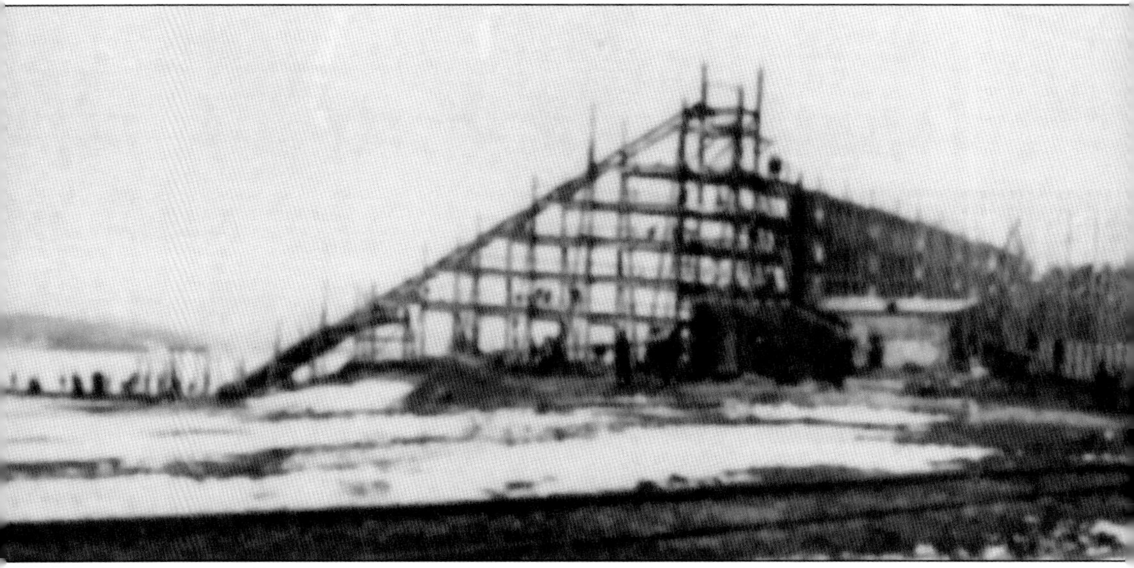

Independent Ice Co. Icehouse, Winter of 1906–1907. This icehouse was one of many such structures erected on the shores of Lakes Paugus, Opechee, and Winnipesaukee—and even on nearby Lily Pond—from which carloads of ice were shipped by rail to Boston, Providence, and even the Caribbean, from the 1890s well into the early years of the 20th century. This gave rise to Lakeport being known as the "Ice City" for a time. Harvesting the vast tonnages furnished employment to hundreds of workers, many of whom were migrants. Sidetracks of the Lake Shore Railroad (center) were used to load ice for shipment to the southern destinations. In 1940, the same tracks were used to unload the sections of the former steamer *Chateauguay* for reassembly as the MV *Mount Washington II*. The Independent icehouse was one of the largest; it was 300 feet wide, 144 feet deep, and 44

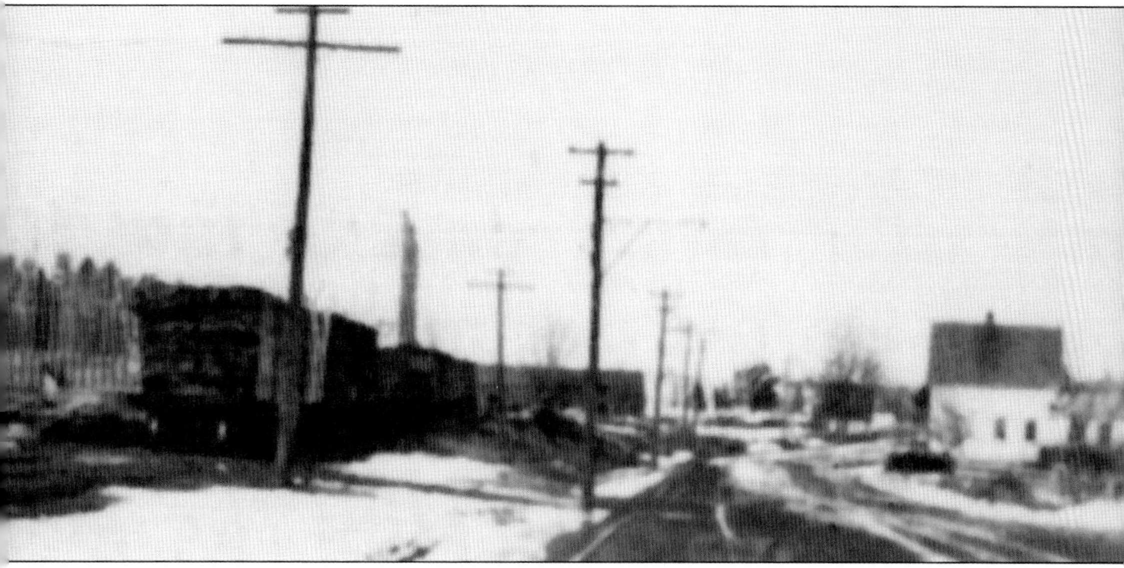

feet high. After the advent of electromechanical refrigeration, its 12 bays were taken over by the New Hampshire Mushroom Co. In 1936, the complex burned in a spectacular fire, fought in subzero weather, with a 45-mile-per-hour gale driving flames across the street. The Chase & Veazey lumber company occupied the site off the photograph at left. At the extreme left is the site of today's Burger King; McDonald's is across the street. Black Brook and the crossing of the main line of the Lake Shore Railroad are behind the photographer. The current site of Barton's Motel is in the distance to the left of the highway. The Paugus Diner and neighboring businesses are today in the distance at right beyond the frame dwelling. Laconia Street Railway tracks (1899–1925) to The Weirs are visible at right, along with a then somewhat primitive Union Avenue.

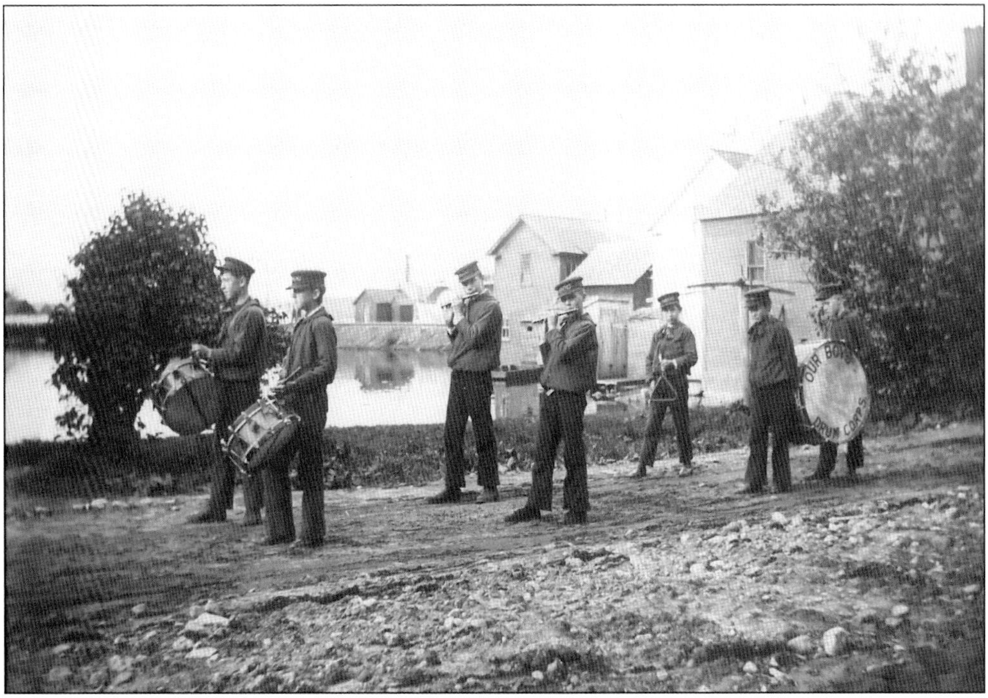

Our Boys Drum Corps. They parade, around the turn of the century, on an unpaved Gold Street, with the railroad track and trestle in the background. Lakeport had a long history of musical organizations, of which Rublee's Band was pre-eminent for several decades.

Acknowledgments

While most of these photographs appear here for the first time in book form, six of them were included in *Slates, Shingles and Shakes*, published by the City of Laconia in 1978. Jo Casey made available the photograph at the bottom of p. 14; Jim Dodge, that at the top of p. 91; Gordon Dubois, those on pp. 93 and 95; Link Fournier, those on p. 13; the family of Sheldon S. Theall, the 1888 panoramic print from which the detail on p. 64 was taken; Charles O. Hopkins, the photographs at the top of p. 87 and bottom of p. 118; George Landry, those on pp. 54, 57, 59, 63, at the top of p. 80, and at the top of pp. 20 and 108; Laurence W. Leonard, those on pp. 50 and 51, at the bottom of p. 86, and at the top of p. 99; Douglas B. McGowan, the photograph on p. 102; the Department of Environmental Services, State of New Hampshire, those at the top of p. 47 and at the bottom of pp. 79 and 81; Arthur A. Tilton, the photograph on p. 115; John Veazey, those on pp. 74–75 and at the top of pp. 39, 104, and 125; Mrs. Norman S. Weeks, the photograph at the top of p. 15; the Earl Welles Collection, that at the top of p. 109; the United Baptist Church of Lakeport, those on p. 52, the bottom of p. 87, and the top of p. 119; and the Laconia Museum Society Inc., those on p. 84, at the top of pp. 110, 118, and 124, and at the bottom of pp. 17, 47, and 108. Photographs on pp. 12, 83, 123, and at the top of pp. 14 and 29 are from the David L. Dickinson Collection of stereopticon views, purchased by the Laconia Historical Society in 1997. The remaining images are from the collections of the Laconia Historical Society and the Laconia Public Library.